Sutured Words
contemporary poetry about medicine

Sutured Words
contemporary poetry
about medicine

Jon Mukand, Editor

AVIVA PRESS
P.O. BOX 1357 • BROOKLINE, MA • 02146

SUTURED WORDS: Contemporary Poetry About Medicine

Cover photograph by Cathy Taylor-Findlay

*Photographs of turn-of-the-century Boston City Hospital
courtesy of Public Relations at B.U. Medical Center.*

Cover design by Dom Iorfino

Aviva Press
P. O. Box 1357
Brookline, MA 02146

Permissions begin on page 391.

Library of Congress Cataloging-in-Publication Data
SUTURED WORDS.

    Includes index.
    1. American poetry—20th century. 2. Medicine—Poetry.
3. Medicine in literature. 4. Medical ethics. I. Mukand, Jon,
1959—   .
PS595.M43S88 1987   811'. 54'080356   87—71549
ISBN 0—9619150—0—5 (pbk.)

MORE COMMENTS ON *SUTURED WORDS*

"This excellent anthology of poems about medicine will be a welcome text for literature and medicine courses. . . If the latest theorists are right, reading poetry will help enhance the skills of observation and interpretation that are so essential in medical diagnosis, as well as help develop the qualities of empathy and compassion that are so necessary in caring for patients."

–Anne Hudson Jones
Editor, *Literature and Medicine*

"This carefully collected assemblage of American poetry informs us that the pageant of modern medicine is more than new procedures, drugs and devices. The poet's vision demands that we recognize the individual patient's personality, and the human dimensions of illness and death. All health professionals will find powerful (and perhaps painful) insights in this unique work; insights that could make their own work more ambiguous, but ultimately more rewarding."

– George Annas
Utley Professor of Health Law
Boston Univ. School of Medicine

"This is a marvelous collection, as full of wonder for medical students touching their first patient as for their teachers more hardened to pain. It should find a place in every hospital ward and floor, so that doctors and nurses can turn from the numbing reality of sickness to the poetry in this book that reminds us how our patients think and hope, pray and love. We owe a debt to Jon Mukand for putting together this extraordinary collection which will bring you to tears at times and may change you utterly."

–Howard Spiro
Director, Humanities in Medicine
Yale School of Medicine

for

my late father

Sushil Kumar Eric Mukand

and my mother

Ivy Vimlu Mukand

TO WAKEN AN OLD LADY

Old age is
a flight of small
cheeping birds
skimming
bare trees
above a snow glaze.
Gaining and failing
they are buffeted
by a dark wind—
But what?
On harsh weedstalks
the flock has rested,
the snow
is covered with broken
seedhusks
and the wind tempered
by a shrill
piping of plenty.

—*William Carlos Williams*

CONTENTS

To Waken An Old Lady . . . . . William Carlos Williams   ix

INTRODUCTION   1

THE MEDICAL ENVIRONMENT
The Hospital Smell Combs My Nostrils   9

Emergency Ward . . . . . Leonard Nathan   21
At The Doctor's . . . . . Robert Watson   22
Waiting Room . . . . . Richard Blessing   23
The Urine Specimen . . . . . Ted Kooser   24
Blood Pressure . . . . . Sandra Gilbert   25
How I Became Fiction . . . . . Joyce Carol Oates   26
In The Hospital For Tests . . . . . Mona Van Duyn   28
The Operation . . . . . W.D. Snodgrass   30
Coma . . . . . Janet Reno   31
Visiting Hour . . . . . Norman MacCaig   32
Corwin Psychiatric Ward, 1972 . . . . . Paul Dilsaver   34
Notes From The Delivery Room . . . . . Linda Pastan   35
The X-Ray Waiting Room
In The Hospital . . . . . Randall Jarrell   36
In The X-Ray Room . . . . . Howard Moss   37
On Seeing An X-Ray Of My Head . . . . . David Wagoner   39
X-Ray . . . . . Celia Gilbert   40
At Nuclear Medicine . . . . . Dixie Partridge   41
Edgewater Hospital . . . . . Albert Goldbarth   42
Metastasis . . . . . Sandra Gilbert   43
A Question Of Memory . . . . . Donald Finkel   45
Having Been Asked
"What Is A Man?" I Answer . . . . . Philip Levine   46
We Shall All Be Born Again
But We Shall Not All Be Saved . . . . . William Matthews   48
Prayer In Fever . . . . . Jean Valentine   50
Hospital View . . . . . Thomas Lux   51
St. Vincent's . . . . . W.S. Merwin   52

PATIENTS' VIEWS OF ILLNESS
The Darkness Within Me Is Growing

55

Fear of *Gray's Anatomy* . . . . . Brendan Galvin   63
The Condition . . . . . Marvin Bell   64
The Doctor Of Starlight . . . . . Philip Levine   65
Nerves . . . . . Howard Moss   67
Tennis Elbow . . . . . Jim Hall   68
Mutterings . . . . . John Ciardi   70
after minor surgery . . . . . Linda Pastan   72
Sack 'A Woe . . . . . Michael S. Harper   73
Tonsils . . . . . Roberta Spear   74
The Leg . . . . . Karl Shapiro   76
Bleeder . . . . . Hollis Summers   77
The Cancer Cells . . . . . Richard Eberhart   80
Seventh Floor: Cancer Ward . . . . . Tom Sleigh   81
The Patient Is Rallying . . . . . Weldon Kees   82
Farmyard At Chassy . . . . . Stephen Dobyns   83
The Parents Of Psychotic Children . . . . . Marvin Bell   84
I Need Help . . . . . Edward Hirsch   85
Insomnia . . . . . Daniel Halpern   87
Insomniac . . . . . Sylvia Plath   88
The Addict . . . . . Anne Sexton   89
Infirmity . . . . . Theodore Roethke   91
You Again . . . . . Beth Bentley   93
A Deathplace . . . . . L.E. Sissman   94

PATIENTS' VIEWS OF DOCTORS
Gentleness And The Scalpel

97

The Doctor Who Sits
At The Bedside Of A Rat . . . . . Josephine Miles   107
Doctor . . . . . David Ignatow   108
Putting Them Down . . . . . William Harrold   109
Transplant . . . . . John Frederick Nims   110
Orthopedic Surgery Ward . . . . . William Matthews   111
Incurable . . . . . Robert Pack   112
My Surgeons . . . . . Stanley Kunitz   114

Monet Refuses The Operation . . . . . Lisel Mueller   115
Pain: 1967 . . . . . Maxine Kumin   117
Pain Work—Up . . . . . Jeremy Nobel   119
The Doctor Rebuilds A Hand . . . . . Gary Young   120
The Persistence Of Memory,
The Failure Of Poetry . . . . . Robert Phillips   121
Lost . . . . . David Fisher   122
"Bed Tablets" . . . . . Michael Benedikt   123
Peau D'Orange . . . . . Marcia Lynch   124
For A Teacher's Wife,
Dying Of Cancer . . . . . Richard Tillinghast   125
The Revenant . . . . . Peter Davison   126
Doctors . . . . . Anne Sexton   127
On The Subject Of Doctors . . . . . James Tate   128
Untitled Poem . . . . . Alan Dugan   129
A Young Doctor
In The Gardner Museum . . . . . S. Ben-Tov   130
The Staff Of Aesculapius . . . . . Elizabeth Bishop   131

PHYSICIANS
Dissecting The Good Lines From The Bad   133

Dannie Abse
    The Doctor   141
    The Stethoscope   142
    Pathology Of Colours   143
    X-Ray   144

John Stone
    Death   145
    Autopsy In The Form Of An Elegy   146
    Amnesia   147
    Getting To Sleep In New Jersey   148
    Confabulation   149

Samuel Stearns
        150
    Autopsy
    The Little Old Man   151
    Resurrection   152
    Epilogue   153

Jon Mukand

    The Son: Returning Home   154
    Words For A Percussion Instrument   156
    The Taste Of The Ocean   157
    First Payment   158

FAMILY AND FRIENDS
Afraid To Name This Dying   161

Commands Of Love . . . . . Molly Peacock   171
Pain . . . . . John Updike   172
Stroke . . . . . Susan Irene Rea   173
Strokes . . . . . William Stafford   174
The Glass . . . . . Sharon Olds   175
The Moment Of My Father's Death . . . . . Sharon Olds   176
Last Elegy . . . . . Stephen Berg   178
Cells . . . . . Phyllis Janowitz   180
Heart Failures . . . . . Richard Howard   181
Death Of A Son . . . . . Jon Silkin   183
Talking To Grief . . . . . Denise Levertov   185
The Dying Friend . . . . . John Hollander   186
The Return: Intensive Care . . . . . Sydney Lea   187
Angina . . . . . James Dickey   190
On Learning Of A Friend's Illness . . . . . C.K. Williams   192
Scar Tissue . . . . . Mary Farrell   194
I'm Terribly Sorry For You,
But I Can't Help Laughing . . . . . Ogden Nash   195
On Tuesdays They Open The Local Pool
To The Stroke Victims . . . . . Robert Hedin   197
Her Stroke . . . . . Jim Schley   198
Nursing Home . . . . . Barry Spacks   200
For My Aunt In Memorial Hospital . . . . . Sandra Gilbert   201
The Night Grandma Died . . . . . Sandra Gilbert   202
The Orchid . . . . . David Bottoms   203
Medicine . . . . . Alice Walker   204
Now, Before The End, I Think . . . . . Edwin Honig   205
Now, My Usefulness Over . . . . . Edwin Honig   206
Moving Into Memory . . . . . Peter Davison   207
Stern Stuff . . . . . Peter Davison   208
Andree Rexroth: Mt. Tamalpais . . . . . Kenneth Rexroth   209

WOMEN
Flowers Of Ether In My Hair   211

One More Time . . . . . Patricia Goedicke   221
At The Gynecologist's . . . . . Linda Pastan   222
Anne: Room 8, No. 2 Biopsy
With Frozen Section . . . . . Kirk Maxey   223
A Story About The Body . . . . . Robert Hass   224
Waiting For The Doctor . . . . . Colette Inez   225
Pregnancy . . . . . Sandra McPherson   226
The Buddha In The Womb . . . . . Erica Jong   228
Soft Mask . . . . . Mary Karr   230
Written On Learning Of Arrhythmia
In The Unborn Child . . . . . Judith Skillman   231
The Recovery Room: Lying In . . . . . Helen Chasin   232
To A 14 Year Old
In Labor And Delivery . . . . . John Stone   233
Giving Birth In Greek . . . . . Judith Hemschemeyer   234
Childbirth . . . . . Anne Perlman   236
Birth . . . . . Constance Urdang   237
Damage . . . . . Ellen Bryant Voigt   238
Seizure . . . . . Jeanne Murray Walker   239
The Choice . . . . . Molly Peacock   240
The Watch . . . . . Marge Piercy   241
Menstruation Rag . . . . . Diane Ackerman   242
Infertility . . . . . Stephen Dunn   243
Mother And Child . . . . . David Axelrod   244
What We Have Now . . . . . David Axelrod   245
Thirty Childbirths . . . . . Millen Brand   246
Couvade . . . . . Michael Blumenthal   247
Rape . . . . . Adrienne Rich   248
Father Of The Victim . . . . . Rae Ballard   249
Change Of Life . . . . . Constance Urdang   250

MENTAL ILLNESS
The Shadow Of The Obsessive Idea   251

Rorschach Test . . . . . Spencer Brown   259
Agoraphobia . . . . . Susan Hahn   261
Panic . . . . . Philip Booth   262

The Mad Scene . . . . . James Merrill   263
To Make A Dragon Move: From The
Diary Of An Anorexic . . . . . Pamela White Hadas   264
Waking In The Blue . . . . . Robert Lowell   267
Preface To A Twenty Volume
Suicide Note . . . . . Imamu Amiri Baraka (Leroi Jones) 269
The Suicide . . . . . David Posner   270
Suicide's Note . . . . . Langston Hughes   271
To A Young Woman
Considering Suicide . . . . . Peter Sears   272
They Call It Attempted Suicide . . . . . Jack Gilbert 273
To D-, Dead By Her Own Hand . . . . . Howard Nemerov   274
Dropping Toward Stillness . . . . . Rose Marcel   275
On A Schizophrenic Frequency . . . . . Jon Mukand   276
Schizophrenic Girl . . . . . X.J. Kennedy   277
Evening In The Sanitarium . . . . . Louise Bogan   278
Counting The Mad . . . . . Donald Justice   280
The Hell Poem . . . . . John Berryman   281
From A Girl
In A Mental Institution . . . . . Diane Wakoski   283
The Invisible Woman . . . . . Robin Morgan   285
At The Hospital . . . . . Carl Dennis   286
Visit To My Committed Grandma . . . . . Leonard Nathan 287
The Asylum . . . . . Hayden Carruth   288

DISABILITY
Their Lockstep Tight As Lilac Buds   289

The Handicapped . . . . . Philip Dacey   297
Rehabilitation Center . . . . . Maxine Kumin   299
The Game . . . . . Harold Bond   300
On The Sidelines . . . . . Lillian Morrison   301
Enid Field: In Memoriam . . . . . Gloria Maxson   302
A Question Of Energy . . . . . Amber Coverdale Sumrall 303
The Stroke . . . . . Christopher Fahy   304
Angles . . . . . Dixie Partridge   305
The Tingle . . . . . Norman Andrew Kirk   306
The Old Hoofer . . . . . Lillian Morrison   308
After Being Paralyzed From The Neck Down

For Twenty Years, Mr. Wallace Gets A Chin-
Operated Motorized Wheelchair . . . . . Ronald Wallace   309
"To: The Access Committee . . . ." . . . . H.N. Beckerman 310
To A Man Going Blind . . . . . John Haines   311
Black Lightning . . . . . Arthur Sze   312
The Blind Always Come
As Such A Surprise . . . . . Ted Kooser   313
Glaucoma . . . . . David Wojahn   314
Out Of Blindness . . . . . Leslie B. Blades   316
Visit To The Institute For The Blind . . . . . Felix Pollak   317
On Becoming Deaf . . . . . S. Soloman   319
The Man With The Hearing Aid . . . . . Ted Kooser   320
Fingers, Fists, Gabriel's Wings . . . . . Michael Cleary   321
How To Sign . . . . . Laurie Stroblas   322
Stutterer . . . . . Alan Dugan   323
Spastic Child . . . . . Vassar Miller   324
Song For My Son . . . . . Marilyn Davis   325
Jenny . . . . . John Mann Astrachan   326
Clinics . . . . . Michael Bachstein   327

SOCIAL ISSUES
Hungry And Frightened By Namelessness   329

The Minneapolis Poem . . . . . James Wright   341
County Ward . . . . . Gary Soto   344
Veteran's Hospital . . . . . Ben Belitt   346
Night Scene . . . . . George Oppen   348
December 24 And
George McBride Is Dead . . . . . Richard Hugo   349
Herrick Hospital, Fifth Floor . . . . . Al Young   350
Jive . . . . . John Wieners   351
In The Waiting Room . . . . . David Bergman   352
Elegy For John, My Student
Dead Of AIDS . . . . . Robert Cording   355
Tarantula or The Dance Of Death . . . . . Anthony Hecht 357
"As My Blood Was Drawn" . . . . . Robert Hayden   358
Plane Life . . . . . Lawrence Ferlinghetti   360
Great Infirmities . . . . . Charles Simic   361
Two Deaths . . . . . joel oppenheimer   362

Deaths . . . . . May Swenson   363
Near The Old People's Home . . . . . Howard Nemerov   364
The Very Old . . . . . Ted Kooser   365
The Old Must Watch Us . . . . . Donald Hall   366
The Ones That Are Thrown Out . . . . . Miller Williams   367
The Retarded Children Find A World
Built Just For Them . . . . . Diana O'Hehir   368
Hard Rock Returns To Prison From The Hospital
For The Criminal Insane . . . . . Etheridge Knight   369
Simple Truths . . . . . William Heyen   371
An Abortion . . . . . Frank O'Hara   374
Abortion . . . . . Ai   375
Resuscitation . . . . . John Stone   376
Accident . . . . . Karin T. Ash   377
Coma . . . . . Beth Bentley   378
Do Not Go Gentle
Into That Good Night . . . . . Dylan Thomas   379
Of Grief . . . . . May Sarton   380
Death Psalm:
O Lord Of Mysteries . . . . . Denise Levertov   382
Lullaby . . . . . Jon Mukand   384

Notes   387

Permissions   391

ACKNOWLEDGEMENTS

This project began at a lunch with Howard Spiro, a professor of medicine at Yale, and Arnold Rampersad, a professor of English at Stanford (now Rutgers), who both urged me to put my ideas into action. On returning from my "sabbatical" in an M.A. program of English at Stanford, I resolved to submit this project as my Honors Thesis for the M.D., and found support for the idea from the Honors Committee, and especially its chairperson, Dean Coryce Haavik. Some of this work was presented at a meeting of the Society for Health & Human Values, organized by Suzanne Poirier, who also kindly offered to comment on this project for the Honor Committee's approval.

I am especially grateful to Kathleen Woodward, director of the Center for Twentieth Century Studies at the University of Wisconsin—Milwaukee, for graciously agreeing to be my supervisor and advisor. This anthology has greatly benefited from her detailed comments and suggestions. Professors and poets William Harrold (English) and John Koethe (Philosophy), also from Milwaukee, have served as readers for this project. My advisors for my work as a poet, W.S. DiPiero and Denise Levertov, have helped me improve immensely as a poet and a critic.

I am grateful to all the poets and publishers who have generously granted permission to reprint some of these poems, and especially to Atheneum Press and Poetry. Clearly, both are intensely committed to the advancement of poetry in America.

Grants from The National Fund for Medical Education, the Marshall and Nellie Alworth Foundation, and the Joseph Collins Foundation were most helpful while this book was being written.

To my friend and colleague, Tony Iorfino, I am grateful for moral support and his artist's eye. Juggling roles as medical student and resident, poet, critic, and friend would not have been possible without the support of my colleague and fianceé, Giselle Corré.

INTRODUCTION

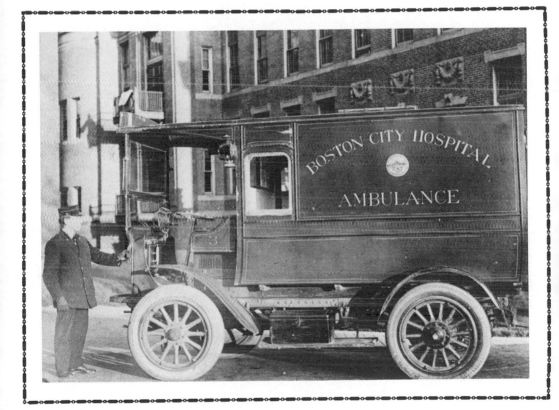

INTRODUCTION

Both Literature and Medicine have the capacity to heal, to help sustain us in periods of physical or spiritual illness. Language and processes common to both domains suggest their affinities: the stress on rhythm in poetry and cardiology, the cleansing process of catharsis, the centrality of narrative in case reports and fiction, poetry therapy in psychiatry, and the prominence of images in radiology and poetry. Both fields utilize diverse methods of studying a work of literature or the patient. Literary criticism can be impressionistic, formal, biographical, psycho-analytic, historical, or social, approaches that are often complementary. Similarly, medicine employs the physical examination, biochemical tests, radiology, histology, and psychological testing. Seeing the patient from a literary point of view may be considered yet another method of study.

Philosphers, poets, and literary critics have emphasized the affinities of literature and medicine. E. D. Pellegrino, a founding member of The Society for Health and Human Values, writes: "Medicine and literature are united in an unremitting paradox—the need simultaneously to stand back from, and to share in, the struggles of human life. . . . Literature gives meaning to what the physician sees and makes him see it feelingly. Whatever enriches the doctor's sensibilities must perforce make a better physician. . . . Linked by a common need to see life bare, to look and see, and to see feelingly, medicine and literature enhance each other. In doing so, they enhance man's capacity to heal himself in spirit and body."[1] The poet Denise Levertov, whose work is included here, has said: "The great power of art is to transform, renovate, activate. If there is a relationship between art and healing, it is that."[2] The recognition of these bonds has led literary critics, such as J. Hillis Miller and Joanne Trautmann Banks, to encourage the pedagogical uses of literature in the study of ethics.

Having received formal training in both medicine and literature, I am often asked about their affinities—or, more tellingly, if there *are* any affinities. Literature has helped me appreciate the *art* of medicine, just as medicine encourages me to see the structure and science of literary criticism. At college, for instance, I studied irony—disparity in points of view—in some major English novels. Captain Gulliver's misadventures, as described by the eighteenth-century satirist, Jonathan Swift, often resulted from his inability to understand another culture's perspective, whether it was the pettiness of the Lilliputians, or the strict morality of the Brobdingnagians. Gulliver's example has often prompted me to stop and see the patient's, the relative's or the nurse's point of view. E. M. Forster's essays on the novel, which plot fictional characters on a spectrum from *flat* to *round*,[3] remind me that our perception of a patient can be either uni- or multi-dimensional. Modern medicine, with its emphasis on the "whole person," has realized the importance of seeing patients as *round* and not *flat*. Similarly, the scientific method used in medicine has often been valuable to me in the study of literature. The frequency of grammatical elements and their combination into syntactical units, role relations, and rhythmic units help to create the final effect of a work of art. I have pointed out some of these linguistic elements in the poems included here.

Choosing to make this an anthology of poetry, as opposed to drama or fiction is, of course, a matter of personal taste. But a more practical reason is that a poem represents a dramatic situation in its entirety, and not an excerpt from a larger work. As a result, a poem can be discussed as an independent entity, providing a satisfying sense of completeness instead of leaving the reader in limbo. At the same time, the dense, multilayered levels of meaning in poetry encourage exhaustive discussion which can take many directions—ethics, language in medicine, social issues, interpersonal relations, personal stances. Poetry has concrete features—a dramatic situation, a character, symbolic objects—which help make it accessible to an audience with a wide range of literary knowledge. As a junior student in Obstetrics and Gynecology, I presented a seminar on post-partum depression, and used Anne Perlman's poem, *Childbirth,* as a touchstone. During my senior clerkship in Internal Medicine, while discussing how to approach a patient with acute leukemia, I turned to a similar situation in Marcia Lynch's *Peau d'Orange,* and suggested that we reveal the patient's grim prognosis instead of minimizing it. (With our advice, she chose not to subject herself to heroic measures, and passed away in less pain than she would have otherwise.) As we know, the case study is an important didactic method in medicine, and a recent editorial in a medical journal emphasized the value of carefully scrutinizing a single case from multiple viewpoints.[4] I believe the same to be true of a single poem, which can lead to a variety of issues and discoveries. As Robert Frost once wrote, "A poem is a journey, from ecstasy to wisdom."

Many professors at my medical school, often remarking that much of what they taught would be obsolete by the time we started practice, emphasized the need for continual self-education. Medical practice has changed dramatically in recent years and continues to change at a rapid pace. Twenty-five years from now, patients, physicians, and relatives may be dealing with very different issues than they are now. Since starting work on this anthology, I have seen many surprising developments: hormone treatments for habitual sexual offenders, a baby with a baboon's heart, an artificial heart, the increasing clinical use of giant magnets in radiology, and the threat of AIDS. The ethical climate will be profoundly affected as we confront the dilemmas surrounding these changes. With these thoughts in mind, I have chosen to limit my selection to contemporary American poetry, going back no more than twenty-five years. (The rare exception will be obvious.) But while dealing with dilemmas peculiar to today's medical environment, these poems also focus on timeless questions.

My criteria for including these poems are simple: that they be good and enjoyable. Admittedly, both are highly subjective, and for some poems, including mine, I asked other poets and friends for opinions. Although many of these works are by well-known poets, many are also by relatively unknown writers, and I feel proud at having made some "discoveries." These more than two hundred poems come from a concordance of poetry,[5] pleasant weekends spent browsing in the fine collections of poetry at the Milwaukee and Boston public libraries, and suggestions from poets and teachers. They represent many movements in contemporary poetry, and the majority would be considered to be in the the mainstream of American poetry. Slightly more than a third are by women. I have divided the poems into nine sections in the following order: the medical environment, patients' views of illness, patients' views of doctors, poems by physicians, family and friends, women, mental illness, disability, and social issues. Each section's sub-title derives from one of its poems.

I have prefaced all the sections with brief commentary: a blend of literary criticism, medical ethics, and personal experience. The criticism combines what is known as "New Criticism"[5] and linguistics.[6] New Criticism, by studying metaphor, irony, tone, rhythm, rhyme, and other structural elements, explores *how* a work achieves its effects. Linguistics, as a method of criticism, examines the detailed semantic, grammatical, and phonological structure of a work. An inherent limitation of both methods is a relative lack of concern with ethical and social values. Recognizing this deficiency, I have tried to comment on these issues whenever possible. As for my own experiences in medicine, I have included them to show that some of the dramatic situations in these poems are very real indeed, and ought to be appreciated as such. Of course, I also hope that my medical comments will help illuminate the poems and serve as a starting point for extended discussion.

Before closing, I would like to acknowledge and comment on some related anthologies. In 1916, a humanist and physician named Charles Dana edited *Poetry and the Doctors,* an annotated catalog of physician-poets and their works dating back to Roman times.[7] (And most of the manuscripts were in the editor's library!) Unfortunately, the anthology of poetry Dr. Dana planned never materialized, but his catalog remains an excellent reference. *Poet Physicians: An Anthology of Medical Poetry Written by Physicians,* appeared in 1945 and was edited by Mary Lou McDonough.[8] Her selections ranged widely over time and came from many countries. Jean and Howard Sergeant edited an anthology of primarily British contemporary poetry about medicine called *Poems From Hospital.*[9] Organized along different lines than my work, this collection includes sections having to do with childbirth, returning home from the hospital, "portraits and appreciations," and other themes. In keeping with contemporary concerns, my anthology has sections dealing with women, social issues, disability, and patients' views of physicians. *Poems From The Medical World,* also edited by Howard Sergeant, spans three centuries of medical poems by Britishers.[10] This collection is more loosely organized than the earlier one. Clearly, my work differs from preceding collections in being an organized anthology of contemporary American poetry with comments that draw upon my medical experiences, literary training, and work as a poet.

I hope that this anthology will help patients, their families and friends, and health care professionals in dealing with the impact of illness on their lives.

THE MEDICAL
ENVIRONMENT
The Hospital Smell Combs My Nostrils

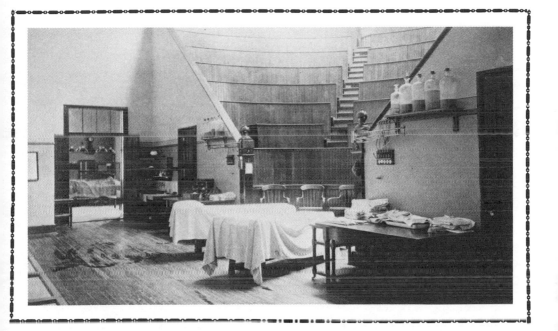

THE MEDICAL ENVIRONMENT
The Hospital Smell Combs My Nostrils

The sliding doors softly glide shut, and now, you are in the hospital. Ahead, the receptionist waits, ready to send you to the correct floor, wing, and room. You are one of the luckier ones, who didn't have to be wheeled in by the paramedics, who didn't need chest compression, oxygen, intravenous drugs, and a siren announcing your condition to the city. Maybe you are a visitor, a rabbi or a priest, an impartial giver of comfort; but the patient might be someone closer to you, a sister or a father or a husband. This may be your first day, or the fortieth. In either case, you know the hospital is a unique place: an island, an oasis, an oracle. Once the border of those deceptively benign glass doors is crossed, a different set of cultural mores comes into effect. Only certain areas can be seen by the layman, such as the waiting rooms, patient rooms, and nursing stations; the procedure rooms, where sterility is essential, where bodies must be invaded in order to heal them, are off-limits. The craft of medicine is not for the squeamish, and certainly not for the relatives of patients undergoing procedures. Exceptions are rare, as in the process of birth, when few complications are expected, and the result is bountiful, usually.

The place has a language of its own also, and the layman must have an interpreter. This may lend an air of mystery or even secrecy, but the hospital cannot function without certain linguistic peculiarities. Phrases such as *IV Push, No Code,* and *Stat Nitro* are integral to rapid and smooth communication. Sometimes this can be quite unnerving to the patient, who must place complete trust in the hospital personnel when there is no time for explanations. (This language barrier can also be a source of some humorous mix-ups. Once an elderly patient, quite concerned about the possibility of Alzheimer's Dementia, asked whether she had *Oldtimer's Disease.)*

To medical personnel, the medical environment rapidly becomes familiar and appears commonplace. As a senior medical student, I was surprised to realize how quickly I had settled into the routine of histories and physicals, intravenous placements, spinal taps, x-rays, and a variety of other procedures and tests. To the layman, however, and especially the patient, the setting of a hospital or clinic hardly seems benign.

If the patient has been abruptly removed to unfamiliar surroundings, he or she may experience disorientation, or perhaps even disbelief at the mere fact of being ill, seriously or otherwise. Patients in Intensive Care Units—exposed to incessant activity and various noises from respirators, intravenous pumps—are often sleep-deprived, and can develop "ICU Psychosis." The majority have to be restrained from pulling out the intubation tube or urinary catheter; reasoning with them appears to be futile. Then there are the *deniers*. Recently, I had to deal with a young man who refused to believe he had suffered a heart attack, and persisted in his "Type-A" behavior by demanding to be discharged because he had to give a lecture at a prestigious university!

The journey through the hospital usually begins at the emergency room. To a layman observing an *Emergency Ward* in Leonard Nathan's poem, the vulnerability of the human body seems astonishing. This catalog poem reads like a literary pathology lecture on trauma, filled with "puncture or slash or scrape or burn."

Medical problems in a doctor's office are often not serious, but may lead to a hospital admission. Patients seem to have an unspoken camaraderie most of the time, but I have seen reactions ranging from sympathy to frank hostility. *At The Doctor's,* the speaker in Robert Watson's poem feels a mixture of pity and repulsion towards a couple and their children. They had "abandoned amenities of attire, diet, soap," and made the other patients "invisible and well" by comparison. Such obvious medical problems in others can make us uncomfortably aware of our own vulnerability. For instance, "The doctor's walls are postered benignly with dangers" in the *Waiting Room* by Richard Blessing. Routine tests are often performed in an office practice. Ted Kooser deals with a fairly benign procedure which can provoke some anxiety. *The Urine Specimen* creates an austere, almost religious mood through careful choice of words and phrases such as "last small chamber" and "chalice," suggesting that a urine test is similar to an oracle, with its attendant rituals. This juxtaposition in itself creates an ironic effect, which peaks in the wickedly humorous conclusion.

Tests, whether academic or medical, have acquired negative connotations: anxiety, difficulty, pain, failure. In medicine, the inverted logic of tests causes a "positive" result to be bad (a disease is diagnosed), and a "negative" one to be good. But it is better to have a "false positive" than a "false negative" since the latter means that the diagnosis was missed! Medical tests may involve some discomfort, such as multiple blood collections, enemas, or fasting. The first thing an elderly lady once told me when I introduced myself as a consultant was "I'm not having any more x-rays"! She still remembered, vividly, her last GI series.

Stress associated with being in a medical setting can affect results of commonplace measurements such as blood pressure. Laboratory tests can also be altered. It may startle some, as it did me, to learn that children can actually go into a toxic diabetic state during temper tantrums, almost as if the acidosis could be willed. The patient in Sandra Gilbert's *Blood Pressure* may indeed be anxious primarily because of his surroundings. "The white-sleeved nurse" is impersonal, and her actions are precise, abrupt, quick: she "steps back, listens, / whistles." On being admitted to a hospital for diagnostic testing, the patient may feel divorced from the body. We see this process in *How I Became Fiction* by Joyce Carol Oates, who writes, "Somewhere, a stranger's fate is being prepared, / to be typed out onto a form." She is afraid of "drifting into fiction," like the old wheel-chaired men. Mona Van Duyn describes the interactions between patients while *In the Hospital for Tests*. Sympathy can change to anger once the patient is "all checked out" and the bond of sickness is broken. Instead of being congratulated, the healthy patient is made to feel ashamed by "staring eyes and their reproaches."

Patients try to comprehend their environment in different ways, through intellectualization or withdrawal or hostility, to name just a few responses. A very intelligent, middle-aged man dying of cancer expected me to know all his lab results on rounds, especially the calcium level, which was related to his nausea and vomiting. Not unexpectedly, his symptoms seemed to wax and wane with the degree of hypercalcemia *reported* to him every day. Another patient, when told that his lungs had crackles, replied that they were only made for so many miles, and asked me if we replaced worn-out carburetors. (He was an auto mechanic.) In *The Operation* by W. D. Snodgrass, the patient makes a careful catalog of medical equipment, including the antiseptic solution's brand name, "Zephiran." Although he is "not frightened," or ashamed, he still appears vulnerable in "delicate sandals" and "thin, loose, light, white garments."

The medical environment is also perceived in a variety of ways by family and friends of the patient. The speaker in Janet Reno's poem *Coma* focuses on how a patient in coma is "aware" of a constant part of the hospital environment—the nursing staff. Nurses, the backbone of the hospital, are nearly always present at the bedside of a patient in the Intensive Care Unit, taking care of intricate equipment, relieving the basic needs of unconscious patients, making notes in charts, and notifying physicians of changes in the patient's status. By repeating the word "shadows" to describe the nurses as perceived by the patient, Reno conveys the notion of a sub-human nervous system insensitive to colors and three-dimensionality. The strategy of this poem is simple, yet highly effective: metaphors which describe the patient's perceptions are followed by an entreaty to "come home."

Although the medical problem appears less serious in Norman MacCaig's poem *Visiting Hour,* his attitude is more pessimistic. In some ways, it is more indicative of how the family and friends of patients may respond to an alien setting where they are disoriented, feel out of place, and may have to confront their mortality. The relative has visited often enough to recognize "the hospital smell," which is, as indicated by the definite article, distinct. (I know of a patient who, after receiving chemotherapy, associated its side-effect of vomiting with "the hospital smell," and invariably became nauseous on returning to the hospital for follow-up visits.) MacCaig perceptively describes her room as a "white cave of forgetfulness," implying a primitive and disoriented state.

And later, when he fully realizes her isolation, there is a confusion of the senses: synesthesia in "the distance of pain."

The public usually associates physicians and other medical personnel with the color *white,* which is an important motif in the poems included in this section. It has obvious associations of purity and sterility; fluorescent lights, uniforms, linen, nurses' notes and other paperwork cover the patient in a white blanket. The patient in *Visiting Hour* is dwelling in a "white cave"; the mind's landscape is "the white of this scene" in *Coma.* Paul Dilsaver takes this idea to a high-pitched extreme in *Corwin Psychiatric Ward, 1972* as he builds up a network of connotations around colors. Setting the poem's tone with a synesthetic line, he writes that "the room reeks of whiteness." The intensity parallels the almost painful sensitivity to light after the pupils are dilated for an eye exam; it is invasive and threatens to empty or "drain the mind"; perhaps he is thinking of electroshock, a white current. The mind, devoid of color both externally and internally, reacts with the suicidal desire to create color from within, from the body's blood-vessels, and "spawns an unmistakable / lust for red."

In a similar manner, we read in Linda Pastan's *Notes from the Delivery Room* that "pain winces / off the walls / like too bright light." Sensory pain is transformed into visual pain, due to the bright fluorescent lights of the delivery room. The patient may feel she is already exposed to all the medical personnel, strapped down under a spotlight. Acutely aware of her surroundings, she feels the "audience" is growing "restive." There is an underlying fear on both sides that the delivery is not proceeding according to schedule, and the possibility of death, even during the event of birth, surfaces: "how much easier it would be later, / returning them to earth."

Behind any medical procedure there lurks a complication which the patient is, or ought to be, aware of. But of all the people I have seen in the medical setting, those about to have x-rays are the most uneasy group; clad in hospital gowns, quiet, cheerless, they are often waiting for the penetrating beams to pinpoint a diagnosis. (Radioactivity, associated with an increased risk of cancer, is often used to *treat* certain cancers that are "radiosensitive"; in other instances, it is essential to a diagnosis; medicine is a logical, but often paradoxical art.) Some patients conjure up all sorts of images about the procedure, especially if a CAT scan or a radiolabeled material is used for the purpose of obtaining contrast. Other patients take them in stride. After carefully examining one of my patients, I said he would probably need an Indium scan. He replied, "Why not? I've already had my *Indian* scan. You've poked and prodded just about every part of me"! A number of poets have written about having x-rays, and illustrate how differently patients can react. Randall Jarrell's wry tone balances anxiety with humor, satirizing the medical establishment, but Howard Moss is serious, filled with anxiety and pessimism. While in *The X-ray Waiting Room in the Hospital*, Jarrell realizes he must look comical in his "big shoes and wrinkled socks / And one of the light blue much-laundered smocks." Rhymes add to the comic effect, especially the double, feminine rhymes: *rotates me, elates me, congratulates me*. But he also honestly admits that "this routine / Misery has made us into cases," pointing to the unfortunate tendency, even today, to describe patients as "the gall bladder," or "the MI."

Jarrell refers to the self-sufficient universe of the hospital, but Moss sets up an early contrast between the benign external world and the dangerous internal one: "The mirror sees you walking towards its knives." There is no place for sympathy, and it is best to "shun / The pain of others" to avoid exposing one's own fears. In the last two stanzas, the speaker imagines his death in an oblique and syntactically complex manner, as if to avoid direct confrontation with the subject. David Wagoner has written a whimsical poem titled *On Seeing an X-ray of my Head*, which he describes as a "madcap, catch-all rattlepot." But the film must have been taken for a reason, which leads to thoughts of mortality: "air, dust, and water as themselves at last." To a mother in Celia Gilbert's poem *X-ray,* the daughter's skull is "a cup: / something is drinking her life up." Clearly, a serious medical problem is being investigated, and the mother views the x-ray as a symbol for that condition. *At Nuclear Medicine*, the patient in the waiting room wonders "if they schedule these elderly together— / an exclusive social club." But this conviviality is soon interrupted by "the ritual" where the scanner, "the eye of a god," stares down at the patient.

During the hospital stay, the foremost thought in the minds of most patients seems to be, "When can I go home"? Some people, after being wheeled through the Intensive Care Unit, the cardiac monitor wards, and finally, the general medical floor, have a right to ask that question. Less fortunate ones may never leave the ICU, and stumble along from complication to complication until, as some put it, the "celestial discharge." Thankfully, for most, the outer world is waiting to be re-discovered. With nothing to do all day except watch soap operas and game shows, patients are prone to become impatient. Time slows down to the rate of the fluid dripping through the intravenous line. The poet Albert Goldbarth writes that "Edgewater Hospital / keeps a different time," governed by the rhythms of "looking / ahead to another visit." That time frame keeps the visitor in "another dimension," but for the patient, "Pain is always outside of time"; the latter is much worse, a temporal limbo. The patient acknowledges this condition by saying "it's half past / cardiac, and stuck." In Sandra Gilbert's poem, *Metastasis*, the passage of time is nearing its conclusion, and the patient accepts this fact by coming to the hospice, "the cancer hotel." Her timeframe has been truncated, and she can look into the future only until "tomorrow [when] she'll carry herself in a plastic bag, / sanitary, disposable, to the recreation room." In addition to suggesting a disposable diaper, a plastic bag could also be used to transport the patient to a morgue. Asking *A Question of Memory*, Donald Finkel shows how an elderly patient with dementia is trapped in the present: "Forgetting backward / she disremembers this morning." Emphasizing her confinement, the poet writes about "the web of her life" and compares her walker to "a portable cage."

What happens when the patient escapes from time's anesthesia? In their poems, *We shall all be born again but we shall not all be saved*, and *Having Been Asked 'What is a Man'? I Answer*, William Matthews and Philip Levine offer contrasting views of convalescence. The latter's poem is a complaint, but manages to arrive at a joyful self-affirmation. The patient is frustrated because it "takes a specialist to tell you how / you look in this place, and none will." When he wakens, "the old man / next to [him] is gone, and the room / is going dark," events which raise the spectre of death. But the peonies brought by his son whisper encouragement: 'this is the place where souls are made.' A burst of vitality in the patient is reflected in the momentum of the long final sentence, which begins with the resolution to "read Keats again." In Matthews' poem, he also feels restricted and needs to be "untethered" from machines. A linguistic observation about the passive role of a patient sets a tone of wry humor: "It would be life as a direct object / for a while." He is probably referring to the passive acceptance of what medical personnel call a *battery* (a word full of implication) of tests and procedures. Like Levine, he appreciates man's potentially active role in the "vale of soul-making." But in contrast to Levine, who affirms "I have no beginning, no middle, no end," he accepts his mortality in a witty paradox, knowing he can leave the hospital "safe to die some other day." Jean Valentine's *Prayer in Fever* is yet another response to illness, an escape through fantasy. In the hospital, she imagines a picnic "on a green edge of the Hudson, / under a cloud of stars." But the earth is deceptively tranquil; it could be an oasis or a grave, "holding us [with] huge curved mosaic hands."

Those who have never been seriously ill simply cannot appreciate the complexities and eccentricities of the medical environment. Thomas Lux gives us a *Hospital View* from just such an outsider. He focuses on the Intensive Care Unit and its "greenly lit / lucidity." With a detached compassion for these patients with tenuous existences, he hopes that their "lives be again and again / limned by dawn." W. S. Merwin presents a series of images garnered after having lived near *St. Vincent's* hospital for some years. We sense a melange of emotions about the institution: acceptance of the routine sirens which the speaker "long / ago . . . learned not to hear"; curiosity about windows that "burn all night"; admiration on seeing the "building drift moonlit through geraniums." Yet, after all his sensitively detailed observation, we are left with speculation, the building remains enigmatic.

Even to the initiate, the hospital is mysterious. While I typed these words, the light in a room on the sixth floor, the cancer ward, went off, leaving a streetlight's fluorescent glare. Was it someone I knew? From my window, I could not tell. Maybe the patient, relaxed after a scheduled dose of morphine, floated down into sleep like a snowflake; maybe the body simply held its breath, refusing to give any more mouth-to-mouth resuscitation to this world, and sank into the depths of white linen. Tomorrow morning, I might find out what happened. But tonight, my pager is off.

EMERGENCY WARD

What is it and how deep? The nurse must know:
Puncture or slash or scrape or burn? There, there,
You bearers of proud flesh in single file
From the boy who holds his hand out, laying bare
The thin nakedness of bone to, O,
The stretcher case that's lain there all this while
But does not seem to care.

What in God's name was it? Fire, dog, car
That went suddenly crazy, or a power saw
That turned on its master? And did these knuckles split
Against that dumb and crooked-hanging jaw?
So nails and glass and hearts were pushed too far,
But what's a distant cause to those who sit
Nursing their new-found flaw?

Sheeted in full-length calm, the stretcher case
Stares at the ceiling while his wife stands by
Holding his one good hand. Stuck in the clock,
Time slows to ticks of pain; a child's keen cry
Ends nothing, but begins another space
Of drifting in the pale deep sea of shock
Under a long white sky.

The boy, held in by bandage, finally goes;
The stretcher case is wheeled far down the hall;
The jaw is wired so hope can still be spoken;
Yet others fill the place; the random call
Of names goes on, no end in sight. God knows
How many ways His image can be broken
And how it hurts to fall!

                                        —*Leonard Nathan*

AT THE DOCTOR'S

Everyone could tell they had given up,
Abandoned amenities of attire, diet, soap;
She lean, face mean with fear or pain;
He obese, socks unmated, belches at the magazine
In which he looks and does not turn a page.
She would cry off and on.
They are themselves, nothing else, too far gone
To soothe our minds with any likeness
To familiar bird, beast, or fish.

　　　　An outrage:

They strung a spell over the doctor's office.
These wretches made us invisible and well,
Pick pocketed our each groomed ill.
They were so cruelly themselves, foreign and other.
Untended, their children bang and rain
Up and down the corridor like a hurricane.
They ruled the waiting room, this crude, poor pair
And they had renounced all that to us is dear.

　　　　　　　　　　—Robert Watson

WAITING ROOM

The three of us wait in the doctor's office. Father
is so long married he has forgotten which of them hurts.
I am the middle-aged stranger who drives them now,
who reminds them this summer how things go.

                           My son, eleven,
waits in the car. Wherever he lives, he misses someone.

The doctor's walls are postered benignly with dangers.
I check my warts, my moles, find they stand out, changeless
on a background of small change. Lumps in the throat,
thickenings at the waist, kill me today so slowly I can smile,
plan a poem, buy furniture or remarry, plant a tree.
Even my pulse is heartening.

                   That's wrong, says Father,
first thing today, like a man waking from a strong dream.
I feel his sentence in my deepest veins, the dissolution,
rankness, and decay, the thoughts wordless as familiar pain.

What is? says Mother, but he's far away, talking I think
to his garden once again, the ripe and ripening beans
strung along his crooked poles, and he soothes us all
with hushing sounds.

                        —Richard Blessing

THE URINE SPECIMEN

In the clinic, a sun-bleached shell of stone
on the shore of the city, you enter
the last small chamber, a little closet
chastened with pearl, cool, white, and glistening,
and over the chilly well of the toilet
you trickle your precious sum in a cup.
It's as simple as that. But the heat
of this gold your body's melted and poured out
into a form begins to enthrall you,
warming your hand with your flesh's fevers
in a terrible way. It's like holding
an organ—spleen or fatty pancreas,
a lobe from your foamy brain still steaming
with worry. You know that just outside
a nurse is waiting to cool it into a gel
and slice it onto a microscope slide
for the doctor, who in it will read your future,
wringing his hands. You lift the chalice and toast
the long life of your friend there in the mirror,
who wanly smiles, but does not drink to you.

—Ted Kooser

BLOOD PRESSURE

The white-sleeved woman wraps a rubber
sleeve around your arm, steps back, listens,
whistles.

        How it pounds in you, how it
urges through you, how it asserts
its power like a tide of electrons

flashing through your veins, shocking your fingertips,
exhausting the iron gates of your heart.
Alive, alive, always alive, it hisses,

crackling like the lightning snake that splits
the sky at evening, *alive,* a black rain
lashing the hollows of your body,

alive, alive.
        You sit quietly on the cold table,
the good boy grown up into

the good man. You say
you want nothing, you'll diet, you
won't complain. Anyway, you say,

you dream of January weather,
hushed and white, the cries of light
silenced by a shield of ice.

Behind your eyes, something
like a serpent moves, an acid tongue
flicking at your cheekbones, something

voracious, whipping your whole body
hard: you're sad, you flush a
dangerous pink, you tell her

you can't understand the fierce rain
inside you, you've always hated that awful
crackling in your veins.

                      —*Sandra Gilbert*

HOW I BECAME FICTION

In the hospital I take care to walk
as if no destination threatened.
I drift with the cool metallic odors,
the creak of carts, the gala energy
of nurses arriving for duty
at eight a.m.

A yeast has arisen in my body.
Somewhere, a stranger's fate is being prepared,
to be typed out onto a form.

My body, see it is eager to please! and innocent
of its own yeast, its poisons and ungirlish discords!
Its product is being carried here
in a brown drugstore jar, prepared
for strangers who will not show offense.
They will charge fourteen dollars.
They will type up forms.

Death will not be simple, say the wheel-chaired
men, khaki-colored with the inertia of the wise.
They are mild beasts now, eyeing me.
Don't stare at me, I am not fiction!
Not your fiction!
My body is a girl's grown-up body, tugging
at their pinpoint eyes. My clothes are miserable
with the strain of possessing
this body so early in the day.

The men's eyes are fixed to me. But no darkness
would recover them, no alley make them male again—
Don't look at me, I am not fiction—
They were men once
but there is no proof of it now.
Unreal now, they brood over old skirmishes.

Like them I am drifting into fiction.
Like them I will be injected with heat and ice.
This morning, sweating, I await my fate
typed out onto a green form.
What further fiction is being imagined? What fee?

—Joyce Carol Oates

IN THE HOSPITAL FOR TESTS

My mother's friend cooked for the drunk-and-disorderlies,
and so, when I was ten, I peeked at a cell,
and that's what I'd swear this room came out of—the county jail.
But here in a sweat lies a strange collection of qualities,
with me inside it, or maybe only somewhere near it,
while all the nonsense of life turns serious again—
bowel movements, chickenpox, the date of one's first menstru-
    ation,
the number of pillows one sleeps on, postnasal drip—
"It has very high arches," I hear the resident note.
He has worked his way down over its ridges and jerks,
its strings and moistures, coursings, lumps and networks,
to the crinkled and slightly ticklish soles of its feet.
"Don't worry, if there's anything going on here," the interne
    says,
"we'll find it. I myself have lots of ideas."

Across the room, over a jungle of plants,
blooming, drooping, withering, withered and dead,
a real face watches, freckled and flat blue eyed.
Sometimes her husband visits, a man of plaid shirts
and apologetic smiles, and sometimes three red-head
little girls in stairsteps, too scared to talk out loud.

In twenty-four hours, the hefty nurse, all smiles,
carries out my urine on her hip like a jug of cider,
a happy harvest scene. My room-mate, later,
gets on a stretcher, clutching her stomach, and it wheels
her off down the halls for a catheter in her heart.
There's one chance in five hundred she'll die in the test. She'd like
to live for two more years for the children's sake.
Her husband waits in the room. He sweats. We both sweat.

She was only fifteen when they married, he says, but she told him
she was past eighteen and he didn't find out for years.
She's wheeled back, after a feverish two hours,
with black crochet on her arm. She was conscious all the time,
and could feel whatever it was, the little black box, go
through her veins to the left of the chest from the right elbow.

The leukemia across the hall, the throat cancer a few doors down,
the leaky valve who has to sleep on eight pillows—
these sit on our beds and talk of the soggy noodles
they gave us for lunch, and the heat, and how long, how soon.
The room stinks of my urine and our greed.
To live, to live at all costs, that's what we want.
We never knew it before, but now we hunt
down the healthy nurses with our eyes. We gobble our food.
Intruders come from outside during visiting hours
and chatter about silly things, no longer our affairs.

"A little more blood, I'm on the trail." He'll go far,
my interne. My room-mate gets on the stretcher again;
she comes back almost dead, but they give her oxygen.
She whistles for breath, her face is swollen and sore
and dark. She spits up white rubber. The bronchoscope,
that's what it was this time, and more tests to come.
She wishes her husband had been here after this one.
They were going to do the other lung too, but they had to stop.

In the middle of the night her bed blazes white in the darkness.
Three red-headed daughters dangle from her lightcord.
The nurse holds a cup to her lips. It is absurd,
she is swallowing my poems. The air knots like a fist,
or a heart, the room presses in like a lung. It is empty
of every detail but her life. It is bright and deathly.

"You can go home this afternoon. You're all checked out."
My doctor is grinning over the obscene news.
My room-mate sits up and listens. "God only knows
what causes these things, but you've nothing to worry about."
In shame I pack my bags and make my call.
She reads a magazine while I wait for my husband.
She doesn't speak, she is no longer my friend.
We say goodbye to each other. I hope she does well.
In shame I walk past the staring eyes and their reproaches
all down the hall. I walk out on my high arches.

—Mona Van Duyn

THE OPERATION

From stainless steel basins of water
They brought warm cloths and they washed me,
From spun aluminum bowls, cold Zephiran sponges, fuming;
Gripped in the dead yellow glove, a bright straight razor
Inched on my stomach, down my groin,
Paring the brown hair off. They left me
White as a child, not frightened. I was not
Ashamed. They clothed me, then,
In the thin, loose, light, white garments,
The delicate sandals of poor Pierrot,
A schoolgirl first offering her sacrament.

I was drifting, inexorably, on toward sleep.
In skullcaps, masked, in blue-green gowns, attendants
Towed my cart, afloat in its white cloths,
The body with its tributary poisons borne
Down corridors of the diseased, thronging:
The scrofulous faces, contagious grim boys,
The huddled families, weeping, a staring woman
Arched to her gnarled stick,—a child was somewhere
Screaming, screaming—then, blind silence, the elevator rising
To the arena, humming, vast with lights; blank hero,
Shackled and spellbound, to enact my deed.

Into flowers, into women, I have awakened.
Too weak to think of strength, I have thought all day,
Or dozed among standing friends. I lie in night, now,
A small mound under linen like the drifted snow.
Only by nurses visited, in radiance saying, Rest.
Opposite, ranked office windows glare; headlamps, below,
Trace out our highways; their cargoes under dark tarpaulins,
Trucks climb, thundering, and sirens may
Wail for the fugitive. It is very still. In my brandy bowl
Of sweet peas at the window, the crystal world
Is inverted, slow, and gay.

—*W.D. Snodgrass*

COMA

Through closed lids you blur
the nurses into shadows.
They speak the sound of pebbles
moved in rain.
You blur the nurses into palest shadows.
Their voices move a thousand fallen leaves.
The nurses blur into shadows,
their voices are the soft collapse of snow.
In the white of this scene
your thoughts feather out, shaking,
or pinch the snow black with their tracks.

Please—from the wisdom of travel
call your animal memory back.
He has squeezed his palms on cobbles
to climb up underground walls.
But when he touches your face,
he is softer than flesh on your bones.
Come home.

—*Janet Reno*

VISITING HOUR

The hospital smell
combs my nostrils
as they go bobbing along
green and yellow corridors.

What seems a corpse
is trundled into a lift and vanishes
heavenward.

I will not feel, I will not
feel, until
I have to.

Nurses walk lightly, swiftly,
here and up and down and there,
their slender waists miraculously
carrying their burden
of so much pain, so
many deaths, their eyes
still clear after
so many farewells.

Ward 7. She lies
in a white cave of forgetfulness.
A withered hand
trembles on its stalk. Eyes move
behind eyelids too heavy
to raise. Into an arm wasted
of colour a glass fang is fixed,
not guzzling but giving.

And between her and me
distance shrinks till there is none left
but the distance of pain that neither she nor I
can cross.

She smiles a little at this
black figure in her white cave
who clumsily rises
in the round swimming waves of a bell
and dizzily goes off, leaving behind only
books that will not be read
and fruitless fruits.

—Norman MacCaig

CORWIN PSYCHIATRIC WARD, 1972

Despite the green drapes,
tan walls,
and brown tile,
the room reeks of whiteness.

And the staff,
dressed in street clothes
as part of the hospital's
"new policy,"
radiates so whitely
that you crave
a pair of those plastic shades
the eye doctor gives
after dilating pupils.

White is the word
of this world,
and white is how
they'll drain your mind
if they can.

So you
lie in your white room
burning eyes
on white ceiling,
listening to
white vibrations,
spine freezing
on white sheets,
while all the time
your hue-thirsty mind,
dwelling on your
nurse-possessed razor
and itchy wrist,
spawns an unmistakable
lust for red.

—Paul Dilsaver

NOTES FROM THE DELIVERY ROOM

Strapped down,
victim in an old comic book,
I have been here before,
this place where pain winces
off the walls
like too bright light.
Bear down a doctor says,
foreman to sweating laborer,
but this work, this forcing
of one life from another
is something that I signed for
at a moment when I would have signed anything.
Babies should grow in fields;
common as beets or turnips
they should be picked and held
root end up, soil spilling
from between their toes—
and how much easier it would be later,
returning them to earth.
Bear up . . . bear down . . . the audience
grows restive, and I'm a new magician
who can't produce the rabbit
from my swollen hat.
She's crowning, someone says,
but there is no one royal here,
just me, quite barefoot,
greeting my barefoot child.

—Linda Pastan

THE X—RAY WAITING ROOM IN THE HOSPITAL

I am dressed in my big shoes and wrinkled socks
And one of the light blue, much-laundered smocks
The men and women of this country wear.
All of us miss our own underwear
And the old days. These new, plain, mean
Days of pain and care, this routine
Misery has made us into cases, the one case
The one doctor cures forever . . . The face
The patients have in common hopes without hope
For something outside the machine—its wife,
Its husband—to burst in and hand it life;
But when the door opens, it's another smock.
It looks at us, we look at it. Our little flock
Of blue-smocked sufferers, in naked equality,
Longs for each nurse and doctor who goes by
Well and dressed, to make friends with, single out the I
That used to be, but we are indistinguishable.
It is better to lie upon a table,
A dye in my spine. The roentgenologist
Introduces me to a kind man, a specialist
In spines like mine: the lights go out, he rotates me.
My myelogram is negative. This elates me.
The good-humored specialist congratulates me,
And I take off my smock in joy, put on
My own pajamas, my own dressing gown,
And ride back to my own room, 601.

—*Randall Jarrell*

IN THE X-RAY ROOM

Beneath a canopy for which the whole city
Seems, this morning, to be painting stripes,
You splash past a glass door while your taxi
Shifts and is off to a thousand other lives;
In the sudden hush of the jaded lobby,
The mirror sees you walking toward its knives.

Ring and Enter. Entering the waiting
Room, doom says that it's polite, that one
Must face the worst alone in unabating
Silence. The news becomes important. Shun
The pain of others, or in contemplating
Theirs the fear you bare will be your own.

The market falls and rises while a ticker
Tape raps out the bedlam of your wits
In a room as brainy as a shrewd, old broker
Inside whose head a stock quotation sits.
Deserted in a cubicle, you wait and stare
At a blank wall, and smoke two cigarettes.

Invisible grower, gardener of alarms,
You lie on a turning table cold as snow.
Down press the camera's praying-mantis arms,
Avid to embrace your negative below;
Your inner organs light their secret farms
Not even lovers come close enough to know.

Deep in the inner landscape of yourself,
You search for contours that the camera plots;
Each mountain is as dangerous as each gulf.
And now you are rising with the speed of jets
To shatter through black glasswork at the top,
As someone says, "You can get up. Get up."

And if that day should dawn, the gradient blue
Be unexceptionable, the cliché birds
Fly up again to where they always flew,
And all the voices sing of large accords,
Whose lone dissenter will be only you,
What justice will there be in just rewards

That day, if running for your life, you run
Into the X-ray of the broken straws
Of all your veins, and pain shoots off its gun
For the last time, and the target knows it knows,
When all the miraculous drugs are gone,
The precious weight of everything that goes?

—Howard Moss

ON SEEING AN X-RAY OF MY HEAD

Now face to face, hard head, old nodder and shaker,
While we still have ears,
Accept my congratulations: you survived
My headlong blunders
As, night by night, my knuckles beat at your brow
More often than at doors,
Yet you were pampered, waved from the end of your stick
Like a bird in feathers,
Wrapped in towels, whistled and night-capped,
And pressed into pillows.
I see by this, the outline of our concern,
What you will lose
Before too long: the shadowy half of chin
And prodding nose,
Thatchwork of hair, loose tongue, and parting lips,
My look as blank as yours,
And yet, my madcap, catch-all rattlepot,
Nothing but haze
Shows on this picture what we had in mind,
The crannied cauliflower
Ready to boil away at a moment's notice
In a fit of vapors
And leave us holding the bag. Oh my brainpan,
When we start our separate ways
With opaque, immortal fillings clenched in our teeth
Like a bunch of keys,
And when your dome goes rolling into a ditch
And, slack in the jaws,
Stops at a hazard, some unplayable lie,
Accept at your ease
Directly what was yours at one remove:
Light through your eyes,
Air, dust, and water as themselves at last. Keep smiling.
Consider the source.
Go back to the start, old lime-pit, remembering flesh and skin,
Your bloody forebears.

—David Wagoner

X-RAY

the bones gleam
out of the dark.
like the ghost of a fern
in stone here
are spine and ribs.

the skull
of my daughter is
a cup:
        something is drinking her life up.
there are islands shadowed
on her brain
        white tides are washing
                    washing them out.

                        —Celia Gilbert

AT NUCLEAR MEDICINE

Sanctum
I am led through heavy doors.
Across the room, a woman in a hospital gown
sits high on a table, white hair radiating
from her head in a baroque halo.
She stares into space, her feet jerking
rhythmically, and will not look at me.
Placed in a curtained cubicle, I wait.

Waiting Room
They have met here before: five old women
and a man who arrives feebly
on the arm of his daughter. One wears accumulating
baldness with a yellow scarf; one smokes incessantly;
one sits apart—an Indian woman in purple,
face stoic but eyes alert. They are joking,
asking after common things—cats and the weather—
their church-toned voices separate
from reception efficiency of typewriters, personnel.

I wait for a diagnostic scan and wonder
if they schedule these elderly together—
an exclusive social club.
A nurse comes in, waits
for a pause in conversation. Then,
her hand on a shoulder like a blessing,
says, "your turn," lightly
as a hairdresser might. There is silence
until they have gone.

I witness for the ritual
I have intruded upon—the low voices,
whirs and clicks removed from me
by design of a grey-striped curtain.
Later, I am brought in my gown
by attendants in baby-blue lead aprons
to the center of the room. There,
mounted in massive stainless steel,
the eye of a god.

—Dixie Partridge

EDGEWATER HOSPITAL

keeps a different time. Across the street, Lake Michigan folds
and unfolds light. It's dawn. It doesn't stop. The light,
the water, meet at a line we know slips into another dimension:
call it forever. They call it that in poems. But in
the linen closets of Edgewater, no matter how intense
and satiated the gift flowers set in window sun, or how
resolutely well-meaning the orderly's smile, something
unfolds, a shadow kept in a deepest crease, and it's

inevitable: we walk from the ward to the radiant world
outside with a part of us dimmed by the visit, the looking
ahead to another visit: we're darkness's octaroons.
Pain is always outside of time. I know two hands across
a face is a clock; and so my father says it's half past
cardiac, and stuck. The doctors have books that call some
futures days. It all depends. The glucose is a note
in a bottle and so it cries for rescue. Writing easy

turns of language on a beach bench is a way of making morning
afternoon. The lake's awaiting. For miles the great
lake drums its fingers—dependable
wash and beat. Like what they call in poems a heart,
they use that simile over and over again, as if the over
and over were reason enough. I think so. A heart.

—*Albert Goldbarth*

METASTASIS

At the cancer hotel, a lobby full of artificial plants,
leaves in the sane green shapes of health,
historical leaves mimicking the past—
and tubes blooming from groins, noses , armpits,
and starved faces in the dayroom
on every floor, thin images
reflecting the clean sheen of the ceiling . . . .

"Just lie down, honey." The nurse's aide,
indifferent as a bellboy, sells the new patient
on a quiet corner. This is it. The last resort.
"Here's your water. Here's your buzzer."
The patient bobs, a courteous guest,
patient, never shows displeasure.
Looking east, over the river, her cousin

watches jets spurt toward Florida, California:
"Kennedy? LaGuardia?" she wonders,
but the patient never turns, never answers.
Unpacking herself like a suitcase,
she sorts, plans, rearranges.
Here's the nightgown, there's the bathrobe.
When are the meals? Where's the soap?

Tomorrow she'll carry herself in a plastic bag,
sanitary, disposable, to the recreation room
at the end of the hall. The Magnavox
will smile, a tour director,
and she'll gaze past sealed panes
at the roof of the children's wing
where roots of September flowers—"autumn color"—

writhe in tubs, trying to get out,
and pigeons settle like insect swarms
among the swings and the desk chairs,
calm as travelers pretending not to see
the musty mugs, the infected
piazzas, the unsavory
kitchens of disease.

—Sandra Gilbert

A QUESTION OF MEMORY

Every morning
the doctor with rimless glances
asks her for the date.

Forgetting backward
she disremembers this morning,
then yesterday,

reels in the years,
undoing the web of her life from the outside in.
Last winter hisses behind her brow, erased.

Caught in her mouth, a memory stirs,
the husk of an enormous moth
that crumbles at the touch.

Voracious, inconsolable, she wolfs it down,
croaks at the doctor, *I know your game!*
 and scowls at the wall.

Under her door she can see the days
pass in the corridor like empty wheelchairs.
An inmate shuffles past,

dragging his walker like a portable cage.

                                        —*Donald Finkel*

HAVING BEEN ASKED "WHAT IS A MAN?" I ANSWER

after Keats

My oldest son comes to visit me
in the hospital. He brings giant
peonies and the nurse puts them
in a glass vase, and they sag quietly
on the windowsill where they
seem afraid to gaze out at the city
smoking beneath. He asks when I
will be coming home. I don't know.
He sees there are wires running
from me to a television set on which
my heartbeat is the Sunday Spectacular.
How do I look? I say. He studies
the screen and says, I don't know.
It takes a specialist to tell you how
you look in this place, and none will.
I must have slept, and when I waken
I am alone, and the old man
next to me is gone and the room
is going dark. This is the Sunday
that will fill the unspoken promise
of all those vanished Sundays
when a shadow on the edge of sight
grew near, enormous, hesitated, and left,
and I sighed with weariness knowing
one more week was here to live.
At last a time and a place to die are
given me, and even a small reason.
The flowers have turned now that
the windows have gone dark, and I
see their pale faces in the soft mirror
of the glass. No, they aren't crying,
for this is not the vale of tears.
They are quietly laughing as flowers
always do in the company of men.
"Because this is the place where souls
are made," their laughter whispers.
I will read Keats again, I will rise

and go into the world, unwired and free,
because I am no longer a movie,
I have no beginning, no middle, no end,
no film score underscoring each act,
no costume department, no expert on color.
I am merely a man dressing in the dark
because that is what a man is—
so many mouthfuls of laughter
and so many more, all there can be
behind the sad brown backs of peonies.

—Philip Levine

WE SHALL ALL BE BORN AGAIN
BUT WE SHALL NOT ALL BE SAVED

"We're going," the paramedics said
(how I burned to be part of that *we*),
"to take you to the hospital."
It would be life as a direct object
for a while. Into the ambulance
they slid me like a loaf of bread.

There would be tests, I understood,
to see why my heart beat in triplets,
and I could see it myself, on TV,
an hour in the afternoon, like a soap
opera. Echo-cardiogram, they
called it. "Narcissus, is there someone

else?" I watched my eager heart
lash and batter for an hour, only
its normal violence, an intern assured
me, but she came back and back
abnormally to see me: "Can I listen
to your heart?" I couldn't trust her.

My green heart on TV looked violent.
This would be an inside job.
Who could break one of those but itself?
It's never been that we *have* bodies:
we *are* bodies. I had to trundle
a kind of aluminum coat-rack

along the hall just to pee, because
of the IV, and I had to eat essence
of junket, and nurses brought me pills
in little paper thimbles. This balm
of obedience and stupor, I thought
while I vomited blood, is all

my docile study. I'd been too sick to take
my own side in a fight, but against whom?
Another day I'd learn the obvious,
that it was me, but that's another story.
In this one I'm untethered from my
machines, my mild, green-faced flock,

and can walk around weakly on my own,
can pack my bags and pills and go out
into Boston safe to die some other day.
"How will this change your life?"
My heart will push me along like a good
rhythm section. I plan to notice everything.

William Matthews

PRAYER IN FEVER

The hospital shuts down to its half-night.

I stand back,
talk in words from some book:
The wall could be the floor.
Everything you look at
is changed by your looking at it

This packed dirt square, these wires . . . somewhere someone must
run for it, black hair, red mouth, burn
strips of flesh on a green edge of the Hudson,
under a cloud of stars, under bridge lights, they must hunch down,
talk to each other, touch each other, the way this thin bright snow
masses, this blind oval pulling

gold   across the ceiling
floating out
off the fold-
back of space

The day does rise. The turning gaze of the river:
So many eyes. So calm.

The gray green curve of earth still
waiting   with us
holding us
huge curved mosaic hands

your hand
—how would you bide so long?

—Jean Valentine

HOSPITAL VIEW

Across an alley, opposite exactly
my window: Intensive Care Unit. At night I sit
in my dark and stare into its greenly lit
lucidity: I can almost read the x-rays hung
on the wall—two bad ghost pears, the lungs . . .
Plasma bottles glister, beep-machines, a blur
of women and men in white frocks.
On starless nights I can read the clock.
I look because it's there. If,
out my window, I could see flax fields
parted like the haircuts of children,
if outside there were wide arenas of air,
if I could look out and up to a long sky
and study a jet's fading headlines . . . But,
Intensive Care is my view.
I never see them wheel anyone in or out.
They're just there, hooked up, in doubt,
trying to come back.   Come back, clear, still shapes;
hang on however, anonymous flesh,
even though you labor with it. I press
my own body back on my own bed, a wish
on my lips that your lives be again and again
limned by dawn.

—Thomas Lux

ST VINCENT'S

Thinking of rain clouds that rose over the city
on the first day of the year

in the same month
I consider that I have lived daily and with
eyes open and ears to hear
these years across from St Vincent's Hospital
above whose roof those clouds rose

its brick by day a French red under
cross facing south
blown-up neo-classic facades the tall
dark openings between columns at
the dawn of history
exploded into many windows
in a mortised face

inside it the ambulances have unloaded
after sirens' howling nearer through traffic on
Seventh Avenue long
ago I learned not to hear them
even when the sirens stop

they turn to back in
few passers-by stay to look
and neither do I

at night two long blue
windows and one short one on the top floor
burn all night
many nights when most of the others are out
on what floor do they have
anything

I have seen the building drift moonlit through geraniums
late at night when trucks were few
moon just past the full
upper windows parts of the sky
as long as I looked
I watched it at Christmas and New Year
early in the morning I have seen the nurses ray out through
arterial streets
in the evening have noticed internes blocks away
on doorsteps one foot in the door

I have come upon the men in gloves taking out
the garbage at all hours
piling up mountains of
plastic bags white strata with green intermingled and
black
I have seen one pile
catch fire and studied the cloud
at the ends of the jets of the hoses
the fire engines as near as that
red beacons and
machine-throb heard by the whole body
I have noticed molded containers stacked outside
a delivery entrance on Twelfth Street
whether meals from a meal factory made up with those
mummified for long journeys by plane
or specimens for laboratory
examination sealed at the prescribed temperatures
either way closed delivery

and approached faces staring from above
crutches or tubular clamps
out for tentative walks
have paused for turtling wheel-chairs
heard visitors talking in wind on each corner
while the lights changed and
hot dogs were handed over at the curb
in the middle of the afternoon
mustard ketchup onions and relish
and police smelling of ether and laundry
were going back

and I have known them all less than the papers of our days
smoke rises from the chimneys do they have an incinerator
what for
how warm do they believe they have to maintain the air
in there
several of the windows appear
to be made of tin
but it may be the light reflected
I have imagined bees coming and going
on those sills though I have never seen them

who was St Vincent

—W.S. Merwin

PATIENTS'
VIEWS OF ILLNESS

The Darkness Within Me Is Growing

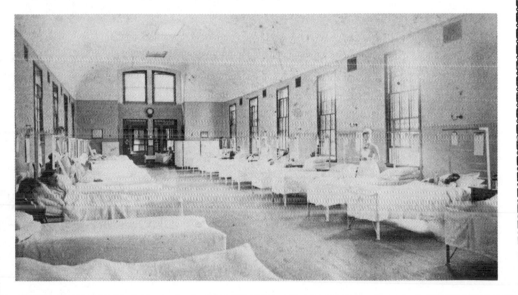

While treating patients on a Spinal Cord Injury unit, I saw a spectrum of emotions ranging from profound depression to incoherent anger, in the same patient. Subtle changes also occur. For instance, in a group of patients with recent paralysis, I found that time appeared to move slowly and be stretched out in the present, the future seemed to be contracted, and the past was remote; in the final analysis, the patient was left in a sort of temporal limbo.

When we are healthy, we rarely think of our bodies at a conscious level. Brendan Galvin is provoked to a meditation on the body because of his *Fear of Gray's Anatomy*. He indulges in mock horror at discovering that he does not fully own himself, but is "Flood's ligaments, the areola of Mamma, & the zonule of Zinn." In spite of his humorous tone, we sense a tear of illness in the resolve to "not open *Gray's Anatomy* again."

The vague fears and uncertainties of being ill are explored in *The Condition* by Marvin Bell, *The Doctor of Starlight* by Philip Levine, and *Nerves* by Howard Moss. These poems deal with the question of identity, each in its own disturbing manner. In Bell's poem, the "darkness within" grows to the point where the patient feels "turned out," as if he were losing himself. While the patient ruminates on his condition as his "thought feeds on it," inexorably "the body is eaten." Levine's surreal poem about the removal of a "perfect little blue star" from a patient may symbolize the necessary loss, or amputation, of a bodily organ. The poet focuses on a different sort of mystery for the layman, that of medical procedures—their rationale and interpretation. On the doctor's table, the patient, "blind / and helpless, thought of all / the men and women who had surrendered," implying that he felt ignorant, completely passive, and even unsure about the benefit of his treatment. The doctor's conversation is unemotional, until he succeeds in extracting the star, and only then does he speak "proudly"; in the meantime he has virtually ignored the patient. The persona of *Nerves* is not afflicted, yet. He imagines all sorts of disasters, triggered by hearing about war in a far away place. He fears the diseases of this industrialized society: cancer, heart disease, catastrophic environmental pollution. There is a vague sense of impending doom, of jittery nerves, and he feels that his "unique fate is grafted/ Onto the general terror," whether it be a "tumor" or a "sudden pain" in his chest.

Jim Hall's *Tennis Elbow* may seem like a minor problem; he realizes the repetitive nature of the game "has worn thin / the cartilage, / has ground it down." But "every exquisite triumph" makes up for the pain, and this condition appears to take on a larger meaning. John Ciardi describes a more serious problem, also in a deft manner. In spite of a whimsical opening—"I have nothing more to say to my left arm"—and the digressive, bantering tone, the speaker admits he is "bone-weary / of being nagged to death from inside."

Linda Pastan conveys the patient's feeling of separation from the body *after minor surgery*. Of course, "minor surgery," a phrase borrowed from medical jargon, may indeed be "major" for the patient. Most operations involve the possibility of complications, however remote, due to anesthesia, infections or blood clots, among other problems. Initially, the body merely "flirts with faithlessness," but in the final stanza, we learn that it deceives her outright, making promises "it knows / it cannot keep." Now, the patient has only a very tentative sense of security in her physical being. Michael Harper describes a "major" surgery in *Sack 'A Woe: Gallstones as History.*' Gallstones are associated with a series of images, including "diamonds to be sorted, / etched in pancreas juice"; they are hard and cutting. The profusion of imagery may help the patient deal with the trauma of surgery. To a child, surgery can be a nightmarish experience, but Roberta Spear remembers having *Tonsils* removed with some nostalgia. In fact, her recollection is "painless . . . / as a root / lifted gently from the mud." Amputations can vary in significance and acceptance of the loss occurs in stages. Karl Shapiro analyzes this in *The Leg*. Starting with a dazed acceptance about the exact nature of the loss, the poem proceeds to a joyful affirmation of the body which remains. The *Bleeder* in Hollis Summers' poem also intends to enjoy life in spite of all the risks of being hemophiliac. Although he does not even "try to swim the lake or play football, he can debate and sing and paint."

Patients with cancer usually have a terminal condition and continually have to re-adjust to its latest ravages. From the patient's point of view, *The Cancer Cells* are "sinister shapes with menacing attitudes." But Richard Eberhart can also perceive them as a poet and see his "own malignance in their racy, beautiful gestures." On the *Seventh Floor: Cancer Ward*, the patients are "lost to the traitor-temples of [their] bodies." Tom Sleigh realizes that the "tumors" are part of the body, yet existing independently, almost like parasites. Although the patient may feel separate from the body, the "routine pain" of cancer is an aching reminder of a corporeal existence. Only with the help of morphine, "a black, comforting spider which spins a web around [the] brain," can the patient achieve distance from the reality of pain. (Cancer pain is like no other, and requires intravenous morphine in severe cases. It *literally* hurts to the bone in some instances.) In Weldon Kees' poem, *The Patient is Rallying*, we find the patient has an even greater sense of disorientation and distance from the body. Experiencing a slightly paranoid state, he hears "unbelieved fanfares / And admonitions from a camouflaged sky." His memory clouded, he questions the very existence of the hospital room: "was there a room like that one, worn / With our whispers?" Similarly, in Stephen Dobyn's poem, a feverish man at the *Farmyard at Chassy* imagines himself outside his body, as a passer-by. Perhaps out of self-pity, he believes that the observer (himself) doubts the farm "could even keep a man alive," and goes on his way.

Occasionally, not only the patient, but also a relative presents a medical problem, as in Marvin Bell's poem. *The Parents of Psychotic Children* are guilt-ridden because their babies move "without compensation / because of them to worlds without them." Yet, they deny any involvement and feel they received 'inadequate safeguards, faulty retribution.'

Not only do they blame others, they also "overcome / their fears of the worst," another kind of denial. This poem has the tone of a sympathetic rebuke to the parents and, in passing, to the "far-fetched" doctors who are "out of touch" and do not give adequate counsel to parents playing the role of patients.

The next three poems in this section portray insomnia, which can have a variety of causes. Young patients usually cannot *fall* asleep, because of anxiety, and especially an anxiety about "letting go" and never waking up again. Depression frequently prevents people from *remaining* asleep, which can also occur during withdrawal from sleeping pills or tranquillizers. And alcoholism can be associated with insomnia.[1] The speaker in Edward Hirsch's *I Need Help* associates sleep with death, but is not insomniac for fear of dying; he wants "help from the six pallbearers of sleep . . . To hoist the body into an empty coffin." The imagery grows out of his urgency in a series of obsessive metaphors. Perception is strikingly altered and even flowers are distorted into "small mouths / Gulping for air like tiny black asthmatics." Daniel Halpern describes the feeling of unreality on first waking up due to *Insomnia.* The eyes are unused to light and "We wake not entirely whole," searching for familiar objects "and a sense of place." The *Insomniac* in Sylvia Plath's poem is oddly ambivalent about insomnia. Although the poem deals primarily with the negative aspects of sleeplessness, in the final stanza, people who have slept well are labeled "brainwashed" and daylight is unpleasantly "Creeping up with her hatful of trivial repetitions." Sleeping medication can deny the body its restful and invigorating stage of sleep (rapid eye movement), and may cause the "sweet, drugged waking." Taking them has become a religious ritual of sorts, since their "influence won for him / A life baptized in no-life for a while."

A similar distortion of religious imagery, also associated with the ritual of taking mood-altering drugs, occurs in Anne Sexton's *The Addict:* "the laying on of hands / or the black sacrament"; "Then I lie on my altar"; "What a lay me down this is." The altar is used for a sacrifice to addiction and for devil-worship. The quasi-religious aspect is intensified in an ironic manner by echoing the children's prayer, "Now I lay me down to sleep."

The addict is tragic and pathetic; once I saw a patient who had recently been weaned from her heroin addiction, but was tearfully demanding opiates, supposedly for a toothache. Her eyes were dilated, and her tone was becoming strident. Opiates have the side effect of constricting the pupils; maybe the light of this world was too bright for her. I had to place an intravenous line, but couldn't find any veins. They were all used up! My attending physician, more experienced at dealing with addicts, showed me a vein in her shoulder, and we managed to start an intravenous line. She was poorly compliant, even in the hospital, and probably went back to her drugs. For her, time stood still until her next dose, or overdose.

To one extent or another, we all have a sense of our own mortality. The aging Theodore Roethke wrote a mock-serious poem about his *Infirmity,* in which he reflects on his body: "There's little left I care to call my own." There is a pure acceptance of mortality in the final lines as the poet realizes "How body from spirit slowly does unwind." Beth Bentley's poem *You Again* presents a more sinister view of infirmity. Mortality is personified as another self, limping because of a "floating cartilage" in the knee and "pale / though not necessarily thinner" due to a diet. Our uneasiness grows as we read this poem and reaches a peak at the macabre conclusion. L. E. Sissman also writes of impending death in a haunting manner. He begins almost casually—"Very few people know how they will die"—and goes on to describe his own demise in graphic detail. Each step is covered, the wasting of his "skimpy chiton" and the anemia as he feels his "blood go thin, go white." What makes his poem so poignant is the fact that he died of Hodgkin's lymphoma just a few years before a cure was discovered.

FEAR OF *GRAY'S ANATOMY*

I will not look in it again.
There the heart in section is a gas mask,
its windows gone, its hoses severed.
The spinal cord is a zipper
& the lower digestive tract
has been squeezed from a tube like toothpaste.
All my life I had hoped someday to own
at least myself, only to find I am
Flood's ligaments, the areola of Mamma,
& the zonule of Zinn, Ruffini's endings
end in me, & the band of Gennari lies near
the island of Reil. Though I am a geography
greater than even I surmised, containing as I do
spaces & systems, promontories & at least
one reservoir, pits, tunnels, crescents,
demilunes & a daughter star, how can I celebrate
my incomplete fissures, my hippocampus &
inferior mental processes, my depressions
& internal extremities? I encompass also
ploughshare & gladiolus, iris & wing,
& the bird's nest of my cerebellum,
yet wherever I go I bear the crypts of Lieberkuhn,
& among the possible malfunctionaries,
floating ribs & wandering cells, Pott's fracture,
mottles, abductors, lachrymal bones & aberrrant ducts.
I will ask my wife to knit a jacket for this book,
& pretend it's a brick doorstop.
I will not open *Gray's Anatomy* again.

—Brendan Galvin

THE CONDITION

The darkness within me is growing.
I am turned out.

Thought feeds on it
even as the body is eaten.

Its goodness is without a face.
But it convinces me to look.

It can fade from now until doomsday.
It will not fade.

In the night I see it shining,
like a thing seen.

—Marvin Bell

THE DOCTOR OF STARLIGHT

"Show me the place," he said.
I removed my shirt and pointed
to a tiny star above my heart.
He leaned and listened. I could feel
his breath falling lightly, flattening
the hairs on my chest. He turned
me around, and his hands gently
plied my shoulder blades and then rose
to knead the twin columns forming
my neck. "You are an athlete?"
"No," I said, "I'm a working man."
"And you make?" he said. "I make
the glare for lightbulbs." "Yes,
where would we be without them?"
"In the dark." I heard the starched
dress of the nurse behind me,
and then together they helped me
lie face up on his table, where blind
and helpless I thought of all
the men and women who had surrendered
and how little good it had done them.
The nurse took my right wrist
in both of her strong hands, and I
saw the doctor lean toward me,
a tiny chrome knife glinting in
one hand and tweezers in the other.
I could feel nothing, and then he said
proudly, "I have it!" and held up
the perfect little blue star, no
longer me and now bloodless. "And do
you know what we have under it?"
"No," I said. "Another perfect star."
I closed my eyes, but the lights
still swam before me in a sea

of golden fire. "What does it mean?"
"Mean?" he said, dabbing the place
with something cool and liquid,
and all the lights were blinking on
and off, or perhaps my eyes were
opening and closing. "Mean?" he said,
"It could mean this is who you are."

—*Philip Levine*

NERVES

Who doesn't have them—bad as the war news
Starting the day off with a little tic,
And you're out of bed, already launched into it:
The announcer stopping to catch his breath
Between two movements of a cello sonata:
"Distant shelling was heard today
In the suburbs of Beirut . . ." What's left of it.
The hungry newsboys touting the death
Of thousands to sell the morning paper . . .
But, no, these are not the true illustrations:
For those, your unique fate is grafted
Onto the general terror, your mirror
Revealing one night in X-ray the tumor
That will kill you, a sudden pain in your chest
Knocking you flat on the bathroom tiles.
And nobody told you the acid rain
Would be fatal today to one who walked
Down to the docks to see the freighters in,
The men in overalls greasing the way
For some new environmental disaster,
A tanker leaking its sick ammonia
Into the Hudson, Liberty at bay,
While last night's hunks of sex weave by,
Still drunk, on their electric rail,
Toward home, wherever those two rooms are
That are dark, though the sun is at the full.

—Howard Moss

TENNIS ELBOW

From having fun
one way only,
doing the same thing,
the same way exactly,
grinding membranes
that once oiled
every movement,
that once made
the fluid glide
of bone on bone,
the thud absorbed,
again absorbed,
until the thin pad
cushioning the heavy
parts of me from
the heavy parts of me
crumbles, disintegrates.
From years of grooving
the stroke: bounce-hit,
bounce-hit, rehearse,
rehearse, racket back,
stroke, strike, follow
through. I know no
other way. The one trick
I know has worn thin
the cartilage,
has ground it down,
until it absorbs no more,
until I am in touch
with myself. Parts
never meant to touch
are touching. They touch
again, crush and grind,

until I am bright with ache.
And every winner I ever hit,
every exquisite triumph
has made me exquisitely tender,
put a twinge in my step,
a shine in every simple act I do.

—Jim Hall

MUTTERINGS

I have nothing more to say to my left arm.
We used to be friends till it took to hanging out
with a cervical pinch. When it doesn't sleep all day
it has taken to needling me. When I try to sleep,

it raises stupid questions. I do not care
to be interrogated by my components.
Especially not when I am trying to sleep.
I don't mind honest questions. —What have I to hide?

(Forgive me: strike that question. It took the race
billions of lives to code me devious.
I will not dishonor my making by pretending
not to know father and mother. I meant to say:)

What can I have to hide from my left arm?
Except what my right is doing. And it is blameless.
It is helping me write this poem. For better or worse,
a poem is exactly where the devious ends.

(Forgive me again. By the split tongues of my people,
there is no point past lying. All saying's bent
to its own forked words, our own, not of our making.
. . . And yet to lie some halfway to a truth!)

But on with it. When my sacro-iliac
blathered me off my legs, a neurosurgeon
harangued them back to me. There can be at times
a winning argument, if only a jargon.

Another logician hanged me from a door
from a slip-on gibbet, a noose from chin to crown,
a counterweight dangling like a corpse from a pulley.
He called it traction. I sat and discussed it with Plato,

stretching myself to noumena till I gagged.
I am tired of the mutterings of my own sub-surfs.
I howled them down, a pink pill under my tongue.
But my speech perfected, I had nothing to say.

And what now? Sometimes I look down at my knuckles
Are they thinking to pop a question? I'm bone-weary
of being nagged to death from inside. And still
the questions come, and one of them is the answer.

—John Ciardi

after minor surgery

this is the dress rehearsal
when the body
like a constant lover
flirts for the first time
with faithlessness

when the body
like a passenger on a long journey
hears the conductor call out
the name
of the first stop

when the body
in all its fear and cunning
makes promises to me
it knows
it cannot keep

—Linda Pastan

SACK 'A WOE: GALLSTONES AS HISTORY

One's still in, a goose's egg's
made its own bile duct;
the 120 wound pearls
season before doctors,
diamonds to be sorted,
etched in pancreas juice;
they photograph this collection
of off-color radishes,
milky and boiled,
for the medical museum.

A gallstone's seed is berry
wild in fuzz, boned
and filleted, cured,
for each special attack.

So many transfusions
have seeded in sediment
the antibodies won't be identified;
a pint of O blood,
pickles from the lab,
a miraculous find;
they pick the unetherized
weedbeds of tissue and stone
for leaks or obstructions;
cut you like mush melon
suckled in worms
picking your liver
and gall bladder
the color of squash.
Jaundice was your tenth
year on the farm;
five conscious hours
they pickax inside;
you float down this aisle
boxed, fingered, eyed.

—Michael S. Harper

TONSILS

1

Two seahorses smiled at me
from a glass of water on the nightstand,
two wishbones of the speech

I wished for.
There were two pink and fibrous roots
picked from a forest

or were they my mother's fingers
pressed twice their size
as she held the glass for me to drink?

I remember it perfectly
though the hospital danced in fog
at 4 a.m.

I was dressed in the blues
of an absent child, to be undressed
by those in gray

calling me back to sleep.
And I swam back, like the small horses,
through the sheets of foam

and water with land on all sides.
The blade trimmed,
mahogany walled and drifted,
glass held water.

2

The hospital is gone,
the rows of small windows sucked out
and scattered over a foundation

that leads back to earth.
Nearly everyone is missing something.
But few remember the colors

or the silence that pushes us away
from its world.
This is a memory of beginnings,

of creatures more exotic
than redworms or stunned flies.
It is to be spoken without swallowing:

a memory painless
as a hen's bone broken for a second time
on a new wish, as a root

lifted gently from the mud,
or clear water
without a name for it.

—*Roberta Spear*

THE LEG

Among the iodoform in twilight sleep,
What have I lost? he first enquires,
Peers in the middle distance where a pain,
Ghost of a nurse, hazily moves, and day,
Her blinding presence pressing in his eyes
And now his ears. They are handling him
With rubber hands. He wants to get up.

One day beside some flowers near his nose
He will be thinking, *When will I look at it?*
And pain, still in the middle distance, will reply,
At what? and he will know it's gone,
O where! and begin to tremble and cry.
He will begin to cry as a child cries
Whose puppy is mangled under a screaming wheel.

Later, as if deliberately, his fingers
Begin to explore the stump. He learns a shape
That is comfortable and tucked in like a sock.
This has a sense of humor, this can despise
The finest surgical limb, the dignity of limping,
The nonsense of wheel-chairs. Now he smiles to the wall:
The amputation becomes an acquisition.

For the leg is wondering where he is (all is not lost)
And surely he has a duty to the leg:
He is its injury, the leg is his orphan,
He must cultivate the mind of the leg,
Pray for the part that is missing, pray for peace
In the image of man, pray, pray for its safety,
And after a little while it will die quietly.

The body, what is it, Father, but a sign
To love the force that grows us, to give back
What in Thy palm is senselessness and mud?
Knead, knead the substance of our understanding
Which must be beautiful in flesh to walk,
That if Thou take me angrily in hand
And hurl me to the shark, I shall not die!

—Karl Shapiro

BLEEDER

The blood in my body weighs
7 lbs. for every 100 lbs. of me;
I weigh 150;
I own 10 lbs of blood;
6 bbls. of bld. pass through my heart
every 2 or 3 min.
my heart manages enough work in 1 hr.
to lift a 160 lb. man 70 ft. into the air;

my bld. keeps me 98.6;
whole bld. can be kept for only 21 days;
I'm 9/10 water,
and men own more bld. cells than women,
than women own, I mean.
Look, I've written a kind of sonnet.

So I write.
So, I'm a *Hee moh Fill ih ack.*
I want you to recognize what I can do.
I don't mean to be hung up on numbs. and abbrvs.

I don't try to swim the lake or play football
or climb even small mountains;
possibly I'm frightened
of the mouths of scratching women;

but I debate and sing and paint;
I read a lot; I meditate;
I dream of unimaginable encounters;
I write a sports clmn. for my town paper.
Blood from animals with backbones differs
from the blood of insects and sponges.

You don't have to blame your mother, for God's sake;
after a while you don't blame your mother,
even if only men boast hemophilia.
It's the disease of kings, for God's sake;

your mother passes it along to you
according to laws.
Mendel's law is as much a law as anybody's law.
A woman has to give bleeding to 2/3 of her sons,
and 2/3 of her daughters give again;
everybody's mother hands him something or other
he doesn't know what to do with;
so does everybody's father.

I would not like to make anything of being
an only child collecting all the thirds.

Factor VIII, that's the secret,
like frozen orange juice, in a refrigerator;
in 10 min. you can inject yourself.

In the old days you had to spend 3 days
in a hospital every time you bled;
if you took a trip, you made your route
where hospitals hovered.

I own a portable refrigerator.
In the old days you blamed your mother.
Factor VIII,
there's nothing mystic about it:
it's not Factor VII,
for God's sake.

Gauze over a wound acts as a network.
Clots form.
Anybody's bruise means
bleeding inside.
We use a lot of gauze in the theater.
Almost everybody uses gauze,
hiding behind laws and factors.

I'm headed for a camping trip now
directing a bunch of kids who bleed;
I'll argue with them and direct them in a play;
we'll sing and take walks,
surrounding a portable refrigerator.
Everybody's an artist and an accident,
for God's sake.

—*Hollis Summers*

THE CANCER CELLS

Today I saw a picture of the cancer cells,
Sinister shapes with menacing attitudes.
They had outgrown their test-tube and advanced,
Sinister shapes with menacing attitudes,
Into a world beyond, a virulent laughing gang.
They looked like art itself, like the artist's mind,
Powerful shaker, and the taker of new forms.
Some are revulsed to see these spiky shapes;
It is the world of the future to come.
Nothing could be more vivid than their language,
Lethal, sparkling and irregular stars,
The murderous design of the universe,
The hectic dance of the passionate cancer cells.
O just phenomena to the calculating eye,
Originals of imagination. I flew
With them in a piled exuberance of time,
My own malignance in their racy, beautiful gestures
Quick and lean: and in their riot too
I saw the stance of the artist's make,
The fixed form in the massive fluxion.

I think Leonardo would have in his disinterest
Enjoyed them precisely with a sharp pencil.

—Richard Eberhart

SEVENTH FLOOR: CANCER WARD

We are the elect in this inverse hell,
Souls lost to the traitor-temples of our bodies.
Familiars of the scalpel, confessors to our tumors,
We know we're dying faster, that each is delivered up

Into the talcummed hands of doctors who visit
Once a day while we smile our wooden smiles:
Our faces frame the question none of them will answer . . .
We are distracted from the truth

By the view of the highway twisting
Off between the hills. Sometimes waking,
I see the clouds lying like dark cattle
Asleep in the fields. Or see the cars

Slither head-to-tail, illumined
Through the blur of fog by the headlights'
Golden beams gilding what destinations,
What untouchable ends . . . But all of that goes on

Outside our days of routine pain. The nurses
Bring us morphine. Like a black, comforting spider
It spins a web around my brain.
The hypodermic's fang on which a drop

Colorless and odorless for a moment clings,
Is like the god I've dreamt who makes
His nightly rounds with a glowing piece of chalk—
He marks an X on my smock like a door.

We sit beneath the reading light that
At a finger's touch sends down its concentrated
Beam, a sword that lays its blade
On the common page we turn:

In the solitary hush
The white shoes whisper room to room
As word by word we lose our lives
In others' hope, others' pain.

                                        —Tom Sleigh

THE PATIENT IS RALLYING

Difficult to recall an emotion that is dead,
Particularly so among these unbelieved fanfares
And admonitions from a camouflaged sky.

I should have remained burdened with destinations
Perhaps, or stayed quite drunk, or obeyed
The undertaker, who was fairly charming, after all.

Or was there a room like that one, worn
With our whispers, and a great tree blossoming
Outside blue windows, warm rain blowing in the night?

There seems to be some doubt. No doubt, however,
Of the chilled and empty tissues of the mind
—Cold, cold, a great gray winter entering—
Like spines of air, frozen in an ice cube.

—Weldon Kees

FARMYARD AT CHASSY

From the window of your sickroom, you look out
across the farmyard to the arch of the front gate.
A man in a blue coat stands in the road. It's raining
and his reflection glimmers in the water at his feet.
To your left and right, the stone farm buildings
seem deserted, although you smell the damp smell
of hay and manure, and sometimes you hear your horse
stamp once in the barn, then fall silent. For a week,
you have lain bored and feverish, and looking out
this wet afternoon, you see no living thing except
the man in the roadway, but he stands so quietly
you begin to doubt him, wondering if he is some
trick of the eye, some accidental configuration
of branches resembling a man. But you know very well
you haven't imagined him and you begin to worry
he might demand something from you, something as
inescapable as taxation or death; and you become so
uncertain, you want to erase the very thought of him
and in your fever you decide it's you standing there,
that you are on your way to warm lands to the south,
and for a moment you have halted at this farmyard
without animals or even wet pigeons ducked beneath
rickety eaves, a farmyard so poor that you doubt
it could even keep a man alive, and you shiver
briefly, glad that you don't live here, and pass on.

—Stephen Dobyns

THE PARENTS OF PSYCHOTIC CHILDREN

They renounce the very idea
of information, they are enamored
of the notion of the white tablet.
Their babies were outrageously beautiful
objects exploding their lives,
moving without compensation
because of them to worlds without them.
They believe they were presented
inadequate safeguards, faulty retribution,
and a concerted retirement into crime
of the many intent on their injury.
No two can agree on the miraculous
by which they were afflicted,
but with economy overcome
their fears of the worst. Their children, alas,
request nothing. And the far-fetched doctors,
out of touch with the serious truth,
are just practical and do not sing,
like the crazy birds, to their offspring.

—Marvin Bell

I NEED HELP

For all the insomniacs in the world
I want to build a new kind of machine
For flying out of the body at night.
This will win peace prizes. I know it,
But I can't do it myself; I'm exhausted,
I need help from the inventors.

I admit I'm desperate, I know
That the legs in my legs are trembling
And the skeleton wants out of my body
Because the night of the rock has fallen.
I want someone to lower a huge pulley
And hoist it back over the mountain

Because I can't go it alone. It is
So dark out here that I'm staggering
Down the street like a drunk or a cripple.
I'm almost a hunchback from trying to hold up
The sky by myself. The clouds are enormous
And I need strength from the weight lifters.

How many nights can I go on like this
Without a single light from the sky: no moon,
No stars, not even one dingy street lamp?
I want to hold a rummage sale for the clouds
And send up flashlights, matchbooks, kerosene,
And old lanterns. I need bright, fiery donations.

And how many nights can I go on walking
Through the garden like a ghost listening
To flowers gasping in the dirt—small mouths
Gulping for air like tiny black asthmatics
Fighting their bodies, eating the wind?
I need the green thumbs of a gardener.

And I need help from the judges. Tonight
I want to court-martial the dark faces
That flare up under the heavy grasses—
So many blank moons, so many dead mouths
Holding their breath in the shallow ground,
Almost breathing. I have no idea why

My own face is never among them, but
I want to stop blaming myself for this.
I want to hear the hard gavel in my chest
Pounding the verdict "Not guilty as charged,"
But I can't do this alone. I need help
from the serious men in black robes

And because I can't lift the enormous weight
Of this enormous night from my shoulders
I need help from the six pallbearers of sleep
Who rise out of the slow, vacant shadows
To hoist the body into an empty coffin.
I need their help to fly out of myself.

—Edward Hirsch

INSOMNIA

It is sometimes the easiest thing
in the world, the world
closing down, lost
to the internal light
of the psychic drama.
The eyes in disuse twitch
like the tripping frames
of a motion picture slowing
to a standstill.
We wake not entirely whole
into the darkness looking
for the light, the glass
of stale water
and a sense of place, our eyes
free to catch the real passing of time.

—Daniel Halpern

INSOMNIAC

The night sky is only a sort of carbon paper,
Blueblack, with the much-poked periods of stars
Letting in the light, peephole after peephole—
A bonewhite light, like death, behind all things.
Under the eyes of the stars and the moon's rictus
He suffers his desert pillow, sleeplessness
Stretching its fine, irritating sand in all directions.

Over and over the old, granular movie
Exposes embarrassments—the mizzling days
Of childhood and adolescence, sticky with dreams,
Parental faces on tall stalks, alternately stern and tearful,
A garden of buggy roses that made him cry.
His forehead is bumpy as a sack of rocks.
Memories jostle each other for face-room like obsolete film stars.

He is immune to pills: red, purple, blue—
How they lit the tedium of the protracted evening!
Those sugary planets whose influence won for him
A life baptized in no-life for a while,
And the sweet, drugged waking of a forgetful baby.
Now the pills are worn-out and silly, like classical gods.
Their poppy-sleepy colours do him no good.

His head is a little interior of grey mirrors.
Each gesture flees immediately down an alley
Of diminishing perspectives, and its significance
Drains like water out the hole at the far end.
He lives without privacy in a lidless room,
The bald slots of his eyes stiffened wide-open
On the incessant heat-lightning flicker of situations.

Nightlong, in the granite yard, invisible cats
Have been howling like women, or damaged instruments.
Already he can feel daylight, his white disease,
Creeping up with her hatful of trivial repetition.
The city is a map of cheerful twitters now,
And everywhere people, eyes mica-silver and blank,
Are riding to work in rows, as if recently brainwashed.

—Sylvia Plath

THE ADDICT

Sleepmonger,
deathmonger,
with capsules in my palms each night,
eight at a time from sweet pharmaceutical bottles
I make arrangements for a pint-sized journey.
I'm the queen of this condition.
I'm an expert on making the trip
and now they say I'm an addict.
Now they ask why.
Why!

Don't they know
That I promised to die!
I'm keeping in practice.
I'm merely staying in shape.
The pills are a mother, but better,
every color and as good as sour balls.
I'm on a diet from death.

Yes, I admit
it has gotten to be a bit of a habit—
blows eight at a time, socked in the eye,
hauled away by the pink, the orange,
the green and the white goodnights.
I'm becoming something of a chemical
mixture.
That's it!

My supply
of tablets
has got to last for years and years.
I like them more than I like me.
Stubborn as hell, they won't let me go.
It's a kind of marriage.
It's a kind of war
where I plant bombs inside
of myself.

Yes
I try
to kill myself in small amounts,
an innocuous occupation.
Actually I'm hung up on it.
But remember I don't make too much noise.
And frankly no one has to lug me out
and I don't stand there in my winding sheet.
I'm a little buttercup in my yellow nightie
eating my eight loaves in a row
and in a certain order as in
the laying on of hands
or the black sacrament.

It's a ceremony
but like any other sport
it's full of rules.
It's like a musical tennis match where
my mouth keeps catching the ball.
Then I lie on my altar
elevated by the eight chemical kisses.

What a lay me down this is
with two pink, two orange,
two green, two white goodnights.
Fee-fi-fo-fum—
Now I'm borrowed.
Now I'm numb.

—*Anne Sexton*

INFIRMITY

In purest song one plays the constant fool
As changes shimmer in the inner eye.
I stare and stare into a deepening pool
And tell myself my image cannot die.
I love myself: that's my one constancy.
Oh, to be something else, yet still to be!

Sweet Christ, rejoice in my infirmity;
There's little left I care to call my own.
Today they drained the fluid from a knee
And pumped a shoulder full of cortisone;
Thus I conform to my divinity
By dying inward, like an aging tree.

The instant ages on the living eye;
Light on its rounds, a pure extreme of light
Breaks on me as my meager flesh breaks down—
The soul delights in that extremity.
Blessed the meek; they shall inherit wrath;
I'm son and father of my only death.

A mind too active is no mind at all;
The deep eye seeks the shimmer on the stone;
The eternal seeks, and finds, the temporal,
The change from dark to light of the slow moon,
Dead to myself, and all I hold most dear,
I move beyond the reach of wind and fire.

Deep in the greens of summer sing the lives
I've come to love. A vireo whets its bill.
The great day balances upon the leaves;
My ears still hear the bird when all is still;
My soul is still my soul, and still the Son,
And knowing this, I am not yet undone.

Things without hands take hands: there is no choice,—
Eternity's not easily come by.
When opposites come suddenly in place,
I teach my eyes to hear, my ears to see
How body from spirit slowly does unwind
Until we are pure spirit at the end.

—*Theodore Roethke*

YOU AGAIN

This time I recognize your limp.
You have aged.
The floating cartilage in your knee
makes you favor your left leg.
Your diet has left you pale
though not necessarily thinner.

If there are auras, yours is gray,
for you abhor violence,
and faint at the sight of blood.
No, it is your habit
of turning away that makes
one shoulder higher than the other; denial
creases your lips with distaste.

On the street, I hear close behind me
your uneven step.
Your long shoe crooks between mine;
I trip, curse.

Someday you'll catch up with me,
your mouth at my ear, hissing.

And you will fit yourself into me
as a corpse into its casket.

—*Beth Bentley*

A DEATHPLACE

Very few people know where they will die,
But I do: in a brick-faced hospital,
Divided not unlike Caesarean Gaul,
Into three parts: the Dean Memorial
Wing, in the classic cast of 1910,
Green-grated in unglazed, Aeolian
Embrasures; the Maud Wiggin Building, which
Commemorates a dog-jawed Boston bitch
Who fought the brass down to their whipcord knees
In World War I, and won enlisted men
Some decent hospitals, and, being rich,
Donated her own granite monument;
The Mandeville Pavilion, pink-brick tent
With marble piping, flying snapping flags
Above the entry where our bloody rags
Are rolled in to be sponged and sewn again.
Today is fair; tomorrow, scourging rain
(If only my own tears) will see me in
Those jaundiced and distempered corridors
Off which the five-foot-wide doors slowly close.
White as my skimpy chiton, I will cringe
Before the pinpoint of the least syringe;
Before the buttered catheter goes in;
Before the I.V.'s lisp and drip begins
Inside my skin; before the rubber hand
Upon the lancet takes aim and descends
To lay me open, and upon its thumb
Retracts the trouble, a malignant plum;
And finally, I'll quail before the hour
When the authorities shut off the power
In that vast hospital, and in my bed
I'll feel my blood go thin, go white, the red,
The rose all leached away, and I'll go dead.
Then will the business of life resume:

The muffled trolley wheeled into my room,
The off-white blanket blanking off my face,
The stealing, secret, private, *largo* race
Down halls and elevators to the place
I'll be consigned to for transshipment, cased
In artificial air and light: the ward
That's underground; the terminal; the morgue.
Then one fine day when all the smart flags flap,
A booted man in black with a peaked cap
Will call for me and troll me down the hall
And slot me into his black car. That's all.

— *L. E. Sissman*

PATIENTS' VIEWS OF DOCTORS

Gentleness And The Scalpel

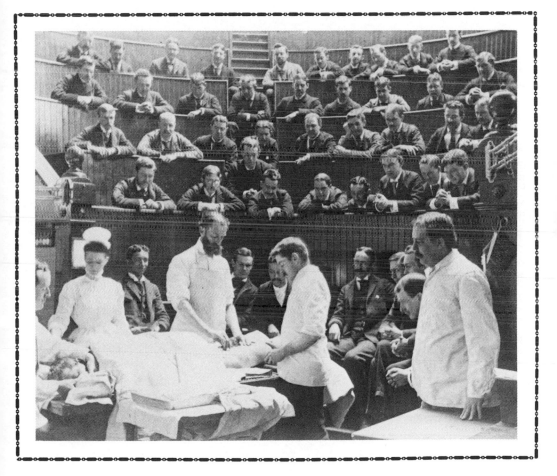

PATIENTS' VIEWS OF DOCTORS
Gentleness And The Scalpel

The examining room is clean, decorated in soft earth tones, and very quiet while you wait for the doctor. You have never been here before, but a friend recommended this physician, and so you made an appointment. Even though you've always trusted your friend's judgment, you feel a little nervous, a little tight in your stomach. After all, who knows what to expect of doctors any more. One of them, a former state governor, was just appointed Secretary of Health and Human Services. But then again, you remember a surgeon recently convicted of practicing surgery in spite of being nearly blind. And of course, the way they abuse drugs! You can't blame them, you suppose; the temptations and such easy access. The local pharmacist caught one of them writing prescriptions for his own narcotics; the stress of the job probably leads them to that avenue of escape. But they get paid well, don't they? And everyone has stresses. Some of them are filthy rich. Like that physician-landlord sentenced to live for a month in one of his own apartment-slums!

The door opens, and you get up to greet the doctor. She appears pleasant enough, and asks how you are feeling. You begin to tell her. Then she starts examining you, warming her cold stethoscope on her hand before placing it on your chest. She seems to ask the right questions, and you pour out your problems as if they could be stored inside an airtight flask and left behind in the clinic's basement, to be analyzed and cultured. She waits until the last drop has fallen, and then asks how your husband feels about all this. You begin to cry, softly and with no embarrassment.

You are the public, and have always had mixed feelings about physicians. If great writers speak for the general public, the doctor as a figure in literature has been much criticized and little praised. As early as Chaucer's *Canterbury Tales,* the doctor was perceived as a superstitious mercenary, who knew "the lucky hours and planetary degrees / For making charms and magic effigies," and had a "special love of gold."₁ Some writers, such as Moliere and Shaw, were especially fond of satirizing the medical profession; the former wrote four plays related to medicine, and the latter's *The Doctor's Dilemma* has a preface titled *Are Doctors Men of Science?* Medicine's history is full of rogues and charlatans, and even today, with fairly strict procedures for licensing, one hears of scandals such as forged diplomas from foreign medical schools and gross incompetence. The profession does have its flaws, but has been steadily improving on a number of fronts such as policing itself, donating medical care to the poor in these times of fiscal inequity, and reviving a humanistic orientation.

In this group of poems, there is a predominantly negative view of physicians. Josphine Miles and William Harrold both use the image of patients as animals to suggest the potentially dehumanizing nature of treatment in the medical system. Miles presents the doctor "who sits at the bedside of a rat" as being excessively concerned with facts such as an "ear tremor, a gain or loss of weight." The patient's 'temper' or psychological state is of less concern to this doctor, although it may be crucial information for the patient's management. Many "purely metabolic" conditions such as hypercalcemia and hypothyroidism may initially have psychological symptoms, and pancreatic cancer is notorious for causing depression. Harrold's poem, *Putting Them Down*, is even more acerbic in its allegorical, absurdist approach to the treatment of a medical condition. He focuses on the frustration a patient often feels in the medical setting. After waiting in a doctor's office "all afternoon" in a state of anxiety, she is referred to a "surgeon for trees." Because of a lack of communication, the surgeon "began pronto to cultivate / her condition" and arranged to have the procedure performed at an entirely unacceptable site. A *Transplant* is also the source of a humorous poem by John Frederick Nims. He imagines the medical establishment, in its excesses, will provide him with "three plastic hearts, or four, / Another's kidneys, corneas," until all that remains is a brain. High technology may do its best, but he still wants two "eyes of glass / To glitter wicked when the nurses pass"! In a different vein, David Ignatow satirizes the *Doctor* who responds to psychic complaints by studying the "latest bulletins / of the Psychiatric Institute." This leads to a bizarre turn of events as the patient rebels against such treatment.

To some extent, the doctor is an object of pity in *Orthopedic Surgery Ward* and *Incurable,* by William Matthews and Robert Pack. The former poem reflects the gloomy ward in the image of the "pale, foreshortened city," suggesting a weak, anemic, stunted place. The speaker realizes, however, that he shares in the suffering whether he wants to or not, and is not immune; the patients are united in "a long / choral breath," even though some are breathing easily and others are "dictated to" by respirators. And the doctors and nurses are also involved in the illness, perhaps because of their environment, for they are "loneliness" personified, which "conducts its brisk, meticulous rounds." (Matthews captures the efficiency of the personnel in the nearly perfect iambic pentameter of the final line.) Patients, trapped in their illness, may not think of physicians with much consideration. I once heard of a patient in a support group for cancer, who became quite annoyed on seeing his physician at a restaurant, when he should have been researching his patient's chemotherapy! On the other hand, some of my patients are very considerate. In a dramatic monologue, Robert Pack elaborates complex relationships between the speaker, his mother, his wife, his daughter, and his would-be son-in-law, who is a surgeon. He has already seen how a surgeon has ignored his mother's condition, confident in "some hidden life reserved inside her head / that he alone could find." That surgeon and his daughter's suitor merge; the latter's lifting a glass symbolizes his holding the speaker's daughter, who will merely be flesh and bone, a collection of organs. The poem moves from criticism to confession to challenge: a "test" to see if the surgeon "too can honor suffering" and agree with the need for euthanasia. This is a test often faced by a physician: families expect a fairly well-defined prognosis and are caught between desires for heroic measures and for cessation of the patient's suffering. (The AMA recently made a public statement in support of withholding treatment if the conditions seemed to warrant the termination of unnecessary suffering.)

My Surgeons by Stanley Kunitz refers to those specialists in a symbolic manner, yet we can sense how he feels about real surgeons. They are "a savage band" and have "squeezed out of my veins / The bright liquor of sympathy." Although the surgeons may symbolize the self-tormenting aspects of human nature, it is significant that Kunitz should have chosen this group. Lisel Mueller shows a more benign skepticism of surgeons as *Monet Refuses the Operation*, probably for a cataract. The artist simply does not want to be "cured" of his ability to "arrive at the vision of gas lamps as angels" and Rouen cathedral as "parallel shafts of sun."

Pain is an important symptom and often its nature can give an almost certain diagnosis. Naturally, the suffering patient does not think of it in this practical manner, and depending on factors like cultural background and temperament, may find it unbearable. A patient and his nurse became quite angry with me one call night because I refused to prescribe narcotics, which would have masked his pain of unknown etiology. Consequently, when his spleen ruptured, we called in a surgeon at once and took him to the operating table. Pain is mysterious, and its "lore is something they keep from you," writes Maxine Kumin in *Pain: 1967*. The patient senses something is being hidden from her: nurses are preoccupied with "tools in the autoclave" and doctors seem to communicate only "into their stethoscopes" in enigmatic words; both nurses and doctors are described in terse sentences, suggesting their own manner of speech. "Rowing out to sea on drugs," she again hopes to find the secret of pain, but is forced to concede its protean nature. (She is adrift, as suggested by frequent participial phrases, a sort of syntactical symbol: *rowing, rowing, crying, Thinking*.) Jeremy Nobel's poem illustrates the medical necessity of describing pain precisely. But this medical history leads to a series of profound questions. Each question in the first half of the poem is designed to associate the pain with a certain organ or disease, but in the second half, the doctor's probing takes on deeper implications, both physical and spiritual.

Jeremy Nobel's poem is written from the perspective of

a practicing physician, but in *The Doctor Rebuilds a Hand*, the poet Gary Young has adopted the role of a physician. The title itself, with its subtle irony, foreshadows a somewhat negative view of physicians. At first the doctor speaks in metaphors, imagining the severed hand as "more wood than flesh," and the "terror / of a man lost in the woods." What remains must be "worked into a hand / using my own as a model," implying that the surgeon is re-creating the hand "in His own image." Not only this, the doctor presumes himself invulnerable: "If I could abandon the vanity / of healing, I would enter the forest of wounds myself." Robert Phillips has also written about a severed hand in *The Persistence of Memory, the Failure of Poetry*. Once again there is an irony directed at physicians, this time with the echo of a nursery rhyme: "all the king's surgeons / put hand and stump together / again." The poet's witty skepticism occurs again in calling the surgery a "miracle," but it can only "scratch and claw." The failure of physicians is clear by the end of this poem; the failure of poetry is not.

During my internship, I encountered the entire spectrum of attitudes towards a physician, from near-deification to hostility in the form of physical violence. At the one extreme, I had managed to convince a family that heroic measures should not be used for a patient with a bleak prognosis; yet, on meeting them in the hall later, I heard the wife say to her granddaughter, "There's the doctor who's going to save Grandpa's life." I was stunned. Everything I had said had been disregarded! The patient died soon, and fortunately I didn't have to face the little girl. Another patient, a young drunk at a County Hospital emergency room, was the most hostile patient I have ever had to face. He had smashed up his car, was tied down on a stretcher with his neck in a cervical collar to prevent spinal cord damage, and was swearing and struggling, all the while stinking of beer and urine. With some trepidation I started an IV and drew blood samples for this gentleman, which at first he refused to allow. Clearly, reasoning was not going to work. But when I casually pointed out that neck injuries could lead to impotence, he became quite cooperative.

David Fisher's poem about physicians is an unusual mix-

ture of surrealism and sarcasm. At one point in the procedure
the patient imagines the doctor wearing "a nacre and ebony
serpent," as though he were a shaman. But in spite of so
"many fine doctors," the patient is *Lost*. Michael Benedikt
makes fun of the unfortunate tendency among some physi-
cians to prescribe a medication for every complaint. So natu-
rally, when the patient's bed started to 'look a little shabby,'
he sprinkled his *Bed Tablets* on it! The conclusion of this
poem continues this absurdity in all its seriousness.

The final poems of this section form a spectrum of
views of the physician. *Peau d'Orange* by Marcia Lynch is a
reference to the way some breast cancers will make the skin
look like an orange peel. Patients sometimes adopt an atti-
tude of helplessness, leaving all the decisions to their doctors,
"the gods / believed in as a child." Overwhelmed by their dis-
ease, patients are rarely in a state of mind which allows them
to decide objectively between 'Surgery, radiation or / death.'
Writing a poem of consolation *For a Teacher's Wife, Dying of
Cancer*, Richard Tillinghast says: "in this lying and cobalt
time, when the doctor has been / Made a god, I had hoped to
offer you truth." Peter Davison's poem *The Revenant* also in-
volves cancer, but here the patient has already passed away,
leaving the grieving husband with memories and a lock of her
hair. Bitter towards medicine and physicians, the speaker un-
dercuts both by juxtaposing "Cytoxin, cure-all" with "not
being able to save her." He also makes a sarcastic comment
about her doctor, who said "of course he could 'make her /
more comfortable' with chemotherapy." Yet another poem
about cancer comments on physicians and their sometimes
callous drive for medical knowledge. In his *Untitled Poem*,
Alan Dugan imagines that the "doctor and his machines /
conduct a long painful diagnosis" of a malignancy, perhaps
with little thought for the patient's comfort.

In contrast, Anne Sexton's poem describing *Doctors* is
bluntly realistic. She recognizes "they are only a human /
trying to fix up a human," and by tersely stating that "Many
humans die," she reminds doctors of their own vulnerability.
She does acknowledge their strong desire to heal, but also
knows they are rationalists: "They would kiss it if it would
heal. / It would not heal." Besides, she subtly juxtaposes the

urge to heal with their "arrogance," implying that the two are connected. Of all these poets, James Tate is most acidic *On the Subject of Doctors*. The speaker in his poem likes "to see doctors cough," because their livelihood depends on the illness of others. He appears to excuse them to some degree in "not saying they enjoy this," but only sets them up for a worse indictment: "they'd rather be playing golf / And swapping jokes about our feet." Like Sexton, he insists "they are only a human," but in a more explicit manner: "Some of them smoke marijuana and are alcoholics." This poem is a caustic reminder to physicians of their human frailties, which cannot be hidden behind a white coat or the surgical mask and gown.

Addressing *A Young Doctor in the Gardner Museum*, S. Ben-Tov may go to the other extreme in her sympathy for physicians. (I'm not denying that her poem comes as a great relief!) It is true that the human details can be too much at times, and we wish to deal only with the medical problems. But then, of course, we would be no better than automatons. I do feel that most physicians are genuinely interested in the patient as a *person*, "a living ruby hidden / in the toad's forehead of our stricken race." Elizabeth Bishop's poem about *The Staff of Aesculapius* is a poetic analysis of this symbol of medicine, and also happens to be generous to physicians. She interweaves research, clinical practice, and the image of the snake, "which by shedding its skin / is a sign of renewal— / the symbol of medicine."

Soon after my patient with the overly-optimistic family died, I found out the autopsy report. My treatment had been correct and aggressive enough; he had been receiving the proper antibiotics and cardiac medications. If I happen to meet his granddaughter again, I will ask her forgiveness and tell her to feel my pulse, with its occasional premature heartbeat. I will tell her it was just such a beat which seduced his heart into a whirling dance out of this life, and his heart, true to himself, must have realized the rhythm of life is only the rhythm of death. Then I will tell her to stay away from Intensive Care Units.

"THE DOCTOR WHO SITS AT THE BEDSIDE OF A RAT"

The doctor who sits at the bedside of a rat
   Obtains real answers—a paw twitch,
   An ear tremor, a gain or loss of weight,
   No problems as to which
   Is temper and which is true.
   What a rat feels, he will do.

   Concomitantly then, the doctor who sits
   At the bedside of a rat
   Asks real questions, as befits
   The place, like where did that potassium go, not what
   Do you think of Willic Mays or thc wcathcr?
   So rat and doctor may converse together.

—Josephine Miles

DOCTOR

The patient cries, Give me back feeling.
And the doctor studies the books:
what injection is suitable for hysterics,
syndrome for insecurity, hallucination?
The patient cries, I have been disinherited.
The doctor studies the latest bulletins
of the Psychiatric Institute and advises
one warm bath given at the moment of panic.
Afterwards inject a barbiturate. At this
the patient rises up from bed and slugs
the doctor and puts him unconscious to bed;
and himself reads the book through the night
avidly without pause.

—*David Ignatow*

PUTTING THEM DOWN

She waited in his office all afternoon
wanting really bad to put them down.
He explained she must lose her complex
and sent her over to see a surgeon for trees.

The surgeon had a butterfly on his forehead
and began pronto to cultivate
her condition.

The butterfly would flutter when she would agree.

"I am becoming more tree-like every day," she said.
"In every way I am getting ready to put mine down."

First the earth was landscaped,
then deep drilling—
for the doctor had explained she had
long ones.

Next day she went out to see the holes
and found they'd been dug in a pig lot.

Furious, she returned to Doctor One.
"My Dear," he said, "You're getting a swine
fixation."
Meantime Doctor Two scheduled a removal
the following Saturday. And Doctor One
sent her out to the sty to eat acorns
and think.

Some weeks later she was more than prepared
and was already putting them down

when a cop in a bacon-striped cap came up
and booked her on a 344—
rooting out of season.

—William Harrold

TRANSPLANT

When I've outlived three plastic hearts, or four,
Another's kidneys, corneas *(beep!),* with more
Unmentionable rubber, nylon, such—
And when *(beep!)* in a steel drawer (Do Not Touch!),
Mere brain cells in a saline wash, I thrive
With thousands, taped to quaver out, "Alive!"—
God grant that steel two wee *(beep!)* eyes of glass
To glitter wicked when the nurses pass.

—*John Frederick Nims*

ORTHOPEDIC SURGERY WARD

And what else? The rain-beaded cars in rows,
the pale, foreshortened city awash on the gray
horizon, two skeletal poplars, an unslaked sky.

On the bed next to mine, an old man dying,
adrift on a thermal of morphine. And I, less ill
by far but rancid with boredom, holding my bad

leg numb and still. The day seems like a long
choral breath—some of us are casual, some wheeze
and strain, a few are dictated to by machines.

Now the rain, and now the light comes at a slant
from the west. At night the hale lie down, too,
though a few are chosen to watch for us all,

to monitor the machines that monitor the sick
while loneliness, complacent and businesslike,
conducts its brisk, meticulous rounds.

              —William Matthews

INCURABLE

I recommend the oysters here! Savoring
good food helps slow me down and pace my thoughts.
      Maybe I've had a prejudice against
surgeons since my mother's operation,
but I believe you're trained not to respond
to suffering: that's why I disapprove
of Margaret's marrying you. I'm sure you think
I'm not prepared to let my daughter go,
but I'm convinced surgeons are trained to learn
how not to grieve. Look at you now—there's not
a ripple on your face to show you don't
like what I've said. You're taught to think of flesh
by feeling with a knife—as if the line
dividing cruelty from cure were drawn
so fine, only a steady hand, and not
the blundering, brave heart, could trust itself.
      I brought you here, this meal's on me, so have
the sirloin steak, the mushroom sauce is done
exactly right. After my mother's stroke
they cut the left side of her neck to clear
the blocked-up artery and get more blood
into her brain. I watched for one whole week;
her speech returned, she could remember me.
But then another blood-clot formed; her chin
drooped to her chest, she drooled, baby sound "oo"s
bubbled upon her tongue. The surgeon said
"We'll go in on the right" as if there were
some hidden life reserved inside her head
that he alone could find. He had the look
your eyes have now when he said "Operate!
We'll try to save her life." What life is it
if she can't think?—humiliation of
poor flesh, gasping its dumb dependency!
      You cut her open and her soul flew out,
leaving a limp creation, an impostor.
I watch you lift your glass, and I can see
my daughter in your hands, numbering

her ribs beneath the skin, naming the organs:
liver, colon, lungs and spleen. How could
your fingers know if *she* is lying there?
Touching like that's no cure for loneliness—
That's why I left my wife, and why I want
my daughter cherished more than hands can do.
    When Margaret was thirteen, we visited
the lake we lived by when she was a child.
Explaining why I had abandoned home,
I said, "Mother and I have fallen out
of touch." We don't touch when our bodies touch
was what I couldn't bring myself to say.
She hugged me as the spindrift loon-calls spread
across the water with the evening mist;
then she pulled back. Softly as possible,
I put my arms around her as we walked,
and yet my love could not reach far enough
inside where love gets recognized as love.
    Then there was nothing I could do except
protect her from my own possessiveness,
and now I must protect her happiness
from you. Maybe I'm wrong, so here's a test
to prove you too can honor suffering:
doctors have professional ways of easing
people out of pain. Release my mother
from the dungeon of her bones; give me a pill
to rescue her. Margaret need never know;
I won't breathe one small sound of what we've said,
but I'll know that you're capable of love.
You'll have a father's blessing if you do.

                        —*Robert Pack*

MY SURGEONS

My surgeons are a savage band.
Surely their patient is ill-fated.
Their tricks are coarse: the small sweet hand
I seized was wax, or amputated.
With the humiliated swollen-footed
And the lost persecuted their traps are baited.

Deftly they opened the brain of a child,
And it was full of flying dreams;
Father was prowling in a field
With speckled tongue and a collar of flame.
They labeled it "Polluted Streams,"
The body floating with the name.

They studied a prostrate fever-chart
With unmitigating eyes; one said,
"Bohemian germs, *Weltschmerz,* bad art
And Spanish fly. Off with his head."
Another, "Fascist. His boot is filled with blood."
They cut me up till I was red.

Lastly they squeezed out of my veins
The bright liquor of sympathy;
I lost the touch of souls, the reins
On white revenge, and I was free
Of pity, a solid man of snow.
But in the night to whom could I go?

Lie down with me, dear girl, before
My butcher-boys begin to rave.
"No hope for persons any more,"
They cry, "on either side of the grave."
Tell them I say the heart forgives
The world. Yes, I believe. In love.

—Stanley Kunitz

MONET REFUSES THE OPERATION

Doctor, you say there are no haloes
around the streetlights in Paris
and what I see is an aberration
caused by old age, an affliction.
I tell you it has taken me all my life
to arrive at the vision of gas lamps as angels,
to soften and blur and finally banish
the edges you regret I don't see,
to learn that the line I called the horizon
does not exist and sky and water,
so long apart, are the same state of being.
Fifty-four years before I could see
Rouen cathedral is built
of parallel shafts of sun,
and now you want to restore
my youthful errors: fixed
notions of top and bottom,
the illusion of three-dimensional space,
wisteria separate
from the bridge it covers.
What can I say to convince you
the Houses of Parliament dissolve
night after night to become
the fluid dream of the Thames?
I will not return to a universe
of objects that don't know each other,
as if islands were not the lost children
of one great continent. The world
is flux, and light becomes what it touches,
becomes water, lilies on water,
above and below water,
becomes lilac and mauve and yellow
and white and cerulean lamps,
small fists passing sunlight
so quickly to one another

that it would take long, streaming hair
inside my brush to catch it.
To paint the speed of light!
Our weighted shapes, these verticals,
burn to mix with air
and change our bones, skin, clothes
to gases. Doctor,
if only you could see
how heaven pulls earth into its arms
and how infinitely the heart expands
to claim this world, blue vapor without end.

—*Lisel Mueller*

PAIN: 1967

The lore of it is something they keep from you.
As with sex, the mechanics are little rehearsed.
Not even among grown men and women the specifics—
yes he unbuttoned her, yes she was a good lay
but how? and in exactly what circumstance?

The nurses will not tell you. They baste and simmer
tools in the autoclave. The doctors whisper
Demerol into their stethoscopes. And the interns,
that volleyball team still challenging its acne,
can only pump up the bag full of blood pressure.

Meanwhile pain comes in dressed up like a spy.
A bearded spy wearing sneakers and murmuring *eat!*
Eat my quick poison. And of course I nibble the edges.
I eat my way to the center of his stem
because something inside it is secret.

At night rowing out to sea on drugs, rowing out
on my little oars, those carefully deployed spoons,
sometimes I think I catch a glimpse of that body
of knowledge. It is the fin of a flying fish.
It is a scrap of phosphorescent plankton
I would take hold of crying *wait!*
Thinking, *tell me.*

Understand that by this time the man next door
is calling *police police police*— his pain
burgles him. *Police,* that kind of father.
Understand that on the other side an old lady
in the thin voice of a music teacher is calling
yoohoo, help me, am I alone in this house?
She is dying with the shades drawn in a deserted villa.

Meanwhile I continue putting out to sea
on my little wooden ice cream spoons.
Although I am not a Catholic, the priest has laid
his hands upon me. He has put God into my pain.
Somewhere in my pineal gland He sits and gloats.

As for the lore, I have learned nothing to hand on.
I go out nightly past these particular needles
and these knives.

—Maxine Kumin

PAIN WORK-UP

Tell me about the pain.
Is it sharp or dull?
What brings it on?
What makes it go away?
Does aspirin seem to help?
Docs it feel better after eating?
Can you tolerate greasy foods?
Does it get relieved when you lie down?
Is it worse in the morning or evening?
Put your finger on the spot that hurts most.
Does it come and go or is the pain constant?
Does it radiate through to your back or shoulder?
Does it crumple you in half when the pain comes?
Do you feel like a small animal is nibbling inside you?
Do you wake in the morning crowned with a halo of pain?
Have you come to depend on the pain to keep you alive?
Do you remember a time before birth when the
rhythm of the universe was your second heartbeat?
Do you remember how green the grass used to be?
Do you remember a time when you remembered no pain?
When you were young did you torture animals?
Were you faithful to your first lover?
Are you afraid of the darkness?
Tell me about the pain.
Is it sharp or dull?

—Jeremy Nobel

THE DOCTOR REBUILDS A HAND
(for Brad Crenshaw)

His hand was a puppet, more wood than flesh.
He had brought the forest back with him: bark, pitch,
the dull leaves and thick hardwood that gave way
to bone and severed nerves throughout his fingers.
There was no pain. He suffered instead the terror
of a man lost in the woods, the dull ache of companions
as they give up the search, wait, and return home.
What creeps in the timber and low brush
crept between his fingers, following the blood spoor.
As I removed splinters from the torn skin
I discovered the landscape of bodies,
the forest's skin and flesh. I felt
the dark pressure of my own blood stiffen within me
and against the red pulp I worked into a hand
using my own as the model. If I could abandon the vanity
of healing, I would enter the forest of wounds myself,
and be delivered, unafraid, from whatever I touched.

                                        —*Gary Young*

THE PERSISTENCE OF MEMORY,
THE FAILURE OF POETRY

The severed hand flutters
     on the subway track,
like a moth. No—

it is what it is,
     a severed hand.
It knows what it is.

And all the king's doctors
     and all the king's surgeons
put hand and stump together

again. Fingers move,
     somewhat. Blood circulates,
somewhat. "A miracle!" reporters

report. But it will only
     scratch and claw, a mouse
behind the bedroom wall. We forget.

At four a.m. the hand
     remembers: intricate musical
fingerings, the metallic

feel of the silver flute.

                              —Robert Phillips

LOST

The bare room,
the table cries,
the doctors harvest the silver vertebrae.
The restraints are terrifying.

"Perhaps you have made of death,"
says the doctor,
"an idea excessively false."

A strange clear dream is born to the poet
in the isolation room.
The doctor is wearing
a nacre and ebony serpent.
The shackled celestial poet
opens the violet of his heart—
forgetfulness uproots the symphony—
a star is feeding.
There is angel strife in the poet's eyes,
o little lost poet with
many fine doctors and one celestial pillow.

—David Fisher

THE REVENANT

Last night, rummaging for scissors
in a back drawer, his fingers touched
something alive, not alive,
a pouch concealed under papers,
an envelope with no address.
In it, a lock of graying hair,
lopped from her head before the Cytoxin, cure-all,
not able to save her,
had struck her bald.
His hand now cradled one part
that had sprouted from her body,
many times assenting to
the touch of his fingers.
Her hair! The only frailty
she'd admit to! Her doctor,
never lowering his eyes,
told her she had a year to go,
adding of course he could "make her
more comfortable" with chemotherapy.
Her hands flew to her head, frightened birds
to save her hair. They fell at once
fluttering to her lap. She had to laugh
at herself, the hands. But not at the hair.
"I'm sorry," she said, aghast at her own reasons.

—*Peter Davison*

"BED TABLETS"

I had been noticing that my sleeping quarters were beginning to look a little shabby lately, so that it was quite a relief when I went to the medicine cabinet and the label on a little bottle of white pills caught my eye. It was marked "Bed Tablets." So, to begin to neaten up the room, I went back to the bedroom and sprinkled Bed Tablets all over my cot and went to sleep on the floor, to allow the room time to recover. And sure enough, the next morning, I noticed a great improvement in the room—in any case, my bed was certainly beginning to look a whole lot better to me! So, lately I've been wondering whether—no questions asked of course—my doctor might be willing to write me out a prescription for "Wall Cream."

—*Michael Benedikt*

PEAU D'ORANGE

We barter the difference
between black and gray.
"Surgery, radiation or
death," you say and leave
the decision to me,

while I insist you are the gods
I believed in as a child.
I prayed you to pull magic
out of your black leather bags
to wave away the rattling
in my bones.

I accept your calling
my breast an orange peel,
let you lay hands on this fruit
my mother said no man
must touch. In this disease
there is no sin.

If you lift the chill
that unravels my spine,
I will send you stars
from the Milky Way,
send them spinning down,
dancing a thousand-fold. Please
let me grow old.

—Marcia Lynch

FOR A TEACHER'S WIFE, DYING OF CANCER

Four-fifteen: a weak snow starts to blot
The city's likeness. I know you are dying.
By tonight chained tires will be churning it,
Headlights plunging into it. No planes will be flying
South from Boston. They will squat in rows
Staring at the snow that grounds them. The mewing
Sea-birds blown inland incuriously rise
Through it all, scorching the flurry with furious eyes.

Your dying glows in my brain: dry light spreading
Through the nerves, converting the cells like cancer
The crab, that pinched your lung once it set in.
I hear the lie scratch like an old record when you answer
You are feeling fine. On the phone your voice
Could almost be a ghost's, half-heard in the tense air.
I dream an ice-storm, poles crashing,
Hot wires sparkling where they loop and cross.

Down South it must seem warm enough for your walk
Today. When your husband asked us over for a drink
You would meet us in your funny walking shoes and sulk.
We talked the modern world to arm's length—
Fireside Agrarians; not even cancer
Could usurp the house's form. You shrank
From our courtesy to closet with the stranger
Whose passion banked your eyes of their gutted fire.

A man can't live in a house with death, your husband
Told me. We shooed the screech-owl off the roof.
But in this lying and cobalt time, when the doctor has t
Made a god, I had hoped to offer you truth.
The storm beats down the birds with an iron grace
And my warm words freeze and shudder in my mouth
The snow swallows my reflection in the window-glass
I can't remember your face.

—Richard Til

DOCTORS

They work with herbs
and penicillin.
They work with gentleness
and the scalpel.
They dig out the cancer,
close an incision
and say a prayer
to the poverty of the skin.
They are not Gods
though they would like to be;
they are only a human
trying to fix up a human.
Many humans die.
They die like the tender,
palpitating berries
in November.
But all along the doctors remember:
First do no harm.
They would kiss it if it would heal.
It would not heal.

If the doctors cure
then the sun sees it.
If the doctors kill
then the earth hides it.
The doctors should fear arrogance
more than cardiac arrest.
If they are too proud,
and some are,
then they leave home on horseback
but God returns them on foot.

—Anne Sexton

ON THE SUBJECT OF DOCTORS

I like to see doctors cough.
What kind of human being
would grab all your money
just when you're down?
I'm not saying they enjoy this:
"Sorry, Mr. Rodriguez, that's it,
no hope! You might as well
hand over your wallet." Hell no,
they'd rather be playing golf
and swapping jokes about our feet.

Some of them smoke marijuana
and are alcoholics, and their moral
turpitude is famous: who gets to see
most sex organs in the world? Not
poets. With the hours they keep
they need the drugs more than anyone.
Germ city, there's no hope
looking down those fire-engine throats.
They're bound to get sick themselves
sometime; and I happen to be there
myself in a high fever
taking my plastic medicine seriously
with the doctors, who are dying.

—*James Tate*

UNTITLED POEM

The patients in the waiting room
are nearly silent like the hanging plants.
Once in a while one rustles or sighs.
A sunbeam moves across the floor,
climbs the wall, hits the *NO SMOKING,
NO MEDICAID* sign, and disappears.
Subjective time collapses and expands
like a new four-dimensional model of the universe.
The doctor and his machines
conduct a long painful diagnosis
in a back room. They have found a new
interesting malignancy, and take their time.

—Alan Dugan

A YOUNG DOCTOR IN THE GARDNER MUSEUM
(for Elizabeth)

You sit down in the cloisters.
Moss speckles the marble basin;
the stone fish glide into your heart.
The fountain diffuses its cool smells.
Light polishes a turned hip, gray patina
on a vault of shoulder; the marbles
are clothed in flawless presence,
and the fountain top sustains its kiss
while your hands remember

patching bones and bloody tatters.
In the vinegar light of the clinic,
you've done too little just to do it all:
sent the sewn arm back to the needle,
and mended legs to prison. The drained knees
are back on the job, mopping water
off the hallway floor; you smiled at her.

Their lives are thin floss jerked
again and again to breaking;
sometimes you long to handle
only the mottled organs spilling their histories.
Will you delegate, finally, someone else to pound
a drunk's tenth life into his stale lungs?

From the galleries' pierced arches
Saint Lucy looks down on you, her body
a garden of enamel, gown and flowers.
Surely it was for this
singing helplessness, music in the water,
in the marble souls and the tenacious moss
that you first set to work
uncovering a robe of blood, a living ruby hidden
in the toad's forehead of our stricken race.

—*S. Ben-Tov*

THE STAFF OF AESCULAPIUS

A symbol from the first, of mastery,
    experiments such as Hippocrates made
        and substituted for vague
   speculation, stayed
      the ravages of a plague.

A "going on"; yes, *anastasis* is the word
    for research a virus has defied,
        and for the virologist
   with variables still untried—
      too impassioned to desist.

Suppose that research has hit on the right one
    and a killed vaccine is effective
        say temporarily—
   for even a year—although a live
      one could give lifelong immunity,

knowledge has been gained for another attack.
    Selective injury to cancer
        cells without injury to
   normal ones—another
      gain—looks like prophecy come true.

Now, after lung resection, the surgeon fills space.
    To sponge implanted, cells following
        fluid, adhere and what
   was inert becomes living—
      that was framework. Is it not

like the master-physician's Sumerian rod?—
    staff and effigy of the animal
        which by shedding its skin
   is a sign of renewal—
      the symbol of medicine.

—Elizabeth Bishop

PHYSICIANS
Dissecting The Good Lines From The Bad

An old woman with mild heart failure is breathing rapidly while lying flat in her bed. I help her up to a sitting position, which provides some relief to her congested lungs. After asking about her symptoms, I begin a mental status exam, which can often give a clue about the brain's oxygenation. "I need to ask you some routine questions, things that I ask everyone. Do you know what month it is"? She replies, "Why, it's fall, doctor." I begin to think about how a ninety-year-old might perceive the passage of time. Maybe she isn't "disoriented" at all. Beyond a certain age, is the season a more convenient and reasonable unit of measurement than the month? I pull out my little green notebook, jot down her response, and begin examining her.

The foremost American physician-poet William Carlos Williams, in the energetic style of his *Autobiography*, wrote: "medicine and the poem . . . amount for me to nearly the same thing. I was permitted by my medical badge to follow the poor, defeated body into those gulfs and grottos . . ., secret gardens of the self. And the astonishing thing is that at such times and places—foul as they may be with the stinking ischio-rectal abscesses of our comings and goings—just there, the thing, in all its greatest beauty, may for a moment be freed . . . . it has fluttered before me for a moment, a phrase which I quickly write down on anything at hand, any piece of paper I can grab."[1] Like Williams, many physicians have felt compelled to write for a variety of reasons, in spite of, or perhaps because of the "abscesses." This section contains the work of four physician-poets: Dannie Abse, John Stone, Samuel Stearns, and myself.

Dannie Abse had his first book of poetry published before 1950, while still a medical student at London's Westminster Hospital. He has written two autobiographical books and edited an annual selection of British poetry. In *The Doctor*, he explores the role of the physician without romanticizing it. He "does not always like his patients, "nor approve of their "politics," but he "must care." Every physician has dealt with patients who are, to put it bluntly, obnoxious. My "favorite" example is an elderly man with heart disease who kept on smoking and seemed to imply that he was too "tough" for tobacco to affect him. He felt there was always the option of another cardiac surgery! (I disliked this man so much that, in trying to compensate for these emotions, I gave him the best care I possibly could.) The physician must also recognize that the patient "expects the unjudged lie . . . some small disease / with a known aetiology, certain cure," and that very often there is none. (In fact, most patients I see do not have just one disease process.) Faced with having to prescribe a panacea, this doctor comes up with a delightful series of "drugs," including the "dew from a banana leaf," "sunlight from waterfall's edge, rainbow smoke," and perhaps most importantly, "tears from eyelashes of the daughter."

The Stethoscope reflects Abse's laudable attitude of humility towards his profession. Though he has heard the "sound of creation" on a pregnant woman's abdomen, he refuses to glorify the instrument. He does not want a mask of ritual and consequent self-glorification. Instead, he can praise his stethoscope in order to "celebrate [his] own ears" and what they hear: "laughter of the sane and insane," moonlight sonatas on a needle; / lovers with doves in their throats." The poet will not allow the stethoscope, a product of man's technology, to interpose itself between the physician and the patient. The very act of listening appears sacred in images that display the wisdom and beauty of sound.

Abse knows the irony of beauty in disease, and can see the vividness of the "color rose . . . when it ripens in a tumor, [the] healing greens . . . so springlike, / in limbs that fester." These deftly composed oxymorons, forcing together images of decay and generation, hint at some of the inherent paradoxes in medical practice. In the midst of a violent car accident, he sees the fragile color "china white" in torn flesh and exposed bone. From the colors of an autopsy, the poet moves to the "terrible beauty" (Yeats on war) of a holocaust, its "criminal, multi-coloured flash." The physician's role in this poem is not limited to medicine, but extends to politics, to a protest against death in both medicine and in war. With the more subtle shadows and densities found in the palette of an *X-ray*, Abse describes a more personal experience, the discovery of cancer (presumably) in his mother. Although he can pry open and dissect bodies for autopsy, his mother's illness is too difficult to face: "I still don't want to know."

John Stone is an American physician-poet who has published three collections of poetry, and is the co-author of a textbook of emergency medicine. His poems are clean, spare, inventive, and show careful attention to form. In his fine poem *Death*, for example, his experiences are distilled to precise similes. Death can be prolonged in its course, move "slowly as rust / sand" or surprise the victim in a moment of terror at being trapped, "as when / someone . . . finds the doorknob / come loose in his hand." The carefully delayed final line comes as a syntactical surprise, just as death arrives in some cases. *An Autopsy in the Form of an Elegy* is similarly refined to its bare essentials. If Abse's autopsy is of global proportions, Stone gives his complete attention to one person who "was very nearly perfect." The poem elaborates a series of relationships that become more and more focused: "In the chest / in the heart / was the vessel . . . [and] the clot / small and slow." But in this dissection are some unexpected "anatomical parts"—the "art" and the "love"—which make these qualities seem integral to the person. The skeleton form of the poem emphasizes parallel rhythmic units which give the poem its music; this typographical structure also makes the poem appear like a headstone.

Another of Stone's poems deals with *Amnesia*, the loss of memory. After any significant injury to the head, the patient cannot, of course, remember the unconscious state. In addition, the periods of confusion just after reviving and just before the injury are lost to the memory. In severe cases, years and even decades can be erased, and the patient absorbs new information with great difficulty. Stone's patient is lucky to have only a mild deficit, as we learn in the first line, which works effectively with the title to set the narrative situation: "Three days black: the day after the fall." Rhyme is a very useful rhetorical device in this poem, and creates associations of meaning that provide cohesion: the mind "leaped out like a pack" through the "crack." leaving "Three days black," a period of time which "is a mirror that follows you back and back." The rhymes of "ledge" and "edge" also suggest a sudden drop, an abrupt loss of memory. The poet describes a different sort of confusion and loss of memory in an old alcoholic who demonstrates *Confabulation*. In an attempt to hide his disorientation, he makes up facts to fit the situation. But the physician makes up his own facts and "out-confabulates" the patient, in the process creating a fictitious character who almost begins to sound real.

The influence of William Carlos Williams on contemporary poetry has been profound, and a number of poets have written poems to him and about him. The list includes Wallace Stevens, Robert Lowell, John Berryman, and Kenneth Rexroth. John Stone has also given an affectionate tribute to Williams, while *Getting to Sleep in New Jersey*. The occasion for writing the poem seems very natural, because "Not twenty miles from where I work, / William Williams wrote after dark." Having established these connections, Stone elaborates upon the similarities between poetry and medicine, which for Williams had great affinities. A pregnant woman's labor and the writing of poetry take on surprising similarities through a pun when Stone speculates if "feet or butt or head-first ever / determines as well the length of labor / of a poem" The way a poem "presents" itself to a poet affects its length, and therefore its basic structural qualities. (Oblique references to Williams' poetry—*red wheelbarrows, the wind / corners the house, his contagious snow*—add a special texture.)

Samuel Stearns is a retired internist in the Boston area. His *Autopsy*, in contrast to the earlier ones, matches the clinical detachment of the pathologists who "cut and weigh / measuring / the diagnosis." In a portrayal of *The Little Old Man* on a commode, we learn how the dying can appreciate the small blessings of life. This physician-poet's perception helps us realize that, instead of being neglected since they are doomed, terminal patients should receive our fullest attention. In a longer narrative poem and character sketch, revival from cardiac failure becomes a metaphor of *Resurrection*. The poet cannot imagine his pathetic patient returning to a life of "rusty rhododendrons and the weeds." Dr. Stearns has written a fine *Epilogue*, which gathers together a variety of ideas and emotions about his profession; even a physician with many years of experience can hope that "wisdom slowly grows with time, / like coral, quietly beneath the waves."

The final poems in this section are my own work. While driving from the Midwest to an interview in New York, I happened to notice a billboard for a tire store in Rutherford, New Jersey. On an impulse, I swerved into the exit lane and managed to get lost on a country road. A few questions later, I was back on the road to Williams' home. Luckily I was able to reach a busy intersection where a policeman was directing traffic, and asked the way to Dr. Williams' house. He knew! At 9 Ridge Road, I stopped to absorb the impact of the house well-shaded by trees. Then I knocked and Dr. Williams, who had continued in his father's footsteps, came out. A very pleasant elderly gentleman, he was glad to hear of my work in progress, a series of poems titled *Letters to Williams*. This literary vehicle has encouraged me to experiment with a variety of poetic forms and devices. In my work, I am trying to articulate the poetry found in medicine and in my Indian experiences, which sometimes come together, as in the long poem *Revisions of a Medical Record*, written for my late physician father. In this poem, a cardiac monitor speaks in a sonnet, a cardiologist in rhymed quatrains, and the wife and son in free verse. One of these sections, *The Son: Returning Home*, is included here. I started writing poetry after my father's death, I suppose as a form of catharsis. Some time after the event, I realized that poetry was still therapeutic, but in a different way; the hysteria and depression were gone, and I was left with the essential pleasures of poetry. I am also working on a series of poems about India, where I grew up. *Words for a Percussion Instrument* is a poem on the diseases of poverty, which have symptoms such as violence. While I was still in India, my father and I stopped to see why a crowd had formed in the street, and discovered a rickshaw-man crouched near the gutter, his hands clutching his genitals. My father offered some help to the man, who could barely tell us that an argument with a passenger had led to blows and a kick in the groin. The lovely music of the *tabla* (small drums) and of rain on the corrugated tin roof of our verandah came together to suggest the image of the rickshaw-man as a beaten percussion instrument. *The Taste of the Ocean* was written for an infant with cystic fibrosis and recurrent pneumonia. His desperate condition evoked the image of delicate poppies by the ocean. The final poem, *First Payment*, was read at my medical school graduation. It is a poem of gratitude for an elderly lady who once offered me a gift of money while I was a sophomore medical student doing an externship in Family Practice. In spite of a chronic and painful condition, she had learned to cope with her disease, and was an inspiration to other patients and to her physicians.

One of my patients, an elderly black lady with a delicious sense of humor, died recently after a cardiac arrest. I started the resuscitation and intubated her before the "code team" arrived, all the while wondering what had precipitated the event. She had been admitted recently, and I was looking forward to chatting with her. A real matriarchal sort, she had migrated with her brood from the deep South, and worked her way up in a factory to a managerial position. During the code, I could feel my green notebook against my chest. There is a blank page waiting for her. Who could have recorded her laughter in it anyway? The poem will write itself one day, without the help of any notes.

THE DOCTOR

Guilty, he does not always like his patients.
But here, black fur raised, their yellow-eyed dog
mimics Cerberus, barks barks at the invisible,
so this man's politics, how he may crawl
to superiors does not matter. A doctor must care
and the wife's on her knees in useless prayer,
the young daughter's like a waterfall.

Quiet, Cerberus! Soon enough you'll have a bone
or two. Now, coughing, the patient expects
the unjudged lie: 'Your symptoms are familiar
and benign'—someone to be cheerfully sure,
to transform tremblings, gigantic unease,
by naming like a pet some small disease
with a known aetiology, certain cure.

So the doctor will and yes he will prescribe
the usual dew from a banana leaf; poppies and
honey too; ten snowflakes or something whiter
from the bole of a tree; the clearest water
ever, melting ice from a mountain lake;
sunlight from waterfall's edge, rainbow smoke;
tears from eyelashes of the daughter.

—Dannie Abse

THE STETHOSCOPE

Through it,
over young women's abdomens tense,
I have heard the sound of creation
and, in a dead man's chest, the silence
    before creation began.

Should I
pray therefore? Hold this instrument in awe
and aloft a procession of banners?
Hang this thing in the interior
    of a cold, mushroom-dark church?

Should I
kneel before it, chant an apophthegm
from a small text? Mimic priest or rabbi,
the swaying noises of religious men?
    Never! Yet I could praise it.

I should
by doing so celebrate my own ears,
by praising them praise speech at midnight
when men become philosophers;
    laughter of the sane and insane;

night cries
of injured creatures, wide-eyed or blind;
moonlight sonatas on a needle;
lovers with doves in their throats; the wind
    travelling from where it began.

—Dannie Abse

PATHOLOGY OF COLOURS

I know the colour rose, and it is lovely,
but not when it ripens in a tumour;
and healing greens, leaves and grass, so springlike,
in limbs that fester are not springlike.

I have seen red-blue tinged with hirsute mauve
in the plum-skin face of a suicide.
I have seen white, china white almost, stare
from behind the smashed windscreen of a car.

And the criminal, multi-coloured flash
of an H-bomb is no more beautiful
than an autopsy when the belly's opened—
to show cathedral windows never opened.

So in the simple blessing of a rainbow,
in the bevelled edge of a sunlit mirror,
I have seen, visible, Death's artifact
like a soldier's ribbon on a tunic tacked.

—Dannie Abse

X-RAY

Some prowl sea-beds, some hurtle to a star
and, mother, some obsessed turn over every stone
or open graves to let that starlight in.
There are men who would open anything.

Harvey, the circulation of the blood,
and Freud, the circulation of our dreams,
pried honourably and honoured are
like all explorers. Men who'd open men.

And those others, mother, with diseases
like great streets named after them: Addison,
Parkinson, Hodgkin—physicians who'd arrive
fast and first on any sour death-bed scene.

I am their slowcoach colleague—half-afraid,
incurious. As a boy it was so: you know how
my small hand never teased to pieces
an alarm clock or flensed a perished mouse.

And this larger hand's the same. It stretches now
out from a white sleeve to hold up, mother,
your X-ray to the glowing screen. My eyes look
but don't want to, I still don't want to know.

—Dannie Abse

DEATH

I have seen   come on
slowly as rust
sand

or suddenly   as when
someone leaving
a room

finds the doorknob
come loose in his hand

—John Stone

AUTOPSY IN THE FORM OF AN ELEGY

In the chest
in the heart
was the vessel

was the pulse
was the art
was the love

was the clot
small and slow
and the scar
that could not know

the rest of you
was very nearly perfect

—*John Stone*

AMNESIA

Three days black: the day of the fall
and one on either side. The crack
in your skull is leaching lime

to put back into place all
the mind that leaped out like a pack
of frenzied dogs. For you the time

since that misstep on the ledge
is a mirror that follows you back and back,
but leaves you at the edge.

—*John Stone*

GETTING TO SLEEP IN NEW JERSEY

Not twenty miles from where I work,
William Williams wrote after dark,

after the last baby was caught,
knowing that what he really ought

to do was sleep. Rutherford slept,
while all night William Williams kept

scratching at his prescription pad,
dissecting the good lines from the bad.

He tested the general question whether
feet or butt or head-first ever

determines as well the length of labor
of a poem. His work is over:

bones and guts and red wheelbarrows;
the loneliness and all the errors

a heart can make the other end
of a stethoscope. Outside, the wind

corners the house with a long crow.
Silently, his contagious snow

covers the banks of the Passaic River,
where he walked once, full of fever,

tracking his solitary way
back to his office and the white day,

a peculiar kind of bright-eyed bird,
hungry for morning and the perfect word.

—John Stone

CONFABULATION

Striding up to his bed, you
know the right questions.
Old with alcohol, yellow
as a lemon, he wrinkles

for a cigarette. He
will lie to you at a moment's
confusion, going along with you

to cover the fact that he can't
remember yesterday.

Do you remember me?

Sure I remember you.

We met in the bar at 8th
and Jackson.

Yeah, sure.

The redhead: you remember her.

Yeah, I remember.

What was her name—started with
an L . . .

Loretta? Laura?

Loretta. That's it. What a
woman. You're a lucky man to
know Loretta.

I know. I know Loretta. I'm a lucky man.

And Loretta is a lucky woman.

—*John Stone*

AUTOPSY

Expressionless,
the recently alive
lies spread and silent
on the dented sink,

the skin green-hued,
the yellow fat
and purple clot
and variegate organs spread out.

The aproned doctors
cut and weigh,
measuring
the diagnosis.

—Samuel Stearns

THE LITTLE OLD MAN

The little old man
on the commode
is content.

It does not matter
he will die
quite soon.

Only
the relief
of the moment

suffuses
his sunken
face.

       —Samuel Stearns

RESURRECTION

He was a wheeler-dealer who had made
his pile by cutting corners, chiseling here
and there, and kicking back a bit of what
he stole. A coronary and a stroke,
two disappointing sons, a nervous wife
who nagged and ailed by turn, extravagance
and generosity, had turned him poor again
at seventy. He humbly asked his sons
to take him in, and, strange to say, they did.

And so he went to live away from home,
abandoning the house that he had built,
the flower beds that he had dug on hands
and knees, the shrubs that he had set with care
for orderly procession of both bloom
and leaf, the copper downspouts from the roof,
the cedared attic and the paneled den,
the parquet floors and antique Persian rugs. . . .

His sons, despite myriad analytic hours,
made him no happier than they had when in
their pimply, selfish teens. He missed and mourned
his home, his friends, his affluence and pride.
He soon was ill again and showed his mood,
when roused from cardiac arrest, by asking,
querulous, the nurse who thumped his chest
to start his heart again, "Why did you hit
me when I merely said 'I'd like another
blanket, please'?" quite unaware that he
had died and resurrection had occurred.

No thump aroused him when asystole
occurred again. Now, when I pass his old
house by, and see the crabgrass in the lawn,
the rusty rhododendrons and the weeds
thick through the flower beds, I think how right
it is that resurrection is a myth
for frightened children on a scary night.

—*Samuel Stearns*

EPILOGUE

Now, after many years of caring for the sick,
I sometimes think on how it all began,
and how I undertook the ancient craft
that had its origin in chant and rite,
in tribal shamans, augurs, oracles and priests,
apothecaries, alchemists and quacks.
This is the lineage I lived each day
in varied acts some men are pleased to call
a science.

God has been very good to me
in granting some small feeling for my art,
for untried knowledge is a fickle friend.
A current fact is often next year's myth
since what we "know" is sometimes less than true,
while what we need to know compounds itself,
accumulates at rates of usury
such as to beggar us, our mouths agape.

The years bring obsolescence to us all.
An old man values as patina
what is rust and crumble at his age;
the pride of old achievement lasts too long,
and art, unaided, makes for charlatans.

To blend a timeless craft with knowledge is
supreme; then wisdom slowly grows with time,
like coral, quietly beneath the waves,
builds islands in a far-horizoned sea.

—*Samuel Stearns*

THE SON: RETURNING HOME
(for Sushil Kumar Eric Mukand)

Moist air crystallizes into morning, shimmers
in the sunrise, cutting my face as I leave the house,
as I leave you.
            You are the medical texts,
the pipes scattered about in empty ashtrays, the sunlight's
dull reflection from the antique brass lamp.
You are gone, resolved
in an electric moment to urned ash, leaving behind
a stray sitar note which resonates
in me with its saffron music.

The respirator's measured, regular breaths
replaced your own cigarette-scarred wheezing.
You tried to quit, but kept on borrowing
cigarettes from patients, as if a smile
was enough payment.

The peaceful hiss and sigh
of your plastic lungs
was incessantly regular.

I tried imagining the incinerator,
but during the funeral
my memory could only filter
the burned fragrance of cumin and cardamom.

Why do we need oxygen
to live and to die,
for metabolism and for combustion?

Was your life
a poorly controlled chemical reaction,
and its by-product your death?

Once, under the heat
of the Indian sun, you lifted me up
to the branches
of a mango tree, caught me when I jumped down.
Now I am left with the fruit of long days,
nights away delivering babies: your heart on

crutches, arteries rusted away.
And you knew, you knew.

90 percent occlusion
of the anterior descending artery,
80 percent of the circumflex.

Hints of self-diagnosis in journal articles
you underlined: *coronary bypass, cardiac
catheters, myocardial infarctions.* Reading
your medical records, I also knew.

We can only walk so far away from home,
from our fathers, who have left us
their lives in each dying cell, each spiral
DNA staircase that ascends
or descends to the next day.

The house holds me
like a kite, reeling me in, taut
against the gusts blowing on this bamboo frame.

You will be waiting:
wire-rimmed glasses, trim moustache, smiling
with my mother, a photograph on the night-stand
before I turn off the brass lamp.

So I turn
homeward, promising to write
a *ghazal* for which you
have left behind a melody.

Someday, I will hear the *tabla,* whose rhythm
no EKG can capture and no cardiologist
can interpret. The music will
take me back to the lotus pond
at our old home in the village of Sultanpur:
then, I will drift away on the fallen petals.

—Jon Mukand

WORDS FOR A PERCUSSION INSTRUMENT

The man crouched
                beside his empty rickshaw
                        ignores the static hum of the shoppers
who gather around, waiting
                for someone to speak, to strike just
                        one phosphorescent word.
He does not care
                about the snake charmer
                        who no longer plays
his gourd, and has let his cobra
                settle down
                        in its wicker basket. The man
crouched near the gutter
                might have felt
                        its curved hypodermic fangs,
for his muscles,
                the ones carved out
                        in all the years
of rickshaw-pulling, are no longer
                his. They are an offering
                        to the statuette of Shiva,
the Destroyer, enshrined in a mud wall;
                they are pieces of unleavened bread
                        dipped in a bowl
of spiced lentil soup.
                And why
                        should he care about the woman
selling her brightly patterned
                cotton saris, embroidered by hand
                        for the past
three months? And in the end,
                he will not even care
                        about the man who has vanished
into the streets as a fly
                disappears from a tray of confections,
                        leaving behind a few
colonies of bacteria; the same man
                who paid his fare
                        with a kick in the groin.

The man crouched
            into himself only cares
                        about the extra rupee
he will not have
                to spend on kerosene oil for
                            lighting up
his hut with a tin roof,
                where the rain
                            keeps playing its *tabla*.

THE TASTE OF THE OCEAN
                                (for Eddie H.)

Your new smile
affects me like my first
solitary orange-burst of poppies by the ocean:

I knelt down to
stroke a silken petal, though afraid
of bruising it.
I shouldn't have
stood up
so quickly: the earth's eager gravity
drained the bright red life
out of my brain's
pulsating blood vessels.

As the sky suddenly
turned a low-pitched
shade of blue,
the sequoias loomed above, offering
their dark green cradles.

Salt air, flecked with
pieces of clouds, flew
easily into my lungs, which will never
be plugged
with swirls of mucus, like yours.

You would not want
a taste of that stringent air. Your body, with its
infant wisdom, knows it has too much salt.

A friend told me he had once diagnosed
cystic fibrosis with a wet kiss.
Holding
your light body in
one arm, listening with a stethoscope
to your collapsed lung, I do not
want to kiss you.

An electrode, sensitive to each
charged atom of salt,
can make the diagnosis.

I have always been afraid of the ocean.

FIRST PAYMENT

In the waiting room, she releases
her white hair from a blue gauze scarf.
Her body has accepted the disease with
no cure, her questions are
empty snail shells. The pain stays,
with the appetite of crabgrass.
She cannot reach
inside, pluck it out by the roots.

Some days, she wants to be only
a gust of winter wind sweeping
the fresh snow
into drifts & whorls on the prairie, filtering
through an apple orchard. She might
linger, wrap herself around
naked branches, wait for spring buds.
She might even learn to be

patient for the orange sun
to drag the bleached skeleton of each day
behind the snow-tinted hills.

The intercom calls. Clenching her
body, she lifts herself up
with a gnarled, polished walking-stick.
In the examining room, her eyes
wander over the fresh table,
the chrome lamp with its fixed gaze.

The student knocks and enters, ready
for her coerced smiles, her
handshake brittle as a curled up leaf.
From her black handbag, a
sealed envelope. *Open it.*
Inside, a new fifty-dollar bill.
To help with school, I know it's expensive.
He can only smile, return her money.
It lies in her palm like a
handful of earth picked up, raised
to the sky
as an offering to the spring wind.

—*Jon Mukand*

FAMILY
AND FRIENDS
Afraid To Name This Dying

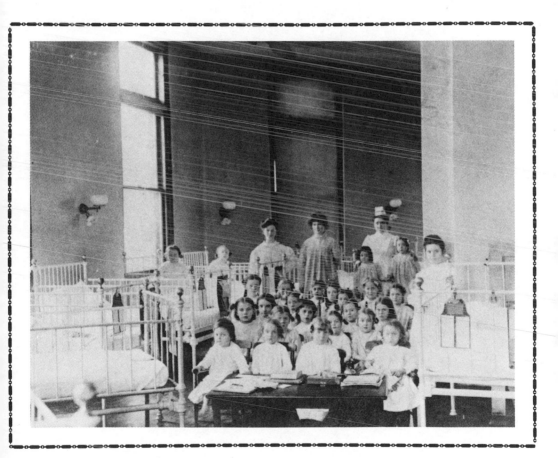

FAMILY AND FRIENDS
Afraid To Name This Dying

I have just finished examining an elderly man whose life is stuttering through a massive stroke, and now, after reviewing his records, I am writing the orders. This is the easy part. Outside, in a dimly lit alcove, his family is talking in soft, bandaged voices. They are transplant candidates for hope. This time, I have to disappoint them all. On other occasions, I have been less pessimistic. But the family room next to the ICU is no place for false hope; it would only be rejected in the end after a severe reaction, a mismatched transplant.

A physician cannot be responsible only for the patient. A common joke heard on pediatric services is that one is "treating the parents," whose anxiety often demands action, any action, preferably a pill of some sort. To some degree, this principle extends to all the other specialties. Relatives & friends also have to be "treated." This consists of frequent meetings to inform them of the patient's condition and to provide reassurance. And in case any problems arise, good relations with the family are invaluable. Fortunately, medical educators are now stressing the importance of maintaining a good rapport with the family; a respected orthopedic surgeon writes that during "the emergency treatment for an injured patient, . . . kindly communication with his relatives is essential, deserved, and appreciated."[1]

Illness is always distressing to a patient's family and friends, but especially so when they see the pathologic process in front of their eyes and have to deal with their own ignorance and fear. The *Commands of Love*, described by Molly Peacock, require us to "hover over those in pain / doing things unasked for and unwanted." When dealing with illness, we are caught in a network of paradoxes, as this poet so deftly elaborates. John Updike also analyzes how the patient with *Pain* interacts with others. He feels isolated from the rest of the world; conversation, smiles and laughter only "slide away / like rain beating on a filthy window / when pain interposes." When a person suffers a *Stroke,* communication can also be severely disrupted. Susan Irene Rea presents just such a situation. The speaker's uncle, losing his ability to speak, leaves the family "word by word." The word "language" is prominently placed, foreshadowing the uncle's inability to express himself and find words for objects (expressive aphasia with anomia). The desperate family members are unable to comprehend the uncle, and "rush at [him] with objects, / determined to interpret what [he] said." With large *Strokes* involving the right hemisphere, as in the poem by William Stafford, language is intact, but spatial reasoning and orientation are affected. In fact, some patients completely ignore everything on the left half of the visual field. We feel the speaker's resigned acceptance in the final line: 'The birthdays of the old require such candles."

Normal reactions of grief include "somatic distress; preoccupation with the image of the deceased; guilt feelings of negligence of the deceased; hostility towards doctors and others, charging them with not properly caring for the deceased before death; restlessness; inability to organize activities or to carry on customary social pleasantries."[2] Many of the following poems show diverse reactions to bereavement. Part of the difference is of course due to the unique relationship in each poem. The pair of poems by Sharon Olds confront the repulsive aspects of a father's death. Perhaps in an attempt to understand and accept the process of his death, the speaker in the poem describes the glass of bloody mucus in a clinical manner. Her "father has to / gargle, hack, cough, and spit a / mouthful of thick stuff." What may initially seem like morbid fascination turns into a process of acceptance in the final line: "spit on the table, these last mouthfuls of his life." This process of letting go is extended in the second poem by Olds. "When he breathed his last breath it was he," in spite of his debilitated appearance. The words *he, him,* and *his* are repeated throughout the poem, to emphasize his living identity, until his silver hair becomes the "unliving glistening / matter of this world."

When a son remembers an estranged father's death in *Last Elegy*, he is confronted with some difficult emotions. Unsure about the meaning of his father's whispered "I love you," the son in Stephen Berg's poem cannot even respond and keeps his 'eyes on the [TV] screen.' Phyllis Janowitz also describes the unreality of seeing a father's death: "tubes / sustaining him, blood and potassium / dripping in, maintaining a proper electrolyte balance." In a complicated poem about *Heart Failures*, Richard Howard examines the relationship between a couple and her father who died of a heart attack. Jon Silkin's much-anthologized poem on the *Death of a Son* also has a complex metaphoric development. Finding it difficult to communicate with his mentally retarded son, the sorrowful father describes this barrier through the metaphor of a house dwelling in silence. Perhaps because the child was "something like a person," the father struggles to define him in less vague terms, and to understand his own reactions; the repetition of "something" many times in the poem suggests the uncertain and ambivalent response to this entity who was his son. In the beautifully simple final lines, the father is convinced that his dying child was able to communicate and to feel emotions. The elaborate descriptions serve a rhetorical function of leading to a modestly sublime ending.

The reaction to bereavement may include denial and guilt at some stage, which, if not overcome, can become pathological. In *Talking to Grief*, Denise Levertov recognizes that, in reacting to a loss, she has treated grief like a neglected pet. Grief must not only be accepted but also be well cared for, given its "own corner, / a worn mat to lie on, / [and a] water dish." "Winter" may symbolize progression to a serious maladjustment, and grief is afraid it will not find its "real place" before then. John Hollander's poem goes even further in reducing the grieving process to its basic elements. In doing so, the speaker acknowledges the depth of grief. *The Dying Friend* becomes separated from the external world and its "cold, continuing light," which "intruded" into the patient's room. Although running the risk of cliché (light vs. dark for life vs. death), this poem is elevated to the level of art by the fundamental emotions expressed in the refrain: "I missed you there, then and now."

Intellectualization often helps in dealing with grief, as in poems by Sydney Lea, James Dickey and C. K. Williams. *The Return*, by the first poet, uses metaphors from astronomy and the motif of circles. We either cannot see ("occultation") or think we see but really do not ("apparition"), and are finally left "searching a sign of perpetuation." The dominant image of circles (*button, breasts, moon, plums*) leads to "the cycling back of things / too cursedly familiar." Moving away from abstractions, Lea realizes the awkwardness of his interaction with his dying friend, and deeply feels the "helplessness" of his "small-talk Yankee palaver" while true communication "frightened" him. A different mode of abstraction occurs in *Angina*—an extended personification of death, "the dreamer" who waits for an old woman to die. Death, resting "in the heart," has an objective view of her surroundings and her past. In deference to her composure, even death is obliged to be "chastened, respectful," and patient. As a tribute and syntactical symbol of her long and full life, a complex and well-paced sentence spans the last four stanzas. C. K. Williams sees pathology reflected in the landscape *On Learning of a Friend's Illness*. The rural scene is being "amputated by freeways and developments" while the horses are "thinning out, reverting." His grief spills over and extends to our societal diseases. (He is also no doubt thinking of his friend James Wright's fine poem about horses, *A Blessing*.)

How do patients respond to the way family and friends react to illness? Mary Farrell describes the interactions of a couple dealing with terminal illness in the wife, who is forming physical and emotional *Scar Tissue*. She sees her illness progressing: "I can only rake the yard / in quarters now." The economic burden of her disease makes her "bark about money," and in her despair, she goes so far as to "ask why you love me." On a much lighter note, Ogden Nash writes how patients with various conditions might be perceived by society. Some people may very well say, *I'm Terribly Sorry for you, but I Can't Help Laughing* because they do not "realize that an affliction can be ludicrous and still be ominous and painful." In spite of his humor, Nash usually has a serious side to his poems, as in this one: Society legitimizes our illnesses, and authorizes physicians to confirm its opinions.

Robert Hedin's *On Tuesdays They Open the Local Pool to the Stroke Victims* is a fine poem, but demonstrates a common problem with our attitude towards the disabled. We can all agree that "Something terrible / Has been bled out of these lives," but disability should not have to be hidden. Stroke victims may not need to "prove to their middle-aged sons / They can still dance"; they may simply want to swim for therapeutic benefits. *Her Stroke*, by Jim Schley, perceptively describes the interactions of a mother, daughter, and the daughter's lover at the sickbed. Although an outsider, he too feels the loss of her past vitality and grace as a dancer, "hot as sunlight criss-crossed / in a handglass"; this contrasts with her "stanchioned" bed, which suggests a support, but also a restraint for animals. In the final lines, the poet implies that this woman's grief may be for herself, completing the identification of daughter with mother: "You love her / for everything, everything / you are." Treatment of a stroke or other condition must not end after the acute management; every attempt must be made to return patients to their homes. Sometimes, there is no recourse but to send patients to a *Nursing Home*, as in Barry Spack's poem about a senile mother. She can only communicate in "a salad of noises," and the speaker's aunt advises him to let go of his grief at seeing his mother demented, to "avoid / abiding mourning."

In the course of an illness, perceptive relatives may come to appreciate the oppressive nature of a hospital room, which only adds to the burden of poor health. Sandra Gilbert has written two sensitive poems on the subject. In the poem, *For my Aunt in Memorial Hospital* the colors of autumn leaves create a stark contrast to the hospital, where "nothing burns, nothing blooms." Not only this, the silence is soporific, and "leaks / like ether from the corridors." The only respite from this atmosphere lies in visits from relatives who are still in touch with leaves that "crackle and fall," instead of being lost in a "forest [that] is still, the growth of a gray day." While trying to console herself on *The Night Grandma Died*, the poet realizes why she cannot: the thought of the hospital bed with its "cold . . . gray rails grating, clanking," just like a cage. In contrast, David Bottoms describes a dying grandmother as "a pale orchid under the oxygen tent," and in spite of her condition, sees her "in bloom." Tenderness may overcome the depressing conditions.

Alice Walker's poem *Medicine* shows the importance of keeping patients in familiar surroundings, if at all medically possible. I have seen a number of elderly patients become acutely disoriented on being transplanted to strange surroundings, especially at night. This phenomenon has even been given a name: sundowning. The grandmother in Walker's poem is sensitive to her husband's needs, and gives him medicine, literally as medications perhaps, but also in the form of her presence, epitomized by her 'long / un- / braided / hair.'

Striking parallels between two stages of grief, before and after bereavement, occur in the pairs of poems by Edwin Honig and Peter Davison. *Now, Before the End, I Think*, by the former poet, shows a couple "holding hands in awe of being / now, together, this moment, now," before they are forever severed. Davison's poem, *Moving Into Memory*, as the title suggests, is also about a transition, the knowledge of imminent death. The speaker addresses his beloved as "dark sunbeam, my bedlight, . . . freshener of shade," creating an interplay of light and dark, of life and death. After the cremation, he is left with *Stern Stuff*: crushed "twigs of brittle, lace-veined wings." Her ashes are still associated with the living form, which 'glowed flowery with every kind of laughter.' The difficult fact of the "cannister" with its ashes is temporarily obscured by this vivid image. In a similar manner, Honig's poem, *Now, My Usefulness Over*, feels the "weight of [her] death / in a handful of ashes." He is also left with a glittering image of his beloved: "this cruel and absolute / jewel of your life." Kenneth Rexroth wrote a poem for *Andree Rexroth* a number of years since they first came to Mt. Tamalpais. The wildlife and scenery are much the same, but some "New sand bars and cobble beds / Have been left where erosion" has attacked the hills. The restrained imagery and emotion of this poem are nonetheless filled with the tension of constancy and change in the poet's physical and emotional landscape.

I have had to console a number of bereaved families, and although each time it is less difficult, I cannot help feeling slightly useless. Every physician, I suppose, must wonder if a death could or should have been avoided or postponed. We are encouraged to attend autopsies of our patients, as if we might learn something to benefit the next patient or to vindicate ourselves. We are not taught that sometimes there is nothing we can do or could have done to prevent death from, in the words of Peter Davison, "chafing the light from smoky diamond eyes."

COMMANDS OF LOVE

The tragedy of a face in pain
is how little you can do for it
because it is so closed. Having lain

outlined in knives, afraid to move,
it cannot move and therefore cannot love.
This is why we say it is a mask,

for the face is so frozen by hurt and fear
it is unable to ask for help.
You can do nothing but stay near.

This is why we hover over those in pain
doing things unasked for and unwanted,
hoping simply with our bodies to cover pain

as if to protect it. Better to go away.
But by asking for help pain is erased,
for the face opens to say what it has to say

and a beauty of concentration overcomes it.
The pain is saying outwardly what it is.
The help it asks for is what overcomes it.

Help me on with this dress.
Get me a glass of water.
Look, I've made a mess.

Both the face of pain and the face of the one
riveted to it in relief believe there's still
something to get, something to be done.

                    —*Molly Peacock*

PAIN

flattens the world—its bubbles
of bliss, its epiphanies, the upright
sticks of day-to-day business—
and shows us what seriousness is.

And shows us, too, how those around us
do not and cannot share
our being; though men talk animatedly
and challenge silence with laughter

and women bring their engendering smiles
and eyes of famous mercy,
these kind things slide away
like rain beating on a filthy window

when pain interposes.
What children's pageant in gauze
filled the skull's ballroom before
the caped dark stranger commanded, *Freeze?*

Life is worse than folly. We live
within a cage wherefrom escape
annihilates the captive; this, too,
pain leads us to consider anew.

                              —*John Updike*

STROKE

After the family dinner, language
is trivial and easy—
until you lose it entirely, Uncle,
asking for something you want
which suddenly has no name.
"Goddamn," you moan, "gimme a . . .
All I want's a . . . Jesus Christ,
ain't you got one?"
The family hands you sweaters,
pills, icepicks, glasses of brandy,
knives. Nothing will do.
Afraid of empty hands,
they rush at you with objects,
determined to interpret what you've said,
afraid to name this dying
and to watch you leave them, word by word.

—Susan Irene Rea

STROKES

The left side of her world is gone—
the rest sustained by memory
and a realization: There are still the children.

Going down our porch steps her pastor
calls back: "We are proud of her recovery,
and there is a chiropractor up in Galesburg. . ."

The birthdays of the old require such candles.

—William Stafford

THE GLASS

I think of it with wonder now,
the glass of mucus that stood on the table
next to my father all weekend. The cancer is
growing fast in his throat now,
and as it grows it sends out pus like the
sun sending out solar flares, those
pouring tongues of fire. So my father has to
gargle, hack, cough, and spit a
mouth full of thick stuff
into the glass every ten minutes or so,
scraping the glass up his lower lip to
get the last bit off his skin, then he
sets the glass down on the table and it
sits there, shiny and faintly
gold like a glass of beer foam, he
gurgles and reaches for it again and
gets the heavy sputum out,
full of bubbles and moving around like yeast he is
like some god producing dark food from his own mouth.
He himself can eat nothing anymore,
just a swallow of milk sometimes,
cut with water, and even then it
can't always get past the tumor,
and the next time the saliva comes up it's
chalkish and ropey, he has to roll it a
long time in his throat like a ball of
clay to form it and get it up and dis-
gorge the elliptical globule into the cup—
and the wonder to me is that it did not disgust me,
that glass of phlegm that stood there all day and
filled slowly with compound globes and then I'd
empty it and it would fill again and
shimmer there on the table until the
room seemed to turn around it

in an orderly way, like a model of the solar system
turning around the gold sun,
my father like the dark earth that
used to be the center of the universe, now
turning with the rest of us
around his death—bright glass of
spit on the table, these last mouthfuls of his life.

THE MOMENT OF MY FATHER'S DEATH

When he breathed his last breath it was he,
my father, although he was so transformed
no one who had not been with him
for the last hours would know him, the gold
skin luminous as cold animal fat,
the eyes cast all the way back into his head,
the whites gleaming like a white iris, the
nose that grew thinner and thinner every minute, the
open mouth racked open with that
tongue in it like all the heartbreak of the mortal,
a tongue so dried, scalloped, darkened and
material. You could see the mucus
risen like gorge into the back of his mouth
but it was he, the huge slack yellow arms,
the spots of blood under the skin
black and precise, we had come this far with him
step by step, it was he, his last
breath was his, not taken with desire but
his, light as the sphere of a dandelion seed
coming out of his mouth and floating across the room.
Then the nurse pulled up his gown and
listened for his heart, I saw the stomach

silvery and hairy, it was his stomach, she
moved to the foot of the bed and stood there, she
did not shake her head she stood and
nodded at me. And for a minute it was fully
he, my father, dead but completely
himself, a man with an open mouth and
no breath, gold skin and
black spots on his arms, I kissed him and
spoke to him. He looked like someone
killed in a violent bloodless struggle, all that
strain in his neck, that look of pulling back, that
stillness he seemed to be holding at first and
then it was holding him, the skin
tightened slightly around his whole body
as if the purely physical were claiming him,
and then it was not my father,
it was not a man, it was not an animal, I
stood and ran my hand through the silver hair,
plunged my fingers into it gently and
lifted them up slowly through the grey
waves of it, the unliving glistening
matter of this world.

—Sharon Olds

LAST ELEGY

Surgeons cutting a hole
in my father's skull
with one of those saws that lift
a plug out of bone also took
a big lump off my spine
in the dream I don't understand
that flickered back
the day before he died.
We were at the shore following
a golf match on TV,
eating, napping. His drained
gray face didn't reveal
any sense of being here,
any desire to live.
The money he made,
the failure he thought he was
in love, in business,
intensified his mood
after the heart attack.
The sky blew flat, smeary gray,
a few fly-like figures
paced the cold beach. Millie,
Clair, Margot, Mom and I
didn't know how to stop his
staring out of nothing into nothing,
so we watched hard
Nicklaus miss two easy putts
and other famous pros tee off
with that quick fluid swing
they have, then stroll down
the fairway to the ball,
the whole world manicured, green.

To say, "I love you"
meant "I know I'm dying,"
but you said it,
at least I think I heard you
whisper it to me. Or was it to yourself?
I kept my eyes on the screen.

—*Stephen Berg*

CELLS

My father, climbing stairs in tenements
to visit his parolees, frightened, a gun
in his holster he knew he'd never shoot.
Two hours a day packed into a subway.
Thirty years. Almost a life sentence.

My father, 74, incarcerated on the 14th
floor of a vast teaching hospital,
wearing striped pajamas and hooked
to a machine lit up like something
you drop quarters into. He raises
his head weakly and whispers,
P.J you have a real hepatitis face.

Intensive Care: My mother, bending
over the bed, one of the tubes
sustaining him, blood and potassium
dripping in, maintaining
a proper electrolyte balance.

I'm leaving, riding back to Boston
on an old Pennsylvania Railroad car.
The air in here is greasy, poisonous.
We pass the Connecticut Sound. Three
bathers, heads teetering on a platter
of scummy water. A billboard
with this graffiti: *Rosie, I Love You.*

The word love, read in a jolt of wheels.
Astonishing. Ineludible. Like a blissful
couple, joined at the chest, thighs,
knees, kissing in the doorway
you're trying to exit through.

—Phyllis Janowitz

HEART FAILURES

My dear, you described it
in such clear detail I should have seen
for myself, suspected from the start.
    You know how we are, though,
all of us, (even yourself, surely?)
about these things: reality comes hard
        and never fast enough
to be the rule . . . I suppose the rain
distracted me, the storm in the air
        but not yet upon us.
Still, just your tone must have meant *something*
at that point—the really awful part
        when your father drove you
all those flat miles out to the new farm
(your voice faltered then), arriving there
        with the rain that came down
soon like dye, darkening everything.
You watched him run, hunched and determined
        between the black puddles
to an ominous haystack, and then
it happened, silent in the blurred lens
        of the Packard windshield:
as if he *meant* to, sliding slowly
into the mud. You had never heard
        of a coronary,
and when he cursed you back to the car
you obeyed, of course. What could you do
        but peer through the downpour
while his limbs twitched, and a kind of mist
—the emanation of pain, it was—
        aureoled his body
where it lay in the rain another
hour until a neighbor took you both
        away. Remembering
how you turned into a child again,

just telling it, *his* witnessing child,
  I guess who I am, too
(it was all so simple, once you set
the scene), lying here awake, lying
  with what is left of you
cold in the sheets against me. The rain
hisses under traffic—it has come
  for good then, so to speak.
I know who I am *for you*. I know,
suffering my private spasm here,
  how anonymously
you yielded when I caught your long legs
in mine: not yours, not mine. From how far
  you must have been staring
through what dim glass, while my foreign nerves
performed! I know who I am—who cares?
  It is as true of this
seizure as of that other: *having*
teaches us little, nothing of love
  whose presence we locate,
and whose power, only in our losses.
You stir in my arms and say, "I thought
  the rain would never come."
Now that it has, my dear, I almost
fear that it will never end. Never.

       —Richard Howard

DEATH OF A SON
(who died in a mental hospital aged one)

Something has ceased to come along with me.
Something like a person: something very like one.
And there was no nobility in it
Or anything like that.

Something was there like a one year
Old house, dumb as stone. While the near buildings
Sang like birds and laughed
Understanding the pact

They were to have with silence. But he
Neither sang nor laughed. He did not bless silence
like bread, with words.
He did not forsake silence.

But, rather, like a house in mourning
Kept the eye turned in to watch the silence while
The other houses like birds
Sang around him.

And the breathing silence neither
Moved nor was still.

I have seen stones, I have seen brick
But this house was made up of neither bricks nor stone
But a house of flesh and blood
With flesh of stone

And bricks for blood. A house
Of stones and blood in breathing silence with the other
Birds singing crazy on its chimneys.
But this was silence,

This was something else, this was
Hearing and speaking though he was a house drawn
          Into silence, this was
                    Something religious in his silence,

          Something shining in his quiet,
This was different this was altogether something else:
          Though he never spoke, this
                    Was something to do with death.

          And then slowly the eye stopped looking
Inward. The silence rose and became still.
The look turned to the outer place and stopped,
          With the birds still shrilling around him.
                    And as if he could speak

He turned over on his side with his one year
Red as a wound
He turned over as if he could be sorry for this
And out of his eyes two great tears rolled, like stones, and he died.

—Jon Silkin

TALKING TO GRIEF

Ah, grief, I should not treat you
like a homeless dog
who comes to the back door
for a crust, for a meatless bone.
I should trust you.

I should coax you
into the house and give you
your own corner,
a worn mat to lie on,
your own water dish.

You think I don't know you've been living
under my porch.
You long for your real place to be readied
before winter comes. You need
your name,
your collar and tag. You need
the right to warn off intruders,
to consider
my house your own
and me your person
and yourself
my own dog.

                    —*Denise Levertov*

THE DYING FRIEND

I visited him at noon.
Even so, he lay in a
Kind of darkening: the light
From outside intruded there,
Part of some other picture.
I missed you there, then and now.

Then I came back here, hoping
To find you, with drawn shades in
Bed, to kindle what we could
Of dark warmth, while outside lay
A cold, continuing light.
I missed you there, then and now.

—John Hollander

THE RETURN: INTENSIVE CARE

I felt for the button . . .
There's a circle of perpetual occultation
at the depressed pole,
within which stars never rise,
and, at the elevated one, one of apparition,
from which they never fall.
I used these facts
to figure the limits of my situation
—mine? or was it yours?—
as again I came back.

Where was I?
I thumbed the button for your floor.
It lit.
Suddenly, I thought,
everywhere there are circles,
as in some new weather or fashion:
the breasts both of a young farm girl
and, sadder, of a fat old orderly
riding up beside me;
the elevator's orbicular lamp bulbs;

and colored like linen,
each drop of snow the night before,
big and round as a saucer—
a night such as we persist in
calling a freak, though it isn't
anything more than the cycling back of things
too cursedly familiar.
Yes, though it was spring,
though it was April,
the moon had worn a great wet halo.

Signifying what?
Why look up
the facts on charts?
How often in history

has everything happened!
The nurse again wheeled away
your tray with its apple, untouched,
and two dark plums,
which precisely matched,
in color and conformation,

the racoon rounds
of valor and exhaustion
through which your eyes peered,
brighter, still, than any planet.
O Jesus Jesus Jesus Jesus Jesus!
Inwardly I cried,
to me the word
recurring like any old habit.
Poor stately Jew, forgive the helplessness
that enforced my genteel outward mode

as you lay there,
my small-talk Yankee palaver
of mercilessness in Mother Nature—
buds in remission,
pathetic birds
spiralling up from the sheeted roads
as if, I surmised, nothing now remained
but vertical migration.
I dropped my eyes. All else, anything
that I might have been moved to say,

anything that might have reached to the heart
of what we may or may not be
here on earth
to do or serve, dismayed
and frightened me.
O David, I couldn't speak
of anything beyond the trivial,
by horror of risk held back,
by horror of saying something
even more banal.

You were on morphine.
You who for the length of this evil illness
had never complained
but had made of yourself a figure—
Look to the light,
or *Don't try to cling* . . .
Shy of prayer,
desperate with my own feckless
impulse to speech, at length I hung
as if in midair

as the dark outside
began again its round.
All so cursedly dignified!
At length, in the distilled absence of sound,
I recalled my *why why why why why!*
at the death of my small terrier.
What a petty thing to remember!
And yet perhaps those yelps
when I was so young
were the only eloquence possible.

As was perhaps the gentle rejoinder
(she had seen more than I)
of my mother's mother;
Revelation helps.
There in the hospital,
lacking for words to tender,
I had recourse to fashion.
Forgive me, I nattered;
then left, once more depressing the button;
then lifted my eyes,

searching a sign of perpetuation.
Would it do any good to tell you that I cried?
There were stars, or there were none,
from wherever it was I stood.
There was, or there wasn't, a moon.

                    —Sydney Lea

ANGINA

That one who is the dreamer lies mostly in her left arm,
Where the pain shows first,
Tuned in on the inmost heart,
Never escaping. On the blue, bodied mound of chenille,
That limb lies still.
Death in the heart must be calm,

Must not look suddenly, but catch the window-framed squirrel
In a mild blue corner
Of an eye staring straight at the ceiling
And hold him there.
Cornered also, the oak tree moves
All the ruffled green way toward itself

Around the squirrel thinking of the sun
As small boys and girls tiptoe in
Overawed by their existence,
For courtly doctors long dead
Have told her that to bear children
Was to die, and they are the healthy issue

Of four of those. Oh, beside that room the oak leaves
Burn out their green in an instant, renew it all
From the roots when the wind stops.
All afternoon she dreams of letters
To disc jockeys, requesting the "old songs,"
The songs of the nineties, when she married, and caught

With her first child rheumatic fever.
Existence is family: sometime,
Inadequate ghosts round the bed,
But mostly voices, low voices of serious drunkards
Coming in with the night light on
And the pink radio turned down;

She hears them ruin themselves
On the rain-weeping wires, the bearing-everything poles,
Then dozes, not knowing sleeping from dying—
It is day. Limbs stiffen when the heart beats
Wrongly. Her left arm tingles,
The squirrel's eye blazes up, the telephone rings,

Her children and her children's children fail
In school, marriage, abstinence, business.
But when I think of love
With the best of myself—that odd power—
I think of riding, by chairlift,
Up a staircase burning with dust

In the afternoon sun slanted also
Like stairs without steps
To a room where an old woman lies
Who can stand on her own two feet
Only six strange hours every month:
Where such a still one lies smiling

And takes her appalling risks
In absolute calm, helped only by the most
Helplessly bad music in the world, where death,
A chastened, respectful presence
Forced by years of excessive quiet
To be stiller than wallpaper roses,

Waits, twined in the roses, saying slowly
To itself, as sprier and sprier
Generations of disc jockeys chatter,
I must be still and not worry,
Not worry, not worry, to hold
My peace, my poor place, my own.

—*James Dickey*

ON LEARNING OF A FRIEND'S ILLNESS

For James Wright

The morning is so gray that the grass is gray and the side of the white
     horse grazing
is as gray and hard as the harsh, insistent wind gnawing the iron sur-
     face of the river,
while far off on the other shore, the eruptions from the city seem for
     once more docile and benign
than the cover of nearly indistinguishable clouds they unfurl to insin-
     uate themselves among.

It is a long time since the issues of mortality have taken me this way.
     Shivering,
I tramp the thin, bitten track to the first rise, the first descent, and,
     toiling up again,
I startle out of their brushy hollow the whole herd of wild-eyed,
     shaggy, unkempt mares,
their necks, rumps, withers, even faces begrimed with patches of the
     gluey, alluvial mud.

All of them at once, their nostrils flared, their tails flung up over their
     backs like flags,
are suddenly in flight, plunging and shoving along the narrow furrow
     of the flood ditch,
bursting from its mouth, charging headlong toward the wires at the
     pasture's end,
banking finally like one great, graceful wing to scatter down the hill-
     side out of sight.

Only the oldest of them all stays with me, and she, sway-backed, over
     at the knees,
blind, most likely deaf, still, when I move towards her, swings her
     meager backside to me,
her ears flattening, the imperturbable opals of her eyes gazing reso-
     lutely over the bare,
scruffy fields, the scattered pines and stands of third-growth oak I
     called a forest once.

I slip up on her, hook her narrow neck, haul her to me, hold her for a
    moment, let her go.
I hardly can remember anymore what there ever was out here that
    keeps me coming back
to watch the land be amputated by freeways and developments, and
    the mares, in their sanctuary,
thinning out, reverting, becoming less and less approachable, more and
    more the symbols of themselves.

How cold it is. The hoofprints in the hardened muck are frozen lakes,
    their rims atilt,
their glazed opacities skewered with straw, muddled with the ancient
    and ubiquitous manure.
I pick a morsel of it up: scentless , harmless, cool, as dessicated as an
    empty hive,
it crumbles in my hand, its weightless, wingless filaments taken from
    me by the wind and strewn

in a long, surprising arc that wavers once then seems to burst into a
    rain of dust.
No comfort here, nothing to say, to try to say, nothing for anyone. I
    start the long trek back,
the horses nowhere to be seen, the old one plodding wearily away to
    join them,
the river, bitter to look at, and the passionless earth, and the grasses
    rushing ceaselessly in place.

                             —*C. K. Williams*

SCAR TISSUE

I can only rake the yard
in quarters now.
Last fall it was halves.
Before we got married,
I could rake my father's
two acres in less than a day.

You talk about lawn services.
 I bark about money.
You ask me where the girl
with all the fight is,
saying she was here only yesterday.

You go back to trying,
talking about this new treatment
with its different needles and tubes,
how it will potentiate and block,
gobble up the swelling.

We'll try it for a while
and, like everything else,
it will have moments of whole, half, fourth.
I am ready to be pushed in a pile,
the good parts along with the rotten.
I know once joy is gone love weakly follows.
The fall will come where I sit.

You go to the linen closet
we've turned into a clinic.
You break out the tubes and plastic.
In the bedroom, looking at the ceiling,
I ask why you love me.

—Mary Farrell

I'M TERRIBLY SORRY FOR YOU,
BUT I CAN'T HELP LAUGHING

Everybody has a perfect right to do what they please,
But one thing that I advise everybody not to do is to con-
    tract a laughable disease.
People speak of you respectfully if you catch bubonic,
And if you get typhus they think you have done some-
    thing positively mastodonic;
One touch of leprosy makes the whole world your kin,
And even a slight concussion earns you an anxious inquiry
    and not a leering grin.
Yes, as long as people are pretty sure you have something
    you are going to be removed by,
Why they are very sympathetic, and books and flowers
    and visits and letters are what their sympathy is
    proved by.
But unfortunately there are other afflictions anatomical,
And people insist on thinking that a lot of them are comi-
    cal,
And if you are afflicted with this kind of affliction people
    are amused and disdainful,
Because they are not bright enough to realize that an
    affliction can be ludicrous and still be ominous and
    painful.
Suppose for instance you have a dreadful attack of
    jaundice, what do they do?
They come around and smile and say Well well, how are
    you today, Dr. Fu-Manchu?
The early martyrs thought they knew what it was to be
    taken over the jumps,
But no martyr really ought to get his diploma until he
    his undergone his friends' witticisms during his
    mumps.
When you have laryngitis they rejoice,
Because apparently the funniest thing in the world
    is when you can't curse and swear at them for
    laughing at your lost voice, because you have lost
    your voice.

And as for boils,
Well, my pen recoils.
So I advise you, at the risk of being pedantic,
If you must be sick, by all means choose a sickness that
    is preferably fatal and certainly romantic,
Because it is much better to have that kind of sickness and
    be sick unto death or anyway half to death,
Than to have the other kind and be laughed to death.

—Ogden Nash

ON TUESDAYS THEY OPEN THE LOCAL POOL
TO THE STROKE VICTIMS

—for my sons

Thank God my own father didn't have to go through this.
Or I'd be driving him here every Tuesday
So he could swim his laps
Or splash around with the others
In the shallow end. Something terrible
Has been bled out of these lives. Why else
Would they be here pulling themselves along on their sides,
Scissoring, having to prove to their middle-aged sons
They can still dance.
                    The last three days I heard water
In the cellar, the rooms below me bumping together
Like dingies. Somewhere back in my sleep
My father splashes in the shallow end.
All these men, even
The balding ones waiting behind the chain-link fence
Watching their fathers, are down there
At the bottom of the stairs.
They are all gliding like sunlight,
Like trout across the cold floors of their breeding ponds.

                                    —*Robert Hedin*

HER STROKE

Even a lover is always, forever,
outside the grip of that gravity
where mother and daughter
interlock. Here she's slipping, on
and back: you clasp at her
as I hover near.
                        I can't
know her, now. There's no time.
Smell of camphor, dust of bromide.
The bed stanchioned with perpendicular
silver rods. The woman we watch there
is not like you; physical echoes,
but all her extensions tied up
and abstracted. The tongue frays
at the edge of the sentence,
the fingers at the hem of the sheet.
I try to imagine the dancer she was,
hot as sunlight criss-crossed
in a handglass.
                        You're impatient—
even angry. I haven't seen, not
exactly. She was elegant and sharp.
    It's not that she's changed
through shadings, like weather
                        but actually
vanished, only halfway returned.

Whatever your fury, you couldn't
have known. Who ever expects
treachery? faults
in the bloodstream, pulse
shut down
                for seconds
while the body is paralyzed, waiting,
    as arteries sieze on a dot

the heart had forgotten.
                    You say
maybe this is not your mother
but someone else, to be cared for
differently.
                    Fear, and exhaustion.
Yet so much of what was
is still clear, in what you do—
your voices, your hair—the ways
you both motion toward the blossoms
in the jar. I love her as I would love
someone wounded. You love her
for everything, everything
you are.

                    —Jim Schley

NURSING HOME

My mother babbles. A salad of noises.
'You know who this is?' asks my aunt and I dread
some horror of an answer, but no,
nothing. She rubs her tray instead.
'It's clean,' says my aunt, 'the tray is clean.
Evelyn, what are you cleaning? Play
with your cards, play *pishy-posh,*' and then she
laughs, that overflowing, tilts
her head at the word and laughs who sits
all day in her chair with her cards in a sweater
embroidered with flowers, all day each day
where the t.v. flickers. My aunt thinks she chose
senility. My aunt says you have to keep
moving, never worry, avoid
abiding mourning,
things that refuse to change.

—Barry Spacks

FOR MY AUNT IN MEMORIAL HOSPITAL

Mid-October. A warm moist day.
The sorrow of the trees, burning
toward winter, flares in the air,
each leaf a little rocket crackling out.

But where you are, nothing burns, nothing blooms.
They've emptied your body of its enemies,
they're filling you with sterile juices.
From your sealed window on the fourteenth floor

you see blank sky, smoke, the doped profile
of a stone forest. Mourning my trees,
I imagine you lying in the silence that leaks
like ether from the corridors:

you imagine nothing, you try to smile.
My leaves crackle and fall.
Your forest is still, the growth of a gray day.
I believe you are waiting for me.

                                      – *Sandra Gilbert*

THE NIGHT GRANDMA DIED

Adrift on the pillows. "She just died," said the nurse.
"A heart attack," the doctor said.
"It was easy, peaceful," I told her daughter.

I tried to picture the pincers of heaven
reaching down and twitching her, a little wrinkled diamond,
from the sweet white cot she lay on.

Tears and sniffles. My consolation
didn't work. Not even for me.
What was it, in the end, that wouldn't go away?

The bed. The feel of the cold rails
sliding up and down when people came with needles,
the gray rails grating, clanking, her fingers

yearning toward them like a baby's lips,
hoping for suction. And the white sheets
stiff as sails, scraping skin as if skin were wind, insubstantial.
And the night light, flashing, going out, flashing again.
And the tough mattress, sullen as a shark's back,
rising toward the nurse's hands

on its steel track.

—Sandra Gilbert

THE ORCHID

What do you remember of me?
The last time I saw you alive you had grown
white as the hospital sheet,
a pale orchid under the oxygen tent,
strange greenhouse.

Grandma, today I saw people on television
who had been revived from death.
They told how they rose
out of their bodies and saw operating rooms,
doctors hovering above white tables.
Others saw their bodies asleep in bed
and roamed their houses as naturally
as they had in life.
Could you see me standing by your shoulder
flower like a crucifix in my hand?

Describe that face for me,
the eyes that saw the orchid bloom.

—*David Bottoms*

MEDICINE

      Grandma sleeps with
      my sick
           grand—
pa so she
can get him
during the night
medicine
to stop
   the pain

       In
     the morning
      clumsily
        I
    wake
      them

Her eyes
look at me
from under—
         neath
his withered
arm

   The
medicine
  is all
    in
her long
  un—
     braided
       hair.

        —Alice Walker

NOW, BEFORE THE END, I THINK

Now, before the end, I think
of how it was when we began:
in holding hands before we knew
each other, in touch there was the silent
awe of what we soon would know
in knowing one another later,
as though to heal the wounds that words
would cause before they were inflicted.

Now, wordless again, you reach to hold
my hand as if to say in silence,
it is healed, we touch, we are together.
We have heard the end, drifting
to the brink of a new silence,
holding hands in awe of being
now together, this moment, now,
now before we part forever.

—Edwin Honig

NOW, MY USEFULNESS OVER

Now, my usefulness over,
the weight of your death
in a handful of ashes
drags at my mind.

My need is the lamp snuffed out
by your absence, and silence
all I have given
my mind to believe.

From ashes I carry you back
to your handsome warm fullness
and alight in a blackness
of time with the burden.

Turning I find myself emptied,
rifled of you and, cored
of my meaning, dumped
in a boneless sack.

Now stuck in my skin to wear,
minded over forever,
is this cruel and absolute
jewel of your life.

                    —Edwin Honig

MOVING INTO MEMORY

As long as those last words are never spoken
we can touch each other lightly
and sit here side by side
in the descending sun.
Our hands often creep
into one another's palms:
every other form of seeking
has gone lame or dry.
O dark sunbeam, my bed light, my cheer,
brightener of houses, freshener of shade,
the only gift I can be sure to keep
is this reaching and touching.
You will be allowed to keep nothing.

I keep unsure memory, and none.
The piano, glittering under delectable mountains,
has lost its way to the center of the music.
Silence gapes to swallow
the provocations of your laughter.
Though our days together are few,
the thunder of syllables
fills a black valley with light
while the wind whistles its own song
from the faraway edge of the glacier.

—Peter Davison

STERN STUFF

The ashes, done up in stiff white paper
with hospital folds sealed over at each end,
lie dizzily beside the hole we've dug.
Tan talcum silt, powdered by two years' drought,
sifts out of a shovel. We watch the cannister
tumble into the hole and lie alone.
Those ashes, while they held their lively form,
glowed flowery with every kind of laughter
and drove an ingenuity of will
to keep her vivid in a fading world.

Is this how we choke, in cataracts of dust?
What stern stuff it is, crumpling
the twigs of brittle, lace-veined wings
and chafing the light from smoky diamond eyes.

—Peter Davison

ANDREE REXROTH

Mt. Tamalpais

The years have gone. It is spring
Again. Mars and Saturn will
Soon come on, low in the West,
In the dusk. Now the evening
Sunlight makes hazy girders
Over Steep Ravine above
The waterfalls. The winter
Birds from Oregon, robins
And varied thrushes, feast on
Ripe toyon and madrone
Berries. The robins sing as
The dense light falls.
                          Your ashes
Were scattered in this place. Here
I wrote you a farewell poem,
And long ago another,
A poem of peace and love,
Of the lassitude of a long
Spring evening in youth. Now
It is almost ten years since
You came here to stay. Once more,
The pussy willows that come
After the New Year in this
Outlandish land are blooming.
There are deer and racoon tracks
In the same places. A few
New sand bars and cobble beds
Have been left where erosion
Has gnawed deep into the hills.
The rounds of life are narrow.
War and peace have passed like ghosts.
The human race sinks towards

Oblivion. A bittern
Calls from the same rushes where
You heard one on our first year
In the West; and where I heard
One again in the year
Of your death.

—Kenneth Rexroth

WOMEN

Flowers Of Ether In My Hair

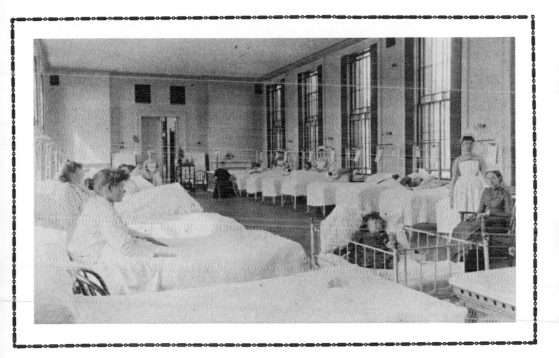

WOMEN
Flowers Of Ether In My Hair

You have come to this clinic for a physical examination, as you have been doing yearly for the last five years. The physician is someone you trust and feel comfortable with. On the examining table, you chat with him, a little nervously, while he examines the heart, lungs, breasts. He agrees there is a lump, small enough and not painful, but worrisome because of your family history of breast cancer. You are slightly relieved when he says it might be a benign cyst, but you suspect he may be trying to decrease your anxiety. Of course, a mammogram and a chest x-ray will be necessary. Next is the part you always wince to even think about: the pelvic exam. You resign yourself to the awkward position, the initial shock of the gloved hand and metal speculum. Then the sample from the cervix. Will it show any signs of cancer on the slide? You must wait to find out. Finally, the bi-manual exam, feeling for the ovaries from above and below. All this time you've been taking some deep breaths, just as the physician directed. Now you take a final breath which resembles a sigh, and sit up on the table. But the mammogram and chest x-ray remain to be done. You make an appointment a week from now, the earliest opening, and walk out of the tastefully decorated clinic into the welcome confusion of a city street.

The preceding scenario might have been written for the speaker of *One More Time*, by Patricia Goedicke. The patient is prepared for the penetrating radiation which feels like "the metal teeth of death." In an effort to escape the situation, "suspended in icy silence," she tries to imagine herself outside her body. But the technician, asking her to breathe deeply once again to obtain the optimum film, interrupts her reverie to remind her she can never be "free . . . not now / Or ever."

The medical needs of women have given rise to the specialty of obstetrics and gynecology. Not long ago, this field consisted almost entirely of male physicians. More than a third of students in some medical schools are women, but the majority of Ob-Gyn physicians are still male. Indeed, until as recently as 1984, the American College of Obstetricians and Gynecologists had never elected a woman president! These facts in themselves suggest potential problems for the doctor-patient relationship, since women may feel that female physicians are more likely than males to understand their problems, both physical and psychological. I never realized this more acutely than during the first pelvic exam I performed. Fortunately, the patient was tolerant of my inexperience and did her best to make *me* feel more comfortable with the procedure. A recent nationwide survey has shown, however, that only ten percent of women preferred a female physician. The most important factor was not gender, but the physician's interest in the patient.[1]

The doctor-patient relationship is sensitively examined in Linda Pastan's *At the Gynecologist's*. The patient, in a vulnerable and embarrassing position, is "caught in these metal stirrups." She also senses the precarious balance of her health, which appears dreamlike in the clinical setting. Perhaps this patient has a chronic problem, and has to return for tests and follow-up visits. These may lead to drastic measures, such as an operation. That thought is very much in the patient's mind as she associates 'stirrups' with "galloping towards death / with flowers of ether" in her hair.

Operations on the sexual organs are especially difficult, since they raise questions about the patient's womanhood. A patient I examined during my clerkship in Ob-Gyn was scheduled to have a hysterectomy for a benign condition of her uterus. She asked the usual questions during the physical exam, but didn't seem overly concerned. Only later, perhaps when she felt more comfortable with me, did she burst into tears about losing her uterus. Unfortunately, her husband had been unable to discuss the subject openly with her, which only made matters worse.

A common operation for women involves the breasts. A mastectomy may cause a patient to feel she is no longer attractive—to her partner, and more importantly, to herself.

Biopsy under local anesthesia is usually necessary to exclude malignant growths, which is probably the situation in Kirk Maxey's *Ann: Room 8 No. 2 Biopsy with Frozen Section*. Yet to the operating room personnel, the biopsy may seem routine. The environment is sterile, orderly, and there seems to be little room for emotions. Disembodied "latex fingers, muffled voices" suggest the distance between the surgeon and the patient. Communication with the patient during the procedure, instead of leaving her "bathed in blue" under the drapes, could have helped alleviate much of her anxiety. Robert Hass, in *A Story About the Body*, shows the effect of a double mastectomy on a romance. The rejected partner, with a true artist's flair, responds to her insensitive suitor in a brilliant manner.

A textbook of Obstetrics and Gynecology emphasizes that "pregnancy and the puerperium are periods of psychologic stress for all women, though some may experience minimal discomfort, and for many it may be the happiest time of life." The emotional state must be evaluated, for it "often has adverse effects on physical well-being."[2] A warning signal can be ambivalence towards the mother, as we see in *Waiting for the Doctor* by Colette Inez. The speaker fears she was viewed by her mother as "female scum, dirty secretions / attendant on woman's time," and this affects her perception of her own unborn child, a "9-lb. load to cart in and out of next year's bed." Mixed feelings about childbirth are even more evident in Sandra McPherson's poem *Pregnancy*. The first lines are a bit too cheerful to ring true, and are in striking contrast to the conclusion.There may be some underlying anger towards the father of the child, which is only hinted at in "I have no decisions to master." Erica Jong's poem on pregnancy is more philosophical. She sets up a dialectic between creation and destruction, recognizing that we are "alive with blood / that will only sing & die." Nonetheless, *The Buddha in the Womb* can have "infinite hope."

Nowadays, medical technology allows the mother to visualize the unborn child on an ultrasound screen. At first, the mother in *Soft Mask* by Mary Karr needs to have the fetus' heart pointed out to her. It seems lost "in his own fluid orbit," and the mother realizes the symbolic nature of their individual heartbeats, "first matching then at odds with" hers. A different sort of pre-natal monitoring gives occasion for a poem *Written on Learning of Arrhythmia in the Unborn Child*. The threat of miscarriage prompts Judith Skillman to meditate on those women who have lost their children, who are "carrying the past in their striated laps." As technology advances, new ethical questions are raised. A recent issue of the *New England Journal of Medicine* (4/87) dealt with the question of using DNA probes to diagnose a certain muscular dystrophy in fetuses. Far from perfect, the technique can only arrive at a probability that the fetus is affected, yet it may lead to a form of eugenics if the information is used to terminate pregnancies.

Helen Chasin depicts the aftermath of labor and delivery in *The Recovery Room: Lying-in*. The patient is disoriented, not only because she "fixes on pain / and breathes it like an element," but also due to the effects of scopolamine, which can cause sedation, delirium, and in toxic doses, hallucinations. (This drug is not widely used today.) As in the poem by Inez, this patient is expressing some undefined anger towards the father of the child, and indirectly at the "mothers-/in-law whose sons brought them to this. / We've been had. The patient's anger towards her sexual partner is perhaps clearest in John Stone's poem *To a 14 Year Old Girl in Labor and Delivery*. The first line, "I cannot say it to you, Mother, Child," avoids the inevitable things people might say in this situation; instead, in the apposition of the last two words, the poet captures the tragedy of her condition. On becoming pregnant, she entered a social "exile," facing the censure of family and friends. Now, caught in the anesthetics, stirrups, and straps of the delivery table, she is in a "cage." Judith Hemschemeyer has written perhaps the most joyful of this group of poems, a celebration of *Giving Birth in Greek*. This very physical poem tells us that initially, there "was a wild animal / stuck inside me," but soon the "beast became my son."

The preceding poems deal with a stage of pregnancy or the period just after delivery. On the other hand, Anne Perlman's poem focuses on the long-term emotional effects of *Childbirth*. The final line in the first section—"They say I will forget labor."—is simple, yet full of implication for the future. Some months later, the patient is "chilled / in the cafe," which may reflect her state of mind. Even her wine glass is "gloomy." We sense that her depression could progress to the point where she "would lose" herself, her sense of identity. Post-partum depression is not a rare phenomenon; once, in a talk on the subject in relation to some of my patients, I used Anne Perlman's poem to illustrate some of the points made above.

As a junior medical student, I learned the standard form to record an obstetric history: the number of term pregnancies, premature deliveries, abortions or miscarriages, and living children. In Constance Urdang's poem *Birth*, this history is described in just enough detail to convey her emotions, but not too much to affect the universality of the poem. An objective statement alternates with a subjective response to the outcome of each pregnancy. The language is simple, yet powerful, because of the understated juxtaposition of event and reaction. Sometimes, the delivery can be uncomplicated, but pre-natal events can *Damage* the child, as in Ellen Bryant Voigt's poem. The mother thinks back to all the bad omens, and, in a poignant yet chilling moment of honesty while bathing him, thinks *How easy to let go*. Yet she does not, attesting to her maternal commitment. In a similar manner, when a *Seizure* strikes a young child, the mother in Jeanne Murray Walker's poem realizes that she "would have struck the bargain, / all my blood / for your small shaking." And this even though she seems to have had physical and emotional problems with her pregnancy.

Molly Peacock's poem is a complex exploration of *The Choice* to have an abortion. The speaker is haunted by the "ghost of [her] pregnancy," a peculiarly ambivalent creature. Call the ghost what you will—superego, conflict, guilt—it clearly has a mind of its own, even though it reflects the speaker's state of mind. The poet cleverly multiplies ambiguities to bring out the subtle drama of the decision: "choice alive with choice, alive with what's not / taken or taken up, both pulsing with direction."

A different form of obsessiveness occurs in *The Watch* by Marge Piercy. Menstruation, along with its other connotations for women, is a "sign of reprieve, the red / splash of freedom." A missed period raises the spectre of an unwanted pregnancy for the speaker of this poem, though she is aware

of the irony when comparing the reactions of childless
women to menstruation. For them, it is "Another month,
another chance missed." In a final series of similes, the poet
triggers a diversity of associations: this monthly event can be
"red as tulips" but also "red as a stoplight." Diane Acker-
man's musical piece is titled *Menstruation Rag*, an interest-
ing pun echoed later in the poem: 'For mankind no jam-rags.'
Not only this, the poet develops the notion of the monthly
event as a performance, especially with her images of a witch-
doctor's ritual, baseball, and the Jewish purification rite, the
mikvah.

Stephen Dunn has written an enigmatic poem on the re-
lationship of a couple dealing with *Infertility*. She is even
counseled to try magic, and if that fails, to "Pass the burden,
lovingly, to him." Paradoxically, their emptiness becomes
heavy, a burden, and raises the question of blame. With fer-
tile couples, pregnancy may enhance *and* disrupt intimacy, as
in the poems *Mother and Child* and *What We Have Now* by
David Axelrod. The husband is aware of the practical conse-
quences of having children: the "sickness you endure, or
pain, / the costs after insurance," but at the moment he is
most conscious of her distended abdomen and "the unbear-
able pressure / stretching you and me apart."

Millen Brand's poem, *Thirty Childbirths*, is about the
experience of having a kidney stone, but shows a man con-
ceptualizing his excruciating pain in terms of a woman's con-
dition. This "description of labor" reveals a certain empathy
with women. Men, at least in Western society and many East-
ern ones, have traditionally been separated from the process
of childbirth. Some "primitive" cultures have a ritual sharing,
in which the man also experiences the pain of labor. This
practice, known as *Couvade*, probably strengthens the bond-
ing between the family, and is described by Michael Blumen-
thal. He praises a man whose bond is so strong with his wife
and child that he literally becomes part of labor and delivery,
entering the "tight tercet / of their togetherness."

Adrienne Rich, in her poem *Rape*, has written about a
subject which many find very difficult to discuss. Physicians
encounter this problem in the emergency room, and may be
seen in the same light as the policeman in the poem if they
are insensitive to the victim's condition. In Rich's poem, the

victim feels resentment towards all men, for the attacker could very well be someone she "grew up with." (A significant number of rapes are perpetrated by acquaintances.) She feels humiliated about having to re-live the experience for a bureaucratic record: "You hardly know him but you have to get to know him." In addition, this situation makes the victim feel she is "guilty of the crime of having been forced." Not only this, she may feel the policeman is deriving some vicarious pleasure: "but the hysteria in your voice pleases him the most." Similarly, the *Father of the Victim* in Rae Ballard's poem sees his daughter as a "Bitch" instead of as a victim. The narrative details are left unclear to good effect, suggesting an incestuous element in the poem. The policeman, again, is portrayed as an unsympathetic observer.

The final poem in this section is about menopause. While giving birth is an event many women experience, most of them experience menopause. Constance Urdang has captured the regrets and uncertainty of this time in *Change of Life*. She sees the post-menopausal state in terms of beautiful, but decayed objects: "Ashes of roses, forsythia bones." The young girl's body is described sensually (reminiscent of Georgia O'Keefe's lush flowers). It is the soil for roses and "ardent tropical blooms / with corollas so deep / you could drown in them." This same body is being transformed into sweet, concentrated honey, "rendered to her essences." Although there is a sense of loss, there is also the sweetness of the honey which remains.

ONE MORE TIME

And next morning, at the medical center
Though the X-Ray Room swallows me whole,

Though cold crackles in the corridors
I brace myself against it and then relax.

Lying there on the polished steel table
Though I step right out of my body,

Suspended in icy silence
I look at myself from far off
Calmly, I feel free

Even though I'm not, now
Or ever:

The metal teeth of death bite
But spit me out

One more time:

When the technician says breathe
I breathe.

—Patricia Goedicke

AT THE GYNECOLOGIST'S

The body so carefully
contrived for pain,
wakens from the dream of health
again and again
to hands impersonal as wax
and instruments that pry
into the closed chapters of flesh.
See me here, my naked legs
caught in these metal stirrups,
galloping towards death
with flowers of ether in my hair.

—Linda Pastan

ANN: Room 8 , No. 2 Biopsy With Frozen Section

Before we started, you were speaking,
Saying something to me;
Golden droplets in the tubing
Caught your eye, held your tongue;
You never finished.

When the drapes were all in place
You cried;
The tears ran sideways;
Glistening streaks upon your temples;
No one noticed.

Latex fingers, muffled voices,
Everything was bathed in blue,
It took no more than half an hour
To cut away a part of you.

                    —*Kirk Maxey*

A STORY ABOUT THE BODY

The young composer, working that summer at an artist's colony, had watched her for a week. She was Japanese, a painter, almost sixty, and he thought he was in love with her. He loved her work, and her work was like the way she moved her body, used her hands, looked at him directly when she made amused and considered answers to his questions. One night, walking back from a concert, they came to her door and she turned to him and said, "I think you would like to have me. I would like that too, but I must tell you that I have had a double mastectomy," and when he didn't understand, "I've lost both my breasts." The radiance that he had carried around in his belly and his chest cavity—like music—withered, very quickly, and he made himself look at her when he said, "I'm sorry. I don't think I could." He walked back to his own cabin through the pines, and in the morning he found a small blue bowl on the porch outside his door. It looked to be full of rose petals, but he found when he picked it up that the rose petals were on top; the rest of the bowl—she must have swept them from the corners of her studio—was full of dead bees.

—Robert Hass

WAITING FOR THE DOCTOR

I hear the doctor's loud success
booming to the anteroom,
my convent girl legs
criss-crossed at the ankles
narrowing the chapel where love huffs
like a wolf in the gray light
of redemptive sex.

Eucharistic body, tasty wafer,
Bristol-Cream sherry tapping through my veins,
Catholic outcome of a priest-father,
medieval mother on the guest bed of the parish,
witnessed by an ivory angel
and a watercolor Christ.

Waiting for the doctor, his loud success,
I think: my mother's breasts at thirty
tightening in my father's palms,
a crack inside her plaster flesh
widening for life,
my infant body's instant flush.

Disgusting girl—female scum, dirty secretions
attendant on woman's time, my mother thought
tying the parcel to mail me away.
I, reared on the assembly line,
factory for molding children into nuns.
Orphanage cookie, my cookie-self

waiting for the doctor
to come and view my masterworks:
assemblages of bone, mid-symphysial stage of decay,
sculptures for love programmed to fail,
but doubling cells under my flesh humming like a laundromat
a 9-lb. load to cart in and out of next year's bed.

—Colette Inez

PREGNANCY

It is the best thing.
I should always like to be pregnant,

Tummy thickening like a yoghurt,
Unbelievable flower.

A queen is always pregnant with her country.
Sheba of questions

Or briny siren
At her difficult passage,

One is the mountain that moves
Toward the earliest gods.

Who started this?
An axis, a quake, a perimeter,

I have no decisions to master
That could change my frame

Or honor.
Immaculate. Or if it was not, perfect.

Pregnant, I'm highly explosive—
You can feel it, long before

Your seed will run back to hug you—
Squaring and cubing

Into reckless bones, bouncing odd ways
Like a football.

The heart sloshes through the microphone
Like falls in a box canyon.

The queen's only a figurehead.
Nine months pulled by nine

Planets, the moon sloping
Through its amnion sea,

Trapped, stone-mad . . . and three
Beings' lives gel in my womb.

—*Sandra McPherson*

THE BUDDHA IN THE WOMB

Bobbing in the waters of the womb,
little godhead, ten toes, ten fingers
& infinite hope,
sails upside down through the world.

My bones, I know, are only a cage
for death.
Meditating, I can see my skull,
a death's head,
lit from within
by candles
which are possibly the suns
of other galaxies.

I know that death
is a movement toward light,
a happy dream
from which you are loath to awaken,
a lover left
in a country
to which you have no visa,
& I know that the horses of the spirit
are galloping, galloping, galloping
out of time
& into the moment called NOW.

Why then do I care
for this upside-down Buddha
bobbing through the world,
his toes, his fingers
alive with blood
that will only sing & die?

There is a light in my skull
& a light in his.
We meditate on our bones only
to let them blow away
with fewer regrets.

Flesh is merely a lesson.
We learn it
& pass on.

—Erica Jong

SOFT MASK

On the ultrasound screen my child curled
in his own fluid orbit, less real
than any high-school-textbook tadpole
used to symbolize birth, till the nurse
placed a white arrow on his heart flicker:
a quick needle of light. Tonight his face

blooms in my window before trees
stripped bare, a moon hung full and red.
That soft mask, not yet hardened in autumn wind,
would hold a thumbprint if I touched him. I hesitate
to touch him. He's not yet felt the burden
of a hand, nor tasted air, nor toddled
toward some bladelike gaze. He is all sweetness,
mouth smudged against the clear silk
that envelops him, webbed hands that reach
and retreat as a cat tests water.

Or like Narcissus, or the great wondering
madonnas, or any beast lost in another, the demon
who kneels to feed at some lily throat.
His pulse first matching then at odds with mine,
that small arrow seeming to tremble
as if striking something true.

—Mary Karr

WRITTEN ON LEARNING OF ARRHYTHMIA
IN THE UNBORN CHILD

I would liken woodsmoke to death
except for the birds which pass through
and emerge intact, and the sky which stands
quietly behind it, white with the chance of snow.

The horse made out of yesterday's snow
loosens its stone eyes and sculpted mane.
In time it will lose everything
except the brave forelegs, those it never had.

I could go on watching these things
until nightfall, which comes each evening
earlier now. I would sit in the inner dark
of a suburban house which burns with life,
my other children lit up from within
by ivory bones and papier-maché complexions.
Their blood flows easy as candle wax
melted from crayon.

I could stay here in the warm pocket
that precedes shock, unlike those women
who don't feel their own faces
anymore. They walk from room to room
in the four perfect chambers
of their own hearts,

staring blankly into the future
as if it were written in chimney smoke,
carrying the past in their striated laps.
Listen as they mouth the name of the child
that was meant to be, while around them
silence widens, and the depths.

—Judith Skillman

THE RECOVERY ROOM: LYING-IN

Diapered in hospital linen,
my public seam stitched back into secrets,
I itch and heal in my crib, wrapped
in scopolamine. My lips like asbestos,
I can't make it
out of the medicine. Something has happened:
my belly has gone
flaccid, ersatz as sponge. Screwed
on this centripetal ache, I fix on pain
and breathe it like an element.
My neighbor-women are bad-mouthing the mothers-
in-law whose sons brought them to this.
We've been had. Joyful and dopey
we roll in our girlish paranoias.
The nurses want to sleep with the doctor; they wait
for my blood pressure to go down.
I try to climb, the walls shrug me off.
In my unique visiting hour I am visited
with guests witty beyond belief; before I can answer
the drug subsides, those pretend bastards are gone.

Back in my skull, out of love with the obstetrician,
I read my tag to prove I'm sensible.
The orderly wheels me upstairs to meet my daughter.

Funnyface, sweet heart,
this ordeal has almost nothing to do with love.

—Helen Chasin

TO A 14 YEAR OLD GIRL IN LABOR AND DELIVERY

I cannot say it to you, Mother, Child.
Nowhere now is there a trace of the guile
that brought you here. Near the end of exile

I hold you prisoner, jailer, in my cage—
with no easy remedy for your rage
against him and the child. Your coming of age

is a time of first things: a slipping of latches;
of parallels like fire and the smell of matches.
The salmon swims upstream. The egg hatches.

—*John Stone*

GIVING BIRTH IN GREEK

Giving birth in Greek
only took two words.

The midwife smoothed my hair,
coaxed my legs into stirrups
and gave me the shot

that sent my head
high into a corner
of that dazzling room

from where I watched it all.

There was a wild animal
stuck inside me,
struggling to get out

and I could see
I was doing everything I could
to help it:

breathing evenly,
exhaling at the crest
of the contractions

not pushing

still not pushing

giving those muscles,
those raw, stubborn snails,
one last chance to break my back

and mold me into whatever shape
it needed to escape.

Then all at once
it was that moment

when I knew if I pushed
I would die

and if I didn't push
I would die
but it would still be inside me

and *'Tora!'* 'Now!' she shouted

and we both bore down
and the beast became my son
and slid into her hands.

'Oraia,' 'Beautiful,'
she said. *'Oraia.'*

Later, in my room, in the dark,
I started to bleed a lot
and I knew I should call the nurse

but I didn't know the words.

Anyway there were no more words.

I lay all night
in that cold, clotting stain,
wide open, wide awake

and falling in love
all over again.

— *Judith Hemschemeyer*

CHILDBIRTH

Comment va-t-elle, Docteur?
Elle est parfaite, Madame.

The distant words
swallowed by my foreign ear.

After pain,
this haze . . . this dazzle?

They say I will forget labor.

*   *   *

It is February now,
and we are chilled
in the cafe until
the winter sun bursts
hotter than August
over the table.
My gloomy wine glass
quickens in the new light,
glistens, casts a shadow,
like the map in myself
filled with common boundaries.
Between my light
and my darkness . . .
those necessary neighbors.

If one of them left,
I would lose myself
in my own house.

                    —Anne S. Perlman

BIRTH

Before. there was one
Without a name

I killed it
It had no heart

One wrenched away
With a single cry

My body floated
Inches above the bed

Another drowned
In freshets of blood

It was warm in the bed
But a cold hand touched my heart

In the eyes of the newborn
I see an ancient woman

She thinks nothing was
Before she came.

—*Constance Urdang*

DAMAGE

It didn't suckle. That
was the first indication.

Looking back, I know how much I knew.
The repetitious bloodfall,

the grating at the door of bone,
the afterbirth stuck in my womb like a scab.

Others were lucky,
response was taken from them.

Each time I bathe him
in his little tub, I think

How easy to let go

Let go

                              —*Ellen Bryant Voigt*

SEIZURE

I gave you what I could when you were born,
salt water to rock you,
your half of nine month's meat,
miles of finished veins,
and all the blood I had to spare.

And then I said, this is the last time
I divide myself in half, the last time
I lie down in danger and rise bereft,
the last time I give up half my blood.

Fifteen months later, when I walked into your room
your mobile of the sun, moon,
and stars was tilting
while your lips twisted,
while you arched your back.

Your fingers groped for something in the air.
Your arms and legs flailed like broken wings.
Your breath was a load too heavy
for your throat to heave into your lungs.
You beat yourself into a daze against your crib.

We slapped your feet,
we flared the lights,
we doused you in a tub of lukewarm water.
But your black eyes rolled.
You had gone somewhere
and left behind a shape of bluish skin,
a counterfeit of you.
                    It was then,
before the red wail of the police car,
before the IV's, before the medicine
dropped into you like angels, before you woke
to a clear brow, to your own funny rising voice,

it was then that I would have struck the bargain,
all my blood
for your small shaking.
I would have called us even.

                              —*Jeanne Murray Walker*

THE CHOICE

The ghost of my pregnancy, a large
amorphous vapor, much larger than me,
comes when I am alarmed to comfort me,
though it, too, alarms me, and I dodge

away, saying, "Leave me alone," and the ghost,
always beneficent, says, "You're a tough one
to do things for." The ghost must have done
this lots, it so competently knows I'm lost

and empty. It returns the fullness and slow
connection to all the world just as it is.
When I let it surround me, the embrace is
more mother than baby. How often we don't know

the difference. It's not a dead little thing
without a spinal chord yet, but a spirit of
the parent we all ought to have had, of
possibility. "I was meant to be dead." Thinking

why it said it was *meant* to be dead brings
the tangible comfort: how I used the foetus
shamelessly, how the brief pregnancy showed us,
its father and me, these choices, not shriveling

but choice alive with choice, alive with what's not
taken, or taken up, both pulsing with direction,
for some mistakes are re-takes, or correction,
past times that were forsaken now held when caught.

I never say goodbye to the ghost for
I've forgotten it's been there. That's what it's for.
The thought of the pregnancy somehow unmoors
the anxiety the choice still harbors.

—Molly Peacock

THE WATCH

At this moment hundreds of women
a few miles from here are looking
for the same sign of reprieve, the red
splash of freedom. We run to check,
squirming through rituals of If I don't
look till two o'clock, if I skip lunch,
If I am good, if I am truly sorry,
probing, poking, hallucinating changes.
Flower, red lily, scarlet petunia
bloom for me. And some lesser number
of women in other bedrooms and bathrooms
see that red banner unfurl and mourn!
Another month, another chance missed.
Forty years of our lives, that flag
is shown or not and our immediate
and sometimes final fate determined,
red as tulips, red as poppies satin,
red as taillights, red as a stoplight,
red as dying, our quick bright blood.

—Marge Piercy

MENSTRUATION RAG

Played if you please
by tamponi and tuba
and accompanied by
an appropriate ritual,
say, snake, obsidian,
or the maw bone
of a buffalo, pouched
in deerskin and rattled
properly with a crisp *ye'ye'*.

But let's consider it
another way, as
theater in the round:
          "I've got dem low-down
          lunar cycle blues, daddy,"
the pitcher at the mound:
          "Two balls, one strike,
          and no outs, buster,"
one small drop for woman,
a hemorrhage for mankind.

For mankind no jam-rags,
powders, sprays, no mikvahs,
tampons, tablets, belts,
no breakthrough bleeding,
no calendar check meticulous
as a tornado watch,
no swearing on your life
in a busy cloakroom
that you're part
of the greatest show
on earth.

                    —*Diane Ackerman*

INFERTILITY

When it gets dark
strip yourself of all garments
and lie down
on the grave of twins.
After you've said
"Springs of water, rise,
myself into myself,"
cover it with candles,
nosegays and ribbons.
You'll want to go home then.
If your husband is asleep
rub his penis with cocoanut oil
and believe
you've done everything you could.
Pass the burden, lovingly, to him.

—*Stephen Dunn*

MOTHER AND CHILD

I kiss your belly
button bursting out like
a silver dollar for your
sixth month. Sleek and
fat you sway before me,
lure me to our conjugal bed
to use each other gently before
the final lay-off.

I kiss your thighs, see
eyes staring at me from
deep inside, that wink to
say we are captured and must
pay ransom for twenty years
before we're free.

You are too sexy to be
pregnant. I am too young
to be a father. We are
too sure we need each other
to let go.

—David Axelrod

WHAT WE HAVE NOW

The reality of you swollen,
tits blue-veined and ready,
abdomen distressed, is not
that you will bear a child,
is not the life we will
surrender—that long-morning
sleep and freedom—or the
sickness you endure, or pain,
the costs after insurance,
the gynecologist (his
finger in you), not the baby
blues or even pinks but
the unbearable pressure
stretching you and me apart.

                    —*David Axelrod*

THIRTY CHILDBIRTHS

In James Street,
as if my pneumonia had not been enough,
I started to have attacks of kidney gravel,
human penalty
for emerging from inanimate matter—pain.
The pain of one daylong attack of gravel
has been compared to the suffering
of childbirth. I must have had
thirty attacks. I thought of suicide.
One time an attack lasted three days
and in my male parturition
I screamed like a woman.
Hospitalized in Jersey City,
I had a doctor, assigned by Uncle Sam Cosgrove,
who without anaesthesia pushed a tube
up my penis, and this scalding insertion
let me be flushed with liquid and the liquid
washed out the gravel, or I peed it out.
No birth, but still
a delivery
giving me back to life.

—Millen Brand

COUVADE
            for H.

When your wife uttered your son
like a large syllable into this world,

you, ever the generous one, took sick too.
You took to bed and, in the large,

violent strokes that heaved beneath your belly,
it was as if you were a woman—as if by

the mere ache and purgation of your wounds
you could return to the place we have all

been exiled from; as if, by mimicking
the motions of your own child's mother,

you could be, to them and to yourself,
all things: child, father, a man so womanly

in his own being that he could, somehow,
bear his own child into the world with his wife

like a duet. It was so kind of you. And I
imagine she, too, must have known it:

How a man aches at times like these toward
places he has left and can never return to;

how he looks into the faces of his own wife
and child and staggers to bed in the sheer

empathy and pain of wanting to become them.
And how, when his wife rises from the dimmed

light of their child's afterbirth, he too
will rise, and all that is good in this world

will speak his name into the tight tercet
of their togetherness. And his son
will call him Father, and his wife: a man.

                              —*Michael Blumenthal*

RAPE

There is a cop who is both prowler and father:
he comes from your block, grew up with your brothers,
had certain ideals.
You hardly know him in his boots and silver badge,
on horseback, one hand touching his gun.

You hardly know him but you have to get to know him:
He has access to machinery that could kill you.
He and his stallion clop like warlords among the trash,
his ideals stand in the air, a frozen cloud
from between his unsmiling lips.

And so, when the time comes, you have to turn to him,
the maniac's sperm still greasing your thigh,
your mind whirling like crazy. You have to confess
to him, you are guilty of the crime
of having been forced.

And you see his blue eyes, the blue eyes of all the family
whom you used to know, grow narrow and glisten,
his hand types out the details
and he wants them all
but the hysteria in your voice pleases him best.

You hardly know him but now he thinks he knows you:
he has taken down your worst moment
on a machine and filed it in a file.
He knows, or thinks he knows, how much you imagined;
He knows, or thinks he knows, what you secretly wanted.

He has access to machinery that could get you put away;
and if, in the sickening light of the precinct,
and if, in the sickening light of the precinct,
your details sound like a portrait of your confessor,
will you swallow, will you deny them, will you lie your way home?

—Adrienne Rich

FATHER OF THE VICTIM

"Rape?" he says.
"Bitch!" he says,
and his lips curl like peeled bark
around the spit-flaked word.
As the child-form huddles on a chair
his eyes slide up and down the curving flesh,
finger the shreds of cloth that hide its breasts.
His hand wipes flat across his mouth,
adjusts his fly.
"Bitch!" he says again,
and "Whore!"
The cop at the door unwraps a stick of gum.

—Rae Ballard

CHANGE OF LIFE

Ashes of roses, forsythia bones
tulips with blackened teeth,
let me read in you
what has become of the young girl in the legend
who so craved honey
that her entire life was changed by it.

When she lay down
roses sprang from her side
her body became a trellis
for ardent tropical blooms
with corollas so deep
you could drown in them,
disappearing in those mysterious caves.

In this way the bees found her;
in the laboratory of the hive
they are transforming her into an old woman,
drained, shrivelled, and unsexual
like a quince blossom mutilated by the frost.
She has been rendered to her essences;
her voice comes to you through the lips of a crone.

—*Constance Urdang*

MENTAL ILLNESS
The Shadow Of The Obsessive Idea

MENTAL ILLNESS
The Shadow Of The Obsessive Idea

I am rushing to an appointment, fighting the eccentric autumn winds with my coat wrapped closely about myself. Suddenly, an elderly woman wearing a light jacket which is inadequate for this weather approaches me. Another autumn leaf from a distant tree? She insists on stopping me, asks if I am cold. "No." I answer, "But what about you"? She's feeling just fine, because of the strawberry jam she had for breakfast. It keeps her warm, she adds, I suppose because of my slightly puzzled look. Then she takes my hands in hers, saying "Oh, aren't you cold? Make sure they give you some strawberry jam when you get inside. Sometimes the honey helps too." After taking a closer look at my face, she says "Are you from India? It's always nice and warm there, isn't it? No wonder you're freezing! You better get inside." And off she went, over a hillock, perhaps to give similar advice to a solitary apple tree losing the warmth of its leaves.

To the casual observer, this woman would hardly seem "sick" and in need of hospitalization. The public usually associates the medical profession with stethoscopes, blood tests, x-rays, or operating rooms. People generally discuss illness in terms of tangible or visible signs, such as scars, casts, lab results. Physicians legitimize illness for patients, making it possible to take sick leave and get disability benefits. But mental illness is not so easily accepted by our society, and sometimes, these patients are actually penalized for their condition. Insurance companies are much more willing to pay for treating an ulcer than for a psychiatric problem which may be contributing to the ulcer. Psychiatric illness is at the heart of many medical problems, and one study has shown that "approximately 50 to 80 percent of general medical patients suffer from some psychiatric disorder."[1]

Diagnosis of mental disease poses some problems since it

continues to be subjective to some extent, even though mod-
ern psychiatry has made great strides in the classification of
mental illness. Certain diagnostic methods were developed
only in this century. Spencer Brown's poem, *Rorschach Test*,
describes a patient's experience with the procedure. Although
"There are no wrong answers," he knows he is being 'tested.'
He is fully aware of the absurdity of his situation: "I must
see enough and not too much." Depending on his behavior
during the testing, he could have been evaluated as "submiss-
ive, challenging, seductive, euphoric, passive-aggressive, or
suspicious—the possibilities are endless."[2]

The spectrum of mental illness ranges from neurosis to
psychosis, agoraphobia to paranoia. Susan Hahn's poem is
about agoraphobia, which can be "one of the most incapaci-
tating of the phobias."[3] Venturing away alone from familiar
surroundings for even a short distance results in such an in-
tense state of anxiety that the patient can go no further. The
woman with *Agoraphobia* feels a perverse vindication when
accidents happen to people who 'travel too far / from home,'
as if these mishaps "secure her place." In Philip Booth's
poem, a patient who has recently been discharged from a
mental institution cannot cope with his *Panic* over the most
minor anxiety-provoking situations. He may be experiencing
a conflict between his healthy and mentally ill selves; there
are clear advantages to both roles, but the sick one may be
easier. A different sort of persona is present in James Merrill's
poem, *The Mad Scene*, which describes a romantic relation-
ship through a dream. The character in the poem feels distant
from the self while observing his own actions. The life they
"were going to share" is reduced to symbolic dirty laundry:
"milk-stiff bibs" are associated with future children, a
"shroud" with death. After their meeting in an opera house, a
paroxysm of violent imagery interrupts the scene, which may
reflect the relationship's turbulent state. His eyes, "enlarged
by belladonna," may have something to do with his percep-
tions: the drug can cause an unpleasant sedation, delirium,
and hallucinations. Pamela White Hadas' poem, *To Make a
Dragon Move: From the Diary of an Anorexic*, describes a
disorder which includes a "disturbance of body image with a
stubborn lack of concern over emaciation, and a pervasive,
paralyzing sense of personal ineffectiveness."[4] Arranged in

eight stanzas of eight lines each, which end in one of eight words, and with a final four-line stanza where all these words appear, this poem has a challenging structure (like a sestina) which is perfect for bringing out the character's obsessive nature. The final word in the series—"disappear"— is especially important, for it hints at the patient's suicidal ideation.

Suicidal thoughts are, of course, common to a variety of mental illnesses beside anorexia. Robert Lowell and Imamu Amiri Baraka (Leroi Jones) have written about this state in *Waking in the Blue* and *Preface to a Twenty Volume Suicide Note*. Lowell is more oblique, hiding the impulse to commit suicide until the last lines: "We are all old-timers, / each of us holds a locked razor." But there are clues to this possibility throughout the poem, which opens with an acutely sensitive line, "Azure day / makes my agonized blue window bleaker," and closes with a horrible premonition as the patient sees "the shaky future grow familiar / in the pinched, indigenous faces" of the veteran cases. Jones' *Preface* has a less ironic tone, and presents a sharper sense of impending doom: the "ground opens up and envelops" him as though he were dead already. Insomniac, he "counts the stars" each night, an obsessive task whose relentless rhythm is suggested by the repetition of "each" in the poem. Jones uses one-line stanzas, which stand out powerfully because of their simplicity, and convey the uneasy energy of disjunctive leaps in meaning. Ambivalence may be a dominant emotion in *The Suicide* patient's mind, as described by David Posner. Clearly, he feels connected with life around him; perhaps in protest, "Gulls scream as [he] dives." Again, the syntax is simple, but meaning is disjointed and under great stress. On the other hand, the *Suicide's Note* in the poem by Langston Hughes is a brief and tranquil acceptance of death, a love-note to the river which asked him "for a kiss."

Patients have to wrestle with their suicidal ideation, but their relatives and friends cannot help being involved, and may even need psychiatric treatment as a result. Imagine knowing that someone you love is on the verge of suicide, as in *To a Young Woman Considering Suicide* by Peter Sears. A friend often has a good chance of helping the patient: He is sympathetic to her condition, acknowledging the monotony of despair, loss of appetite, insomnia. Yet, a rhetorical turn, the incentive to "go on living," follows the sympathy. And by involving her with small details of the lives of others, he asserts her importance. Sometimes a friend may deal with mental illness through minimizing, as in *They Call it Attempted Suicide*, by Jack Gilbert. The poet reflects on the act of defining or naming, as if they can make the incident "into something manageable." Ironically, the "mess she had made of his room" becomes the major concern. Howard Nemerov's poem, *To D—, Dead by Her Own Hand*, has a more complicated strategy: first he wonders if a friend, before committing suicide, had "thought about a children's game" which simulated death; then follows a fine description of the game; finally, the game takes on aspects of the adult world, where one is committed to staying "balanced on the ledge above the dark," even if there is a fear of falling. (An interesting formal aspect of Nemerov's poem is the harmony of syntax and meaning in the second stanza: the interposition of *where* near the middle mimics a balancing act!)

   Dropping Toward Stillness by Rose Marcel and one of my own poems, *On a Schizophrenic Frequency*, show similar views of the mentally ill. Marcel's image of the mind as a stone resonates with the title of her poem, implying that the patient's mind is "dropping toward" silence and catatonic immobility. The poet seems skeptical about the medical care the patient is receiving from "people who say / they know her," and who "believe / that shock is therapeutic." (In defense of electro-convulsive therapy, I might note that it is used primarily for certain types of depression, when benefits can be significant; [5] this patient could have either.) The patient in my poem, in addition to having some insight, is also more articulate. He knows he "belongs in the / italicized fine print of a textbook case." His account is so compelling that when he describes his auditory hallucinations, the "thousand voices perfectly loud," I am tempted to hear them and "almost ask the janitor to / stop his vacuuming for a moment." A *Schizophrenic Girl* described by X. J. Kennedy exemplifies a different form of the illness—catatonic withdrawal. "Involved around some point we can't see," she cannot communicate with anyone and is lost in a "perpetual free-fall."

   While strolling past an outpatient psychiatry clinic, I happened to glance inside. These people appeared perfectly healthy, no different than any other patients with minor medical problems. Returning that way, I once again looked in, this time more carefully. A young girl's hair was in disarray and she looked a little *too* casually draped over the armchair; a Hispanic gentleman had just kissed an orchid with a flourish; a young man's gaze was transfixed on a blank part of the wall, as though he was hallucinating. People who have never been inside mental hospitals or browsed through a textbook of psychiatry may be surprised at the variety of mental illness, which we see in Louise Bogan's *Evening in the Sanitarium* and Donald Justice's *Counting the Mad*. Both poems use the device of the catalog. Bogan sees the "blunt-faced woman," "the manic-depressive," "one paranoiac," and provides just enough detail to hint at causes and effects, leaving the patients enigmatic. The series of details is ironic, often sarcastic: "Everything will be splendid," "The fruit salad will bloom," "The cats will be glad." Their future may appear well-regimented, but the present is still dangerous; suicide is insinuated throughout the poem, as the "safe bone needles" resonate with the "splinter of the suicide to be." Unlike the preceding poet, Justice uses very simple diction, syntax and imagery, along with a refrain that prepares for a surprise ending: The man who "cried No No No No" in the refrain did not have hallucinations or delusions. He was merely an "ordinary man," someone who could be one of the so-called sane. The poem tellingly questions our standards for labeling people as *sane* or *insane*.

From a chronic patient's eyes, a mental ward is an appropriate setting for *The Hell Poem*, by John Berryman (who was hospitalized a number of times and died by leaping off a bridge). This patient can understand the anguish of his fellow patients, along with his own: "Will day glow again to these tossers, and to me"? Diane Wakoski has written a poem *From a Girl in a Mental Institution*, who imagines herself as a "gull, sitting on the mast." This apparent freedom is soon marred by her paranoia about the waves, which say "odious things" and "have torn the sleeping children to bits."

Robin Morgan, in *The Invisible Woman*, adopts the point of view of a patient, reducing our distance and making us more sympathetic. The patient is the active agent *and* the commentator in most of the poem. In the closing four lines, she thinks, with a long-suffering attitude, "Better to suffer this prominence / than for the poor young doctor to learn / he himself is insane." And the confident last line—"Only the strong can know that"—effectively invites us to share her perception. Similarly, a visitor *At the Hospital*, by Carl Dennis, explores how a patient perceives other patients with a superior attitude. They are "reaching out, needy and ignorant," but he refuses to establish any connections with them, perhaps because he is afraid to see himself reflected in their condition. (This is in striking contrast to John Berryman's poem.) During a *Visit to my Committed Grandma*, by Leonard Nathan, the visitor is struck by his grandmother's lack of recognition. This loss of "kinship" may lead him to see her more objectively as an "ancient being," not his "grandma."

Hayden Carruth gives us a comparison of a patient's initial reactions with his present condition in *The Asylum*. At first, it seemed like a haven, its "Mauve walls rose up then tranquilly." But even then, his disturbed mind could "read dismay . . . in a twisted beech." Now, the illusion of the place as a refuge has dissolved, its walls are "thin against the dense insistent gale." The poet does not state directly how the symbolic wind affects the patient's illness, but we feel sure that it does, for there is a progressive weakening of the walls' ability to provide protection: they "Are thin," "No good," and finally, "Useless." Carruth's confessional poem arises from the impulse to comprehend, to understand the present in terms of the past. This poet shows how the act of writing a poem can in itself be therapeutic.

RORSCHACH TEST

I am to hold the pictures as I wish,
Look as long as I wish, and tell you all
I see—wholes, parts, details, or anything.
There are no wrong answers. Anything goes.
Yet you will not say what my answers tell you,
And I am being tested knowing so.
I launch a boomerang at a shadowy mark
Of indefinite size at an unknown distance.

    I see a bat with islands and a bear,   I
But mostly pelvis. Then bears join snouts in a V;   II
Though they are gentle teddy bears, their feet
Stand in blood, and a blood-cloud floats above.
(Viewed upside down, there are bloody little puppets;
Satan leers; there is a cave in the middle.)
Twin footmen bow over a roasted crab,   III
With hovering blood in the sky. (Seen from above,
Always the pelvis, sutured with a zipper.)
    Then looms King Darkness, zip-sex at the bottom. IV
A pelt laid out on a slab, and little lizards.
Another zippered bat, clam-valves, proboscis.   V
A dead goose with a few neck-feathers clinging.   VI
Its soft racoon-fur zippered all the way;
Clouds, with an elephant, pelvis at the top,   VII
With faces. Bison-foxes going down,   VIII
With blue, green, pink, and lurid; liver ice-cream
Dripping down from the top. (I do not see
The lampshade—not very commonly observed—
Perhaps only by the gifted or disturbed.
Nor do I note the Grand Lama, seen
By one in a million—idiot or Einstein?)
    The stimuli are being switched on me;   IX
Things are no longer quite symmetrical:
An arc-halo over green, orange, and rose;
Tree-witches with fingers; the face of Mark Twain;
Blood boils up through a tube (perhaps Fallopian).
Then drunken fireworks in all colors, loud
As the last salvo on the Fourth of July;

Yellow elephant-butterflies and a blue crab,
Pink shad-roe at the side; green caterpillars
Join heads or tails to make a fertile rabbit;
And sepia monsters out of Jerome Bosch
Converse in eighteenth-century rhymed couplets,
Erecting in the sky a pole-and-hole.
     Take them away. I have told you enough.
They are like rain-stains on my childhood ceiling,
Unchanging, but never twice suggesting
The same shadows, and always ominous.
I am to go over them a second time?—
Pointing out where I saw things and then listing
Others I have forgotten—or repressed?
You have found out too much about me already.
One horned beast more, one zippered pelvis less,
Would smoke me out of sepia into sunlight.
Though you do not say so, where there are no wrong
Answers, there can be no right answers.
     I must see enough and not too much, must talk
Enough and not too much, must say I see
What the well-adjusted person says he sees.
I want to be like everybody else.
Though I may have failed this test you set for me,
I am not compelled to go through it again.

                                        —*Spencer Brown*

AGORAPHOBIA

It isn't that she doesn't
want to go to the marketplace, if only
to buy one small
compliment. She can remember each
time she went,
got one, took it
home, put it in
a porcelain cup she kept
beside her bed.
She stopped
going out for fear

of wanting too much to fill
the fragile container,
decorated her house in muted
stripes
and moved onto her bed
a color TV

which she watches
steadily.
She likes the news, especially
the accidents that happen
when people travel too far
from home.
They secure her place.
And when she faces
a scene filled with a good
time, she wanders—
but only in her mind.

                   —Susan Hahn

PANIC

It is to be out
of familiar walls
with no place left
but the Halfway
House far up
the block: it is,
this first after-
noon, to carefully
ask your new self
for a walk beyond
the drugstore around
the block, but then
to have to refuse;
it is to remember
how trees grow out
of the sidewalk, to
figure how this time
to face him: the one
with hair like old vines,
who steps out of
nowhere, trying to
take you over, back
where he always
comes from; it is
having moved here
instead: here to
sleep, to learn
to get up: it is,
at supper the always
first night, to
try to ask for
the salt. And having it
passed, it's to weep.

—Philip Booth

THE MAD SCENE

Again last night I dreamed the dream called Laundry.
In it, the sheets and towels of a life we were going to share,
The milk-stiff bibs, the shroud, each rag to be ever
Trampled or soiled, bled on or groped for blindly,
Came swooning out of an enormous willow hamper
Onto moon-marbly boards. We had just met. I watched
From outer darkness. I had dressed myself in clothes
Of a new fiber that never stains or wrinkles, never
Wears thin. The opera house sparkled with tiers
And tiers of eyes, like mine enlarged by belladonna,
Trained inward. There I saw the cloud-clot, gust by gust,
Form, and the lightning bite, and the roan mane unloosen.
Fingers were running in panic over the flute's nine gates.
Why did I flinch? I loved you. And in the downpour laughed
To see us wrung white, gnarled together, one
Topmost mordent of wisteria,
As the lean tree burst into grief.

—James Merrill

TO MAKE A DRAGON MOVE:
FROM THE DIARY OF AN ANOREXIC

> *It would have starved a gnat*
> *To live so small as I—*
> *And yet I was a living Child—*
> *With food's necessity*
>
> *Upon me like a Claw*
> *I could no more remove*
> *Than I could coax a leech away—*
> *Or make a Dragon—move—*
>
> —*Emily Dickinson, No. 612*

I have rules and plenty. Some things I don't touch.
I'm king of my body now. Who needs a mother—
a food machine, those miles and miles of guts?
Once upon a time, I confess, I was fat—
gross. Gross belly, gross ass, no bones
showing at all. Now I say, "No, thank you," a person
in my own right, and no poor loser. I smile
at her plate of brownies. "Make it disappear,"

she used to say, "Join the clean plate club." I disappear
into my room where I have forbidden her to touch
anything. I was a first grade princess once. I smile
to think how those chubby pinks used to please my mother.
And now that I am, Dear Diary, a sort of magical person,
she can't see. My rules. Even here I don't pour out my guts.
Rules. The writing's slow, but like picking a bone,
satisfying, and it doesn't make you fat.

Like, I mean, what would I want with a fat
Diary! Ha ha. But I don't want you to disappear
either. It's tricky . . . "Form in a poem is like the bones
in a body," my teacher says. (I wish he wouldn't touch
me—ugh!—he has B.O.—and if I had the guts
I'd send him a memo about it, and about his smile.
Sucking the chalk like he does, he's like a person
with leprosy.) I'm too sensitive, so says Mother.

She thinks Mr. Crapsie's Valentino. If my so-called mother
is getting it on with him behind my back, that fat
cow . . . What would he see in her? Maybe he likes a person
to have boobs like shivery jello. Does he want to disappear
between thighs like tapioca? His chalky smile
would put a frosting on her Iced Raspberry, his "bone"
(another word for IT, Sue said) would stick in her gut,
maybe, bitten right off! Now why did I have to touch

on that gross theme again, when I meant to touch
on "thoughts too deep for tears," and not my mother.
That Immortality thing, now—I just have a gut
reaction to poems like that—no "verbal fat"
in poems like that, or in "the foul rag and bone
shop of the heart." My God! How does a person
learn to write like that? Like they just open to smile
and heavy words come out. Like, I just *disappear*

beside that stuff. I guess that's what I want: to disappear.
That's pretty much what the doctor said, touching
me with his icy stethoscope, prying apart my smile
with that dry popsicle stick, and he said it to Mother.
And now all she says is "What kind of crazy person
would starve herself to death?" There I am, my gut
flipflopping at the smell of hot bread, my bone
marrow turning to hot mud as she eases the fat

glistening duck out of the microwave, the fat
swimming with sweet orange. I wish it would disappear,
that I . . . If I could just let myself suck a bone—
do bones have calories?—I wouldn't need to touch
a bite of anything else. I am so empty. My gut
must be loopy thin as spaghetti. I start to chew my smile.
Is lip-skin fattening? I know Hunger as a person
inside me, half toad, half dwarf. I try to mother

him: I rock and rock and rock him to sleep like a mother
by doing sit-ups. He leans his gargoyle head against the fat
pillow of my heart. But awake he raves, a crazy person,
turned on by my perpetual motion, by the disappearing
tricks of my body; his shaken fist tickles drool to my smile.
He nibbles at my vagus nerve for attention. Behind the bone
cage of my chest, he is bad enough. He's worse in my gut
where his stamped foot means binge and puke. Don't touch

me, Hunger, Mother . . . Don't you gut my brain.
Bones are my sovereign now, I can touch them here and here.
I am a pure person, magic, revealed as I disappear
into my final fat-free smile, where there is no pain.

—*Pamela White Hadas*

WAKING IN THE BLUE

The night attendant, a B.U. sophomore,
rouses from the mare's-nest of his drowsy head
propped on *The Meaning Of Meaning.*
He catwalks down our corridor.
Azure day
makes my agonized blue window bleaker.
Crows maunder on the petrified fairway.
Absence! My heart grows tense
as though a harpoon were sparring for the kill.
(This is the house for the 'mentally ill.')

What use is my sense of humor?
I grin at 'Stanley,' now sunk in his sixties,
once a Harvard all-American fullback
(if such were possible!),
still hoarding the build of a boy in his twenties,
as he soaks, a ramrod
with the muscle of a seal,
in his long tub,
vaguely urinous from the Victorian plumbing.
A kingly granite profile in a crimson golf-cap,
worn all day, all night,
he thinks only of his figure,
of slimming on sherbet and ginger ale—
more cut off from words than a seal.

This is the way day breaks in Bowditch Hall at McLean's;
the hooded night lights bring out 'Bobbie,'
Porcellian '29,
a replica of Louis XVI
without the wig—
redolent and roly-poly as a sperm whale,
as he swashbuckles about in his birthday suit
and horses at chairs.

These victorious figures of bravado ossified young.
In between the limits of day,
hours and hours go by under the crew haircuts
and slightly little too nonsensical bachelor twinkle
of the Roman Catholic attendants.
(There are no Mayflower
screwballs in the Catholic Church.)

After a hearty New England breakfast,
I weigh two hundred pounds
this morning. Cock of the walk,
I strut in my turtle-necked French sailor's jersey
before the metal shaving mirrors,
and see the shaky future grow familiar
in the pinched, indigenous faces
of these thoroughbred mental cases,
twice my age and half my weight.
We are all old-timers,
each of us holds a locked razor.

—Robert Lowell

PREFACE TO A TWENTY VOLUME SUICIDE NOTE

Lately, I've become accustomed to the way
The ground opens up and envelops me
Each time I go out to walk the dog.
Or the broad edged silly music the wind
Makes when I run for a bus—

Things have come to that.

And now, each night I count the stars,
And each night I get the same number.
And when they will not come to be counted
I count the holes they leave.

Nobody sings anymore.

And then last night, I tiptoed up
To my daughter's room and heard her
Talking to someone, and when I opened
The door, there was no one there . . .
Only she on her knees,
Peeking into her own clasped hands.

—*Imamu Amiri Baraka*
(Leroi Jones)

THE SUICIDE

I drink this whiskey from a window overlooking the sea,
The fierce plunge
Fixed at the back of my skull.
Bicycles roar like breakers down the shore.
In twos and threes the riders disappear,
Taking my life in their wheels.
Gulls scream as I dive.
Oh, fish, have I hated enough?
Let's sleep in silence. This is no dream.
The birds have murdered the trees.

—David Posner

SUICIDE'S NOTE

The calm,
Cool face of the river
Asked me for a kiss.

—*Langston Hughes*

TO A YOUNG WOMAN CONSIDERING SUICIDE

When everything you touch is already touched,
you can't sleep, can't eat, can't even
remember when you could, you go on living;

When everywhere you are you want to leave,
it's so stupid, stupid not to go down
with the sun, down with leaves spiralling,

Down with the duck pulled under
by the muskrat, waves, they don't roll in,
they roll down and die—even now, you go on living.

Would you help me with my plant?
See, it's not doing well at all, and out
there in the snow my friend's car is stuck.

He needs a hand. What do you think?—
More light? A bigger pot? And what do I say
to my child, to your child perhaps someday,
if she goes out, as you have, under the long shadow?

—Peter Sears

THEY CALL IT ATTEMPTED SUICIDE

My brother's girlfriend was not prepared for how much blood
splashed out. He got home in time, but was angry
about the mess she had made of his room. I stood behind,
watching them turn it into something manageable. Thinking
how frightening it must have been before things had names.
We say *peony* and make a flower out of that slow writhing.
Deal with the horror of recurrence by calling it
a million years. The death everywhere is no trouble
once you see it as nature, landscape, or botany.

                                             —Jack Gilbert

TO D—, DEAD BY HER OWN HAND

My dear, I wonder if before the end
You ever thought about a children's game—
I'm sure you must have played it too—in which
You ran along a narrow garden wall
Pretending it to be a mountain ledge
So steep a snowy darkness fell away
On either side to deeps invisible;
And when you felt your balance being lost
You jumped because you feared to fall, and thought
For only an instant: that was when I died.

That was a life ago. And now you've gone,
Who would no longer play the grown-ups' game
Where, balanced on the ledge above the dark,
You go on running and don't look down,
Nor ever jump because you fear to fall.

—Howard Nemerov

DROPPING TOWARD STILLNESS

Her mind is a stone   dull
and smooth at the edges

Even the voices she loves
sound strange   and muffled
passing through phones
and long-distance handkerchiefs

There are people who say
they know her   attendants
who fix the wires   and believe
that shock is therapeutic
that the first principle
is to keep moving   to stay
awake   not to go mute

Inside it gets quieter
and the secret box she lives in
makes motion harder

She means to tell them that
but the words latch in
Her throat is shutting down

—Rose Marcel

ON A SCHIZOPHRENIC FREQUENCY

The stubble growing on his pale cheeks
is the remnant of a fall harvest, and snow
will settle
on the leached-out earth until it
melts
into stagnant pools. He has returned
for his fifth admission
to the hospital. Again he is
losing
his voice among all the other
voices in a fugue, whose notes
swarm like bees driven
from their hive.

When we shake hands, his palm isn't sweating.
There is no reason to
be nervous, and I don't have to
tell him that.
He knows, as even the old black janitor
in his pressed uniform knows, that he
belongs
in the italicised fine print
of a text-book case.

The janitor goes on
vacuuming the carpet, where
someone has crushed out a cigarette,
someone who knows
today will not catch fire, and has left
the lounge to find another smoke.

Meanwhile, the stubble keeps
growing, and when he tells me
about the Beatles, their *fool on the hill*
hearing
a thousand voices perfectly loud,
I almost
ask the janitor to
stop his vacuuming for a moment.

—*Jon Mukand*

SCHIZOPHRENIC GIRL

Having crept out this far,
So close your breath casts moisture on the pane,
Your eyes blank lenses opening part way
To the dead moonmoth fixed with pins of rain,
Why do you hover here,
A swimmer not quite surfaced, inches down,
Fluttering water, making up her mind
To breathe, or drown?

All the fall long, earth deepening its slant
Back from the level sun, you wouldn't quit
That straitbacked chair they'd dress you in. You'd sit,
Petrified fire, casting your frozen glare,
Not swallowing, refusing to concede
There are such things as spoons. And so they'd feed
You through a vein
Cracked open like a lake they'd icefish in—
Can no one goad
You forth into the unsteady hearthlight of the sane?

Already, yawning child
At some dull drawn-out adult affair,
You whimper for permission to retire
To your right room where black
T-squares of shadows lie, vacuity
A sheet drawn halfway back.

If you'd just cry. Involved
Around some fixed point we can't see, you whirl
In a perpetual free-fall.
Come forth. We cannot stand
To see turned into stone what had been hand,
What had been mind smoothed to a bright steel ball.

—*X. J. Kennedy*

EVENING IN THE SANITARIUM

The free evening fades, outside the windows fastened
    with decorative iron grilles.
The lamps are lighted; the shades drawn; the nurses are
    watching a little.
It is the hour of the complicated knitting on the safe bone
    needles; of the games of anagrams and bridge;
The deadly game of chess; the book held up like a mask.

The period of the wildest weeping, the fiercest delusion,
    is over.
The women rest their tired half-healed hearts; they are
    almost well.
Some of them will stay almost well always: the blunt-
    faced woman whose thinking dissolved
Under academic discipline; the manic-depressive girl
Now leveling off; one paranoiac afflicted with jealousy.
Another with persecution. Some alleviation has been
    possible.

O fortunate bride, who never again will become elated
    after childbirth!
O lucky older wife, who has been cured of feeling
    unwanted!
To the suburban railway station you will return, return,
To meet forever Jim home on the 5:35.
You will be again as normal and selfish and heartless as
    anybody else.

There is life left: the piano says it with its octave smile.
The soft carpets pad the thump and splinter of the
    suicide to be.
Everything will be splendid: the grandmother will not
    drink habitually.
The fruit salad will bloom on the plate like a bouquet

And the garden produce the blue-ribbon aquilegia.
The cats will be glad; the fathers feel justified; the
     mothers relieved.
The sons and husbands will no longer need to pay the bills.
Childhoods will be put away, the obscene nightmare abated.

At the ends of the corridors the baths are running.
Mrs. C. again feels the shadow of the obsessive idea.
Miss R. looks at the mantel-piece, which must mean
     something.

—Louise Bogan

COUNTING THE MAD

This one was put in a jacket,
This one was sent home,
This one was given bread and meat
But would eat none,
And this one cried No No No No
All day long.

This one looked at the window
As though it were a wall,
This one saw things that were not there,
This one things that were,
And this one cried No No No No
All day long.

This one thought himself a bird,
This one a dog,
And this one thought himself a man,
An ordinary man,
And cried and cried No No No No
All day long.

                              —Donald Justice

THE HELL POEM

Hospital racket, nurses' iron smiles.
Jill & Eddie Jane are the souls.
I like nearly all the rest of them too
except when they feed me paraldehyde.

Tyson has been here three heavy months;
heroin. We have the same doctor: She's improving,
let out on pass tonight for her first time.
A madonna's oval face with wide dark eyes.

Everybody is jolly, patients, nurses,
orderlies, some psychiatrists. Anguishes;
gnawings. Protractions of return
to the now desired but frightful outer world.

Young Tyson hasn't eaten since she came back.
She went to a wedding, her mother harangued her
it was all much too much for her
she sipped wine with a girl-friend, she fled here.

Many file down for shock & can't say after
whether they ate breakfast. Dazed till four.
One word is: the memory will come back.
Ah, weeks or months. Maybe.

Behind the locked door, called 'back there,'
the worse victims.
Apathy or ungovernable fear
cause them not to watch through the window starlight.

They can't have matches, or telephone. They slob food.
Tantrums, & the suicidal, are put back there.
Sometimes one is promoted here. We are ecstatic.
Sometimes one has to go back.

It's all girls this time. The elderly, the men,
of my former stays have given way to girls,
fourteen to forty, raucous, racing the halls,
cursing their paramours & angry husbands.

Nights of witches: I dreamt a headless child.
Sobbings, a scream, a slam.
Will day glow again to these tossers, and to me?
I am staying days.

—John Berryman

FROM A GIRL IN A MENTAL INSTITUTION

The morning wakes me as a broken door vibrating on its
hinges.
We are drifting out to sea this morning. I
can barely feel the motion of the boat as it rocks me.
I must be a gull, sitting on the mast,
else why would I be so high above the world?
Yes.
I see everything down there—
children tucked, sleeping, into the waves,
their heads nestled in foam

> *AND I DON'T LIKE THE WAVES THEY*
> *DISTINCTLY SAY THINGS*
> *AGAINST ME.*

The wind is blowing my feathers. How good
that feels. If the wind
had always blown my feathers, I would
never have cried
when the waves spoke
that way—
taking my brother away, when he dove in and never came
back.

> it was because he loved the seashells
> too much
> i know
> and broken water foams in my hair
> in its new color—the color of my wing

Why don't we hear the fog-horns today?

> *IF I AM TO SIT HERE ALL DAY I MUST*
> *HAVE SOMETHING TO LISTEN TO.*

The waves have torn the sleeping children to bits. I
see them scattered on the crests now.
There—an arm floating by.

> leave me alone, i have not hurt you
> Stop pulling my wings,
> my beak, *DON'T YOU HEAR STOP IT.*

There is nothing more horrible than hands
like ancient crabs, pulling at one. And they cannot
hear because they have no ears.
                          I have no ears.
I am a gull. Birds have no ears. I cannot hear
Them
or anyone.
The fingers on the dismembered arm, floating
in the waves,
can point and make signs,
but I will not hear
the waves
telling the fingers odious things about me.
I will not watch their obscenities
pointing to the bottom where the children are buried;
where he is buried;
where I am buried.

Slam the door as often as you like—you will
not wake me.
I am a gull
sitting on the mast, and I feel the ocean rocking
because I can hear nothing
but silent voices the wind carries from the past—
                          gently rocking.
The ocean is as still as a newly made bed,
rocking.

—Diane Wakoski

THE INVISIBLE WOMAN

The invisible woman in the asylum corridor
sees others quite clearly,
including the doctor who patiently tells her
she isn't invisible,
and pities the doctor, who must be mad
to stand there in the asylum corridor,
talking and gesturing
to nothing at all.

The invisible woman has great compassion.
So, after a while, she pulls on her body
like a rumpled glove, and switches on her voice
to comfort the elated doctor with words.
Better to suffer this prominence
than for the poor young doctor to learn
he himself is insane.
Only the strong can know that.

—*Robin Morgan*

AT THE HOSPITAL

On the garden bench of the hospital,
Resting behind trim hedges in the shade,
My friend looks peaceful for the first time.
"Good thoughts," he explains, "make a good life.
So I sit here all day thinking good thoughts:
How many more little threads
Reach out by evening from this bench
To tie themselves to fences and barns.
The faintest twitching of my hand,
The ghost of a wish to haul them in,
Would break each one. So I sit still,
My fingers like stone, my bench
The quiet tether of the world.

"Do you see those patients over there,
How they wedge their faces between the fence bars
To stare at the road? These are the ones
Who wake me at night with crying.
Should I make myself join in out of fellowship,
Pretending to cry so they won't feel alone?
That would be a thread from my bench to theirs.
But they, reaching out, needy and ignorant,
Would break what might have held for years."

—Carl Dennis

VISIT TO MY COMMITTED GRANDMA

Though she is small and clean and neat,
Standing before me, whom I greet
I fear, as if the old could see
Something terrible in me
And cry it out. Her dress, her skin
(No starch can smooth) conceals within
What will not let us recognize
Our kinship, though her chewing eyes
Come close; I have another name,
Am "dear," and "fool," have loved, caused shame,
Until she, begging, cries to me
For failure of identity . . .
His, or hers, or mine? I come
To pity, but am finally dumb
Before this ancient being where time
Is nothing, fear, or its sublime
Of love is lastly all. The nurse
Insists today is somehow worse
And brings her milky glass of drugs
For what beneath those wrung-out dugs
Went wild, headlong, back and deep,
And needs, returning, childlike sleep
And not my pity; yet I claim
More kinship than a dubious name,
To show her (if I could) the mark,
This family wears, most bright in dark,
And, stranger though I seem, I bear:
The self like one bad dream we share.

—Leonard Nathan

THE ASYLUM

1.

I came to this place one November day.
Mauve walls rose up then tranquilly, and still
Must rise to wind-burned eyes that way—
Old brickwork on a hill,
Surfaces of impunity beneath a gray
And listed sky. Yet I could read dismay
There rightward in a twisted beech
Whose nineteen leaves were glittering, each
A tear in a rigid eye caught in the pale
Deep-pouring wind. Now these walls
Are thin against the dense insistent gale,
No good when the wind talks in our halls,
Useless at night when these high window bars
Catch every whisper of wind that comes and falls,
Speaking, across my catacomb of stars.

—Hayden Carruth

DISABILITY
Their Lockstep Tight As Lilac Buds

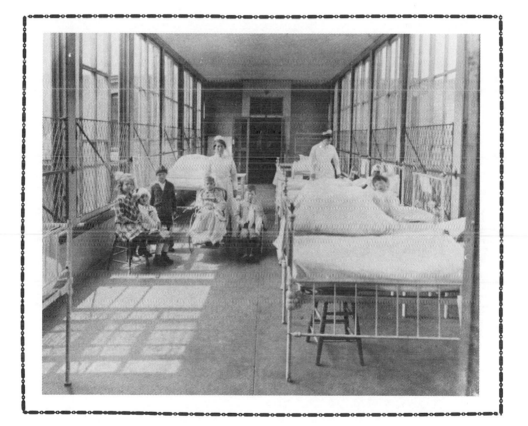

DISABILITY
Their Lockstep Tight As Lilac Buds

A young man is crying noiselessly; he seems lost among
the empty shells of the other wheelchairs parked in the rec-
reation room. His mother has just left, though visiting hours
have just started. She is angry that he is not walking, that he
is not *trying* hard enough. He had better stop being lazy! she
has told him. I do not know what to say. I feel as paralyzed
psychologically as he is physically; we are both helpless.
When I recover, we begin to talk. Words are inadequate dress-
ings for this wound, but they are all I can offer.

These poems are related to my field, Physical Medicine
and Rehabilitation, a relatively new specialty which was born
after World War II. As the population ages, conditions such
as arthritis, strokes, and cardio-respiratory problems will be-
come more common. These conditions require specific modes
of rehabilitation, which physiatrists are trained to deliver. In
addition, physiatrists must be especially sensitive to social
and psychological complications, which can be just as, if not
more, disabling than physical complaints. For instance, one
of my patients, a young man with an exotic "cocktail" in his
drug screen, fell/jumped from a building and suffered serious
brain damage. After intensive physical, occupational and
speech therapy, he made a fairly good recovery. But every-
one felt he had to begin drug rehabilitation, or else he would
eventually come back to us, via the neurosurgeons. Only
when he showed signs of reforming his lifestyle, of being re-
habilitated in the fullest sense, was he allowed to go home.

Most of my patients have external signs of disability,
and are very self-conscious. One quadriplegic felt that people
avoided looking at him, and another complained of people
staring too much! In fact, the latter once refused to go down
to Radiology for an x-ray, because he resented the looks
some people gave him. But I had to coax the reason for his

refusal out of him. He cooperated only when I promised his film would be taken as soon as he reached Radiology.

The way society perceives the disabled often contributes to their psycho-social problems. Through the poetic act, Philip Dacey succeeds in reversing some of our perceptions of *The Handicapped*. Our conventional prejudices are stripped away in his descriptions of the blind, the deaf, the paralyzed. His parallel between "repetitions of the stutterer" and "flickering of the stars" is particularly apt. In *The Rehabilitation Center*, by Maxine Kumin, there is a reversal of a different sort. Describing the "newly maimed," she writes: "Curbs curse them. / Puddles damn their simplicity." This pointedly suggests how society sometimes blames the handicapped merely for *being* handicapped; Kumin is probably referring to "curb-cuts" or ramps for sidewalks which allow mobility in wheelchairs, only a recent development. But the poet also realizes they must learn to navigate for themselves as much as possible, making sure that "distance, depth, doorsills / are ridged on their maps." One of the most common stumbling blocks in rehabilitation is the natural but misguided desire of relatives and friends to "help" patients as much as possible, which only perpetuates a state of dependence. Harold Bond decries this tendency in a direct and humorous manner. The disabled speaker allows friends to play *The Game* of dependency with him, but makes fun of their anxiety by saying, "You embrace my shoes with your / compassion."

In Lilian Morrison's poem the speaker also uses the metaphor of a game, and is *On The Sidelines*. She confronts disability in a defiant manner, as though she could express self-control through description: "If I ransom my injuries / with poems / will my joints harmonize"? This person appears to be struggling with questions of self-image, unlike the woman eulogized by Gloria Maxson in *Enid Field: In Memoriam*. Her "grace was consummate, her footstep light," in spite of being "upheld by brace and crutch." To her, "calamity was just a kind of cloak," instead of a shroud. The patient in Amber Coverdale Sumrall's *A Question of Energy* is similarly "not diminished / by this loss of limb." In fact, with a clever paradox, the speaker asserts that "to deny my scars / is to deny my power." In contrast, for *The Stroke* victim in Christopher Fahy's poem, the pre-morbid personality may interfere with adjustment to disability: "His fractured will / his vanity / can't thaw his frozen wrist."

Most disabilities strike unexpectedly, but some are familial. In these instances, the patient may have a sense of doom but adjustment may also be easier. *Angles*, a poem by Dixie Partridge, refers to a hereditary deforming arthritis. With "Joints frozen / At right angles," the speaker's grandmother and father are reminders of the future, a landscape where even the "trees grow at a slant."

Spinal cord injury usually results from violent accidents, and consequently these patients seem especially susceptible to psychic trauma. Part of this undoubtedly derives from their feelings about how society perceives them. During my first physical examination of a quadriplegic patient, *I* was the one who felt disabled. His involuntary movements (spasms) only seemed to worsen with my attentions, which may or may not have been desired. Fortunately, we both appreciated the comic relief when I bent over to check the blood pressure and a spasm caused my glasses to end up askew on my face!

Norman Andrew Kirk gives a fine description of spasticity and abnormal sensations associated with nerve re-growth in *The Tingle*. Nerve recovery is usually unpredictable and may occur over varying periods of time. Each new movement is a joyful event; I will never forget a patient who excitedly called me over to see his toe twitch, and who came to mind on reading Lilian Morrison's *The Old Hoofer*. Perhaps he too would be able someday to perform "intricate dances with [the] toes." But when the legs cannot move, there can still be wheels, as we see in Ronald Wallace's poem *After Being Paralyzed from the Neck Down for Twenty Years, Mr. Wallace gets a Chin-operated Motorized Wheelchair*. The irony is that this patient's new-found mobility leads to escape, a suicide attempt. Mobility for the paralyzed is seen in a more positive light by the "Juliet" of H. N. Beckerman's delightful poem *To: The Access Committee* . . . . To many laymen and physicians, the disabled seem asexual, when in fact they can have very fulfilling sex lives. I realized this fully after hearing the tenderness with which a paraplegic patient described his relationship. And he had no sensory function below the level of his abdomen!

Spinal cord injury appears most devastating in its effect

on motor function. Blindness, on the other hand, is primarily
a sensory disability. Consequently, the other senses begin to
compensate, as in *To A Man Going Blind* by John Haines.
"Streets smell / of leafsmoke and gasoline," but this sharp-
ened olfactory perception gives way to the synesthesia of
summer as a "curse / or a scar." Similarly, Arthur Sze ima-
gines the exotic perceptions of a blind girl typing in braille,
which could refer to "garlic, / the sun, a silver desert rain."
And ironically, sighted people such as the speaker in the
poem "feel / the world as black lightning." In contrast to
these sympathetic views, Ted Kooser allows himself to ex-
press our uneasy tolerance. *The Blind Always Come As Such
A Surprise*, tapping out paths with canes like "cracks travers-
ing our favorite china." The patient with *Glaucoma* in David
Wojahn's poem can sympathize with those at "the home for
the blind." Seemingly trivial acts, such as pouring milk for a
cat, become charged with the intensity of effort. As with the
poems by Haines and Sze, the speaker imagines the "visions"
of the blind, but in a more concrete manner: 'She's decided
his eyes are green, his fur / is brown and streaked with silver.'
From a blind person's perspective, "transactions" with the
sighted involve mildly resentful acceptance, as depicted by
Leslie Blades in *Out of Blindness*. Even for the blind, "Lan-
guage of the sight is current coin." The poet, however, imp-
licitly asks which is preferable, "airplane" or "noise oblitera-
ting bird-song," the language of sight or of blindness. During
a *Visit to the Institute for the Blind*, the character in Felix
Pollak's poem becomes caught in a crowd of sighted people.
Naturally, they assume he needs "steering . . . like a ship-
wreck," and in spite of all their good intentions, "heave me
off my feet so that I / stumble and slip."

During rounds with a neurologist, I learned that of the
five senses, loss of hearing had the worst consequences. Des-
cribing her isolation and loneliness after going deaf, an elder-
ly lady said to me, "I can't laugh at people and I can't laugh
with them. How can you expect people to keep shouting at
you"? Then her syntax broke down in her emotion: "It feels
me so alone . . . it feels me so sad . . . you tired of talking to
me"? *On Becoming Deaf* by S. Soloman is an economical, ex-
tended metaphor of how vision must replace hearing. The
faded voices of others seem obscured: "There are clouds / in

your voice." Words become the "beating of wings," foreshadowing the necessity for lip-reading. *The Man With The Hearing Aid*, by Ted Kooser, shows the darker side of deafness. His ear is clogged with "thousands of bats," which fly out at night but return at dawn when "his ear is thick with fur and silence." As with my patient, the ability to "flutter and dive / through laughter" is a significant loss. Like some of the poems on blindness, the following poems attempt to show the positive aspects of deafness. Both describe sign language as an almost magical form of communication. For Michael Cleary, "conversation" with a deaf girl takes on a sacred quality, as suggested by the title, *Fingers, Fists, Gabriel's Wings*. A teacher of sign language addresses a student in *How to Sign*. Laurie Stroblas tries to convey a sense of wonder at the power inherent in signing: "Make an island, start a river. / Build a floodgate and walk the width." Alan Dugan also uses the image of flowing water to describe the speech of *The Stutterer*. The tongue, buffeted by the "rapids of the breath," must learn to relax. The poet realizes that is easier said than done, and in spite of being the "sound advice / of experts" it is a "true despair."

Patients with cerebral palsy often have speech deficits. Distorted production of sounds and uncontrolled salivation may occur because of abnormal oral muscles. The *Spastic Child* in Vassar Miller's poem cannot produce intelligible speech because his tongue is a "slight mollusk broken in its shell." Perhaps with the help of speech therapy, "his mind, bright bird, [will not remain] forever trapped in silence." Another child, with "feet prancing," does a "crazy puppet dance" when he is happy. His joyful mood is infectious and his family joins in; Marilyn Davis does a beautiful accompaniment in verse for this dance in the poem *Song for my Son*.

Cerebral palsy may involve intellectual deficits of varying degrees. The lay public, however, has a deplorable tendency to label anyone with speech and swallowing dysfunction as "retarded." In fact, in some quarters, the words *spastic* and *retarded* have become synonymous. On of my most intelligent patients is a stock market analyst with cerebral palsy. Others are less fortunate, such as *Jenny* in John Mann Astrachan's poem. The speaker is worried about his daughter who has a learning disability "and so she glides and looks sad and bewildered / at those who can both skate and sing." The insistent repetition of "song" and its verb forms suggests the extent of her father's concern. Conversely, a four-year-old child looks at the relationship between handicapped children and parents in *Clinics* by Michael Bachstein. He imagines the parents are "as unnerved as I am to see / Their mangled only son stripped from their love." But the parents do not face a child's fear: "and what / If I never get my legs and they forget me"?

Successful rehabilitation depends on constant vigilance and on having a safety net in medicine and the community at large. On rare occasions, a patient will find the perfect physician. One of my teachers, a blind physiatrist who also happens to be a superb pianist, once treated another musician who had sustained a head injury and developed spasticity in one hand. Her hand was beginning to take the shape of a claw, so he tested the range of motion, tone, and strength of each finger; then he began to prescribe exercises, certain pieces of music which could be performed in spite of her disability. In the future, if he tries his hand at composition, I hope he will write a piece titled *Sonata for a Spastic Hand*.

THE HANDICAPPED

1
The missing legs
Of the amputee
Are away somewhere
Winning a secret race.

2
The blind man has always stood
Before an enormous blackboard,
Waiting for the first
Scrawl of light,
That fine
Dusty chalk.

3
Here
The repetitions of the stutterer,
There
The flickering of the stars.

4
Master of illusion,
The paralytic alone moves.
All else is still.

5
At Creation,
God told the deaf,
"Only you will hear
The song of the stone."

6
Dare not ask
What the dumb
Have been told to keep secret.

7

When the epileptic
Falls in a fit,
He is ascending
To the heaven of earth.

—*Philip Dacey*

REHABILITATION CENTER

In the good suburb, in the bursting season,
their canes awag in the yellow day,
the newly maimed mince back to danger.

Cave by cave they come to build their hearing
hard as fists against the jangling birds,
the slipslop of car wheels, walls' mimicries,

the hollow rebuttal of planes. Curbs curse them.
Puddles damn their simplicity. At lot lines
forsythia is a swipe across the face.

Under a wide sky let them cry now
to be coddled, misread a tree, black shins,
or crack their knees on countermands;

the downgrade is uncertain for us all.

In time they will grow competent,
love us, test and correct, feel words
on their quiet skin, begin to light our lamps.

Six weeks and they will swing around these corners,
grotesque and right, their appetites restored.
It is true the sun is only heat,

but distance, depth, doorsills
are ridged on their maps until
they know exactly where they are now.

I see their lockstep tight as lilac buds.

—Maxine Kumin

THE GAME

You are my friends. You do things
for me. My affliction is
your hangup. It is yours more
than it ever could be mine.
You spread my affliction thin

enough to go around once
for all of us. You put my
coat on for me when I ask
you. You put my coat on for
me when I do not ask you.

You embrace my shoes with your
compassion. You tell me I
would be less apt to fall with
rubber soles. You carry things
for me. You tell me they are

heavy things, how it would be
difficult for anyone
to carry them. You open
mustard bottles for me. You
tell me how hard it is to

open mustard bottles. I
agree with you. I will not
destroy our game. At night I
dream I am Samson. I will
topple coliseums. I

will overwhelm you with my
brute power. I will knock you
dead. I will open mustard
bottles for you. I will show
you how easy it really is.

—Harold Bond

ON THE SIDELINES

If I ransom my injuries
with poems
will my joints harmonize?
muscles, in the act of singing,
embrace them?
Will torn ligaments marry
and support me
in moving toward you?
Perhaps if my words are strong
I, too, will be,
knowing again
the marvelous mute scrimmages.

—Lillian Morrison

ENID FIELD: IN MEMORIAM

An agile voice, quick smile, and leaping eyes:
among the verities that bore her name,
and these things made one slow to realize,
quite incidentally, that she was lame.

The way she laughed if someone pitied her!
Calamity was just a kind of cloak
that one should wear akimbo, as it were,
with easy nonchalance—a kind of joke
was tragedy, that postured like a clown:
a trouble gone theatrical with age,
a grief got up in greasepaint, whose renown
depended on trick lighting and a stage.

Upheld by brace and crutch to common sight,
her grace was consummate, her footstep light.

—Gloria Maxson

A QUESTION OF ENERGY

I'm not diminished
    by this loss of limb
I'm more than
    the sum of my parts
to deny my scars
    is to deny my power
the core of heat in each cell.

I've got wires humming
    juice surging
        detours on the path
it takes less time now
less resistance
to complete the circuit

        I'm well grounded
            you can touch me
                without a shock.

—Amber Coverdale Sumrall

THE STROKE

attacks while he's on the toilet,
thin dull pain and yellow stars.
The bright world dies.

His new self wakes contracted
dry.
He starts again
can't finish.

His numbness struggles
with oatmeal, loses to
his once fastidious chin.
Words are boulders
that roll on his tongue,
burst.

Gray shadows of family
gather
in too loud blurred TV.
Decisions
hang in the closet,
time rusts shut.

He dozes with half a world
in each eye
waits with animal cries
on the collar of hope.

His blazing pride
his fractured will
his vanity
can't thaw his frozen wrist.

—Christopher Fahy

ANGLES

Gram died with most of her joints frozen
  At right angles. My childhood watched
    Her form brittle until she couldn't walk;
      After that her frame assumed unchosen

    Angles of the wheelchair and cracked like deadwood.
      When I see my father now, I feel
        A bloodrush back: his spine congeals
          From the hips a rigid angle forward.

        As in some half-forgotten dream
          I've lived a future; it persists
            In hard lumps on my wrists,
              A bamboo gait and a grip growing lame.

          Here where I live the trees grow at a slant
            To northeast with the wind; they calcify
              In traction. Across from my early
                Years, trees grow straight along the ditchbank,

              Each shaped like an ostrich feather.
                Enchanted child, I think they've volatile
                  Powers to create the wind as they will
                    By fanning still air.

—Dixie Partridge

THE TINGLE

My body fell asleep years ago. Cut off
at my neck by shattered bone fragments,
the line of my spine was bizarre. Alert,
my mind and soul prayed over my body's comas
for the burial of the dead, for the body's
resurrection. Spasms were electro-therapy
that increased its voltage as my muscles
twitched in an embryonic retreat to gain
again the lost dance of running grass anew.
Fire. My bed on fire! Quick, get a nurse!
"Is my bed on fire? Don, is my bed on fire?"
My skin was blazing. I tossed myself just
inches about with spasms, with arms a-fire,
flaying at imagined fires burning beneath me
burning through the mattress and rubber sheet,
burning the returning nerves into finite
disaster and no hope of repair. Time. Hurry.
Doctor help me. Doctor see me. Doctor. Doctor.
They came in answer to my pounding heart,
with white faces of care as we all feared
destruction beyond control. The sheets were
flung. The mattress shoved and bent. Ten arms
help me above the floor away from the fire.
I was saved. I felt saved. I felt love. All
of the faces of my friends began to smile.
Saved. We all loved our saving gift. All
having done all that there was to do. Fire?
Not a spark. Not a singe. No smoke. My spine
was a flaming tree within me with the flames
reaching my flesh, as I healed into wakefulness.
My body awakening in a flash from hell and
I lay burning in bed. All touch was flame but
I was a mystic lying on hot coals, not fearing
fires that eased into a tingle, the awakening
of sleeping hands. Today the slight tingle

of my body is a sensation few will know.
Unlike electric sparks, my skin does not dazzle
from the fire within and hands, all kinds of hands,
are like warm water, a kiss that takes fire's hot
melting into the warm glow of a natural comfort
as snug as body love, relaxed without release,
without the climactic claim of final conquest.
Hold me, if only in illusion. Feel the kicking stop.

—*Norman Andrew Kirk*

THE OLD HOOFER

If my legs cannot move
I will wriggle my toes
Till they learn
To do intricate dances.

—*Lillian Morrison*

AFTER BEING PARALYZED FROM THE NECK DOWN
FOR TWENTY YEARS, MR. WALLACE GETS A
CHIN-OPERATED MOTORIZED WHEELCHAIR

For the first time in twenty years
he is mobile, roaring through corridors,
bouncing off walls, out of control,
breaking doorways, tables, chairs,
and regulations. The hallways stretch out
behind him, startled, amazed,
their plaster and wallpaper gaping,
while somewhere far off,
arms spastically flailing,
the small nurses continue to call:
Mr. Wallace . . . Mr. Wallace . . .

Eventually he'll listen to reason
and go quietly back to his room,
docile, repentant, and sheepish, promising
not to disappoint them again.
The day shift will sigh and go home.
But, in the evening, between feeding and bedtime,
when they've finally left him alone,
he'll roar over to the corner
and crash through the window
stopping only to watch
the last geese rising,
rising by the light of the snow.

—Ronald Wallace

"TO: THE ACCESS COMMITTEE . . ."

"To:
    The Access Committee,
Attention:
    Handicapped Romeo.
        There is now a suitable ramp
installed at my balcony.
        Impatiently,
            Miss Juliet

        —H. N. Beckerman

TO A MAN GOING BLIND

As you face the evenings
coming on steeper and snowier,
and someone you cannot see
reads in a strained voice
from the book of storms . . .

Dreamlike, a jet climbs
above neighboring houses;
the streets smell
of leafsmoke and gasoline.

Summer was more like a curse
or a scar, the accidental blow
from a man of fire
who carelessly turned toward you
and left his handprint glowing
whitely on your forehead.

All the lamps in your home town
will not light the darkness
growing across a landscape
within you; you wait
like a leaning flower, and hear
almost as if it were nothing,
the petrified rumble
from a world going blind.

                        —*John Haines*

BLACK LIGHTNING

A blind girl
stares at me,
then types out ten lines
in braille.

The air has a scent
of sandalwood and
arsenic; a night-blooming cereus
blooms on a dark path.

I look at the
short and long flow
of the lines:
and guess at garlic,
the sun, a silver desert rain,
and palms.

Or is it simply
about hands, a river of light,
the ear of a snail,
or rags?

And, stunned, I feel
the nerves of my hand flashing
in the dark, feel
the world as black
lightning.

—*Arthur Sze*

THE BLIND ALWAYS COME AS SUCH A SURPRISE

The blind always come as such a surprise,
suddenly filling an elevator
with a great white porcupine of canes,
or coming down upon us in a noisy crowd
like the eye of a hurricane.
The dashboards of cars stopped at crosswalks
and the shoes of commuters on trains
are covered with sentences
struck down in mid-flight by the canes of the blind.
Each of them changes our lives,
tapping across the bright circles of our ambitions
like cracks traversing the favorite china.

—Ted Kooser

GLAUCOMA

1.

There's an olive grove inside the fence
that circles the home for the blind.
I drive each day past the gate
where they come to the crosswalk
in mismatched couples,
having one great thing in common.
I'm braked, the motor off,
making up names.
There's sightless Elena leaning
on the stoplight, twelve-year-old Samuel
gripping her wrist. Redhead Anya
drops her cane to the curb,
stops the traffic as she searches.
I always picture their dorms at night.
Roommates, Anya and Elena
drink wine after lights-out.
The gray, forbidden cat
nudges their knees for food.
Elena pours too much milk,
filling the bowl from fingertip to knuckle.

2.

At first the drops sting.
The nurse holds my pulse and offers me gum.
This is the third test
in a month, various lenses.
I watch the doctor's forehead underwater:
G P X R. I have to correct myself twice.
Glaucoma, pressure on the retina's
subtle nerves; some,
like my grandmother, go crazy from it,
more than blind. I can't concentrate—
I'm five again at midnight,
wake to grandmother carrying blankets
to my bed. In the morning,
I'll stare at smudges her hands
have made for years along the walls,

see her turn from the dress pattern
laid out clumsy on the table,
her mouth full of pins. . . .

3.

After bourbon all night,
we undress with the lights on,
do it in front of the closet mirror.
You're on top with eyes halfclosed
when I ask you to look at my face,
grab my neck and look
at my face. Your back's arched
forward, hair across my chest.
The first warm night this winter,
we open windows to the lights
in the valley. No one should be
permitted to love the moon, you say.
And each night it's smaller for me.
Even tonight, full.

4.

I wake from the dream
where grandmother leads me
along the walls of an endless house,
stucco cutting our palms.
I sit up, touch
your sleeping face, try
to imagine blindness. One hand
across my eyes, the other
on the oranges, the wicker basket.
Still life in darkness. Oranges:
dwarf stars colliding. In the valley,
Elena's asleep in her chair.
Anya wraps her arms
around the cat. She's decided
his eyes are green, his fur
is brown and streaked with silver.

—*David Wojahn*

OUT OF BLINDNESS

Give names to sounds,
if it so please you:
call the abrupt tumultous thrum
of gasoline explosion—"airplane."
But it is not.
It is noise obliterating bird-song.

Call wind among invisible leaves,
"rustling whisper of the trees."
But it is not.
It is an oval defined by silence,
wherein a multitude
of faint staccato clicks
sound magically.

Say—if you like—the weightless warm
against my cheek is sunlight,
and the cool my cheek feels
(penetrating yet leaving undisturbed
the film of warmth) is wind.
I will agree and we will play our game.
But do not ask me to believe
that *name* and *feel* are quite the same.

Your language of the sight is current coin
for our transaction, I agree.
But in my *real*
seen things do not count
but sound and what I feel.
I link these, each to each
within the brain until—
thought alien in your world—
my tongue can speak your speech to a degree
that buys me privilege of your company.

                                   —*Leslie B. Blades*

VISIT TO THE INSTITUTE FOR THE BLIND

I. The Walk

Swimming against the coarse grain
of sun-streaked air, I am intercepted
by the crisscross of fins, the sparkle
of black diamond scales and the greetings
of strangers of long standing, who slip
their arms under mine, steering me like
a shipwreck. *Watch out!* they cry, *there's
a step!*, and heave me off my feet so that I
stumble and slip, leaving my arm behind.
When they finally leave me and dissolve
into fibres of mist, my thankyous damn
their eyes.

II. The Institute

All objects have evaporated here, turned into
sounds and echoes. Walls are white vibrations
nesting on fingertips, doors are brown currents
of space. The lounge is traversed by whispers
in various keys of blackness, with occasional
glints and flickers under closed lids—
memories stalking the scents of rows upon rows
of roses. The hum of stirred-up bees inside the
soft-drink automat: all the black spectacles turn
towards it—opaque shades drawn over milky windows:
Eyes are an endangered species here, grapes into
raisins.

In a corner, a woman stretches the feelers of her
private night across a page, caressing meaning.
A young man, chin on his chest (contemplating existence?),
suddenly rises and begins to pace the floor,
in a time-charted curved line, avoiding the reverberations
of shadows. Wherever he moves is the dark side
of the moon.

III. The Dream

That night, I dreamed of quicksand.
There was no longer any pain in sinking,
now that my fear of drowning was
drowning with me. It was the anti-climax
of a firstnight, after too many
dress rehearsals.

—Felix Pollak

ON BECOMING DEAF

There are clouds
in your voice
and I do not
always hear.
Your words
take a direction
that is unfamiliar.
Out of your mouth
comes a beating of wings
and my tongue burns,
I can only pretend.
My eyes cling to your song,
the silent flight of birds.

                    —*S. Soloman*

THE MAN WITH THE HEARING AID

A man takes out his hearing aid
and falls asleep, his good ear deep
in the pillow. Thousands of bats
fly out of the other ear.
All night they flutter and dive
through laughter, catching the punch lines,
their ears all blood and velvet.
At dawn they return. The weary squeaks
make the old stone cavern ring
with gibberish. As the man awakens,
the last of the bats fold into sleep.
His ear is thick with fur and silence.

—Ted Kooser

FINGERS, FISTS,
GABRIEL'S WINGS

My voice, plucked from the air,
clasped in the interpreter's hands:
fists bloom, close,
pulse of hothouse flowers;
supple fingerpuppet dancers
move to unsounded strains.

Watching the deaf girl listen,
I think there is more to words
than sound ever knows,
brimming handfuls of speech
tempered by secondhand grace.
The word, unutterably, made flesh:
fingers flutter, hover, fold,
the whisk of Gabriel's wings.

—*Michael Cleary*

HOW TO SIGN

Invent and *father* are said at the forehead.
Mother comes out from the chin.
On the bumpy nose sits *fool.*
You won't learn the sign for yes until page 112.
No is a beak prattling to its shadow.
In front of the mouth scratches *bird.*
Squeeze the bird once or twice in your hand
to get *orange.* Now you can do anything.
Teach your fingers to spell without you.
Make an island, start a river.
Build a floodgate and walk the width
to let it know your weight.
Test the water with your toes.
Now you can say almost anything.
The line for the past moves back
over the right shoulder.
Stop flailing your arms.
When you finally learn *yes*
it will be a fist knocking.

—Laurie Stroblas

STUTTERER

Courage: your tongue has left
its natural position in the cheek
where eddies of the breath
are navigable calms. Now
it locks against the glottis or
is snapped at by the teeth
in mid stream: it must be work
to get out what you mean:
the rapids of the breath
are furious with belief
and want the tongue, as blood
and animal of speech,
to stop it, block it, or come clean
over the rocks of teeth
and down the races of the air,
tumbled and bruised to death.
Relax it into acting, be
the air's straw-hat
canoeist with a mandolin
yodelling over the falls.
This is the sound advice
of experts and a true despair:
it is the toll to pass the locks
down to the old mill stream
where lies of love are fair.

—*Alan Dugan*

SPASTIC CHILD

A silk of flame composed his hair to fleck
His cheeks with freckles dappled on his pallor,
Misplaced like cartoons on a pall, to spatter
His chin laced with a silver thread of spittle
His wax doll hands cannot wipe off. Subsuming
The muted tragedies of moth and mote
Like crucifixes wrought in ivory,
His tongue, slight mollusk broken in its shell,
Is locked so minnows of his wit may never
Leap playing in our waterspouts of words
For the sheer luxury of diving back
Into the pools of quietude, inlaid
With leaves the autumn-umber of his eyes—
His mind, bright bird, forever trapped in silence.

—Vassar Miller

SONG FOR MY SON

a wooden puppet with tangled
strings   he bobs and bounces
in mid-air   head flopping
arms waving   my hands
under his arms sustain
his spastic stiffness
the Blue Fairy cradling
sweet Pinocchio

He loves to rock and roll
feet prancing   a crazy
puppet dance   his face glows
with the light   of the wishing
star   and borrowing his
brilliance   we too dance
heads bobbing   arms waving
faster and faster until
cast off puppets all
we fall to the floor   laughing
while the fading light
of the wishing star
caresses his face

                    —*Marilyn Davis*

JENNY

You see it's that she can't remember songs
and when friends come to play and want to sing,
you know, songs that children always sing,
she can't remember the songs she sang
even the day before, songs all children sing.

She plays with younger ones,
one little girl really,
and she is so much quicker than my child
and screams at her and calls her stupid
because she can't remember songs.

She can ice skate,
there's nothing wrong with her balance,
and so she glides and looks sad and bewildered
at those who can both skate and sing,
songs that all children know and sing.

And when she is older and the songs are harder
and she needs songs to sing
if she is hurt or loves or isn't sure,
what will she do;
my child who can't remember songs.

—John Mann Astrachan

CLINICS

When I am four a crippled hospital
Peels me out of my parents' arms
To make me better. I wring my mother's neck

For safety, knowing this is not
What they said would happen, that they
Are as unnerved as I am to see
Their mangled only son stripped from their love
Into the cracking-plaster bowels
Of this place, into a row of endless cages
Where children no stronger than their parents'
Worst fears lie writhing, waiting for the legs

The doctors have promised. I have made it
Perfectly clear ever since breakfast
That I want to stop there again on the long
Way back, at that same roadside place
Where I slurped up my hungry hot oats this morning
And they said we'd be sure to, but now
They just stand there growing smaller as some
White-headed woman with her glasses on a chain
Around her neck takes me down the long green
Hallway frowning, and they are still waving goodbye
As we turn the ugly corner and disappear, and what
If I never get my legs and they forget me?

—*Michael Bachstein*

SOCIAL ISSUES
Hungry And Frightened By Namelessness

In the lobby of the Milwaukee County Hospital, a black man in an oversized tweed overcoat which has been through minor surgery is smoking a cigarette, punctuated by erratic rings of smoke and a dry cough. Judging from his posture, his salt-and-pepper beard, and his cough, I would put his age between an old fifty and a young seventy-five. But it is 8 o'clock and there is no more time to speculate; I am on my way to the night shift at the E. R., and keep walking, past the row of wheelchairs lined up in the hallway, slowing down only to wonder which one has been reserved for this man in the lobby.

Medicine has always posed ethical problems, but medical education has only recently emphasized the importance of discussing these issues early in the careers of physicians. Courses on medical ethics are now well-established in a number of medical schools, journals are devoted to the subject, and ethicists are often consulted by their colleagues in medicine. Laymen are also increasingly concerned about ethical issues in medicine, as seen in the sharp criticism of the role doctors have played in some well-publicized cases. Some have accused physicians of taking unnecessarily heroic measures to prolong life, others of not providing the ultimate in medical care. Worst of all, in the legal struggles that ensue, the wishes of the patient and the family sometimes become secondary.

One of the most personal forms of communication is poetry, an appropriate medium for some of the most personal of medical problems. The reader should remember that my comments are made only in the spirit of literary criticism: the "objective" appreciation of technique and imagination, without any attempt to take sides on an issue. In one of my own poems included here, my ethical stance is clear.

Americans generally take for granted their right to

health care, but should we, and more to the point, can we? The World Health Organization's *Constitution* states:

1. Health is a state of complete physical, mental and social well-being and not merely the absence of disease or infirmity.

2. The extension to all peoples of the benefits of medical, psychological and related knowledge is essential to the fullest attainment of health.

3. Governments have a responsibility for the health of their peoples which can be fulfilled only by the provision of adequate health and social measures.[1]

This egalitarian view is obviously difficult to maintain in an era of fiscal restraint. Who decides when a man with a severe stroke and end-stage renal failure should be allowed to die instead of undergoing costly dialysis? In a summary of medical news in 1984, we read that "as hospital finances become stretched, the commitment to indigent care was questioned at non-profit as well as for-profit hospitals. Theorists began to wonder how, in an increasingly price-sensitive market, hospitals would be able to provide free care."[2] Physicians sometimes get caught between the corporation and the patient, and may face a conflict of interest. A recent editorial in the *New England Journal of Medicine* (4/87), titled "Practicing Medicine in the New Business Climate," addresses this issue in a cogent manner.

James Wright is one of the most articulate poets of this century on the subject of social injustice. *The Minneapolis Poem* encompasses many of his themes. The poet's impulse is not to romanticize, but to sympathize and to identify in a natural and un-heroic manner with his "brothers" as he wishes them "good luck / And a warm grave." Their anonymity is a strong motif, an indictment of how society refuses to acknowledge them: "How does the city keep lists of its fathers / Who have no names"? Gary Soto also develops this theme in his poem about a *County Ward*, where patients are referred to as "the cough / That rises like dust" and "the blond one / Who bites a smile" and has a stroke. Similarly, Ben Belitt describes the "prosthetic world" of a *Veteran's Hospital*. He suggests that this is a place where society can hide its "expendables," the fighters who are now reduced to a "junkpile of used parts." Clearly, the poet feels we can do better for them.

The preceding poems show society's tendency to shun the medical problems of others. Sometimes, this attitude appears as a refusal to recognize an entity as a disease; the very nature of disease has been an important ethical and social question in the history of medicine. For instance, only recently has alcoholism been re-defined as a disease which requires treatment and can be treated. A disproportional number of patients at county and veteran hospitals are alcoholics and drug abusers. This makes them subject to a unique spectrum of medical and psycho-social problems. In a photographic *Night Scene* by George Oppen, we see a "drunken man / On an old pier" who is on the verge of suicide. Richard Hugo has written an elegy for an alcoholic friend, *December 24 and George McBride is Dead*. Ambivalent towards his friend, he is angry that McBride could not control his alcoholism. Ironically, his grief leads to the same medical problem as he sits "in the kitchen, / fat and writing, drinking beer and shaking." The musician who has been admitted to *Herrick Hospital, Fifth Floor* has "finally OD'd on Blackness." Al Young may be referring to mental illness, drug abuse or both; in any case, his choice of metaphors suggests the high incidence of drug abuse among the musician sub-culture.

Both intravenous drug abusers and male homosexuals are at high risk for AIDS. The poet John Wieners has written some painfully honest poems about his lifestyle. "Tomorrow some motel with a guy, / Who'd have thought my dreams would come to this"? Today, we should add: Who expected we would ever encounter an organism such as the "Human Immunodeficiency Virus"? David Bergman describes the sense of doom in a patient *In the Waiting Room* of a research center; a "study of the life cycle / of the adult homosexual" is being carried out, as if they were exotic organisms. These patients may begin to feel like outcasts, lepers of a sort, driven from the "walled, polluted city / that cast them out." In an *Elegy for John, my Student Dead of AIDS*, Robert Cording realizes the isolation inflicted by the disease. More than likely, the student's "nobleness of living with no one / To turn to ended in dishonor." The condition seems to arouse some intense emotions from heterosexual people. At an E. R. I once saw a patient with documented AIDS, who was complaining of fevers. Naturally, I didn't look forward to drawing blood from this man, but I donned two pairs of gloves and did the job. Sure enough, the lab called back a little later to say "Insufficient Quantity." When I told a fellow-resident about having to draw yet some more blood, he said, "Just kill the fag"! I was shocked and simply unable to respond.

Since AIDS appears to be our "modern plague," it might be useful to read a poem about the Black Death; Anthony Hecht has written a macabre poem titled *Tarantula or The Dance of Death*, which shows how "Half Europe died" and was "powerless against contagion." Our medical interdependence on each other has rarely been so well described. A similar theme arises from a different occasion, in a poem by Robert Hayden titled *As my Blood was Drawn*. The patient's condition becomes parallel to the pathology of the world, which contains "horrors multiplying / like cancer cells." Although at first, there seems to be no direct connection between the individual and the world, near the poem's conclusion the poet asks the world: "is it your sickness / luxuriating / in my body's world"? In a more oblique manner, *Plane Life* by Lawrence Ferlinghetti questions our involvement in the illnesses of others. The disparity between the woman having a heart attack and the other passengers is sharpest in the juxtaposition: "*I am going to die* / and the passengers all still roaring." The poet, however, has the last laugh, with his ironic final image of the plane as it "sails on / carrying its helpless passengers."

Charles Simic realizes how our lives are inescapably intertwined with the rest of society through our *Great Infirmities*. We all are vulnerable, are disabled to some extent: "we are almost blind, / And a little deaf in both ears." The poet may be implicitly urging us to be more sensitive to the medical problems of others. Sometimes the ills of society seem magnified by personal loss and vice versa, as in a reaction to *Two Deaths* by Joel Oppenheimer. The assasination of Robert Fitzgerald Kennedy, coupled with the death of a grandfather, intensify "the private grief and the public grief." May Swenson has written a catalog poem about the multiplicity of *Deaths* which can overtake us. Poems of this genre derive most of their strength from careful juxtaposition, which the poet has succeeded in achieving. Ironies abound in this poem. Someone "will die while driving a hearse," which "will detour the traffic in which / a cab containing one about to give birth will die."

Statisticians have estimated that more than twelve percent of Americans will be over sixty-five by the year 2000. This graying of America will create a number of issues now and in the future. (We are only thirteen years away!) Already the health care industry is wondering how we will provide adequate geriatric care. In my own field, Physical Medicine and Rehabilitation, geriatric rehabilitation is becoming an important sub-specialty. Howard Nemerov is an observer *Near the Old People's Home*, where everyone is "Wearing some decoration of his damage, / Bandage or crutch or cane." They are susceptible to many problems, including wandering onto the road and "getting hit by cars." *The Very Old* in Ted Kooser's poem are also "forever / hurting themselves." (Falls are common in the elderly. I am currently carrying out a research project on peripheral nerve damage in these patients.) Still, they manage to recover and can be seen in their gardens, "perennial, / checking their gauges for rain." These poems show markedly different reactions to the elderly, with the latter being more hopeful. Donald Hall imagines how *The Old Must Watch Us* with envy, and even "hate." His poem is quite negative about the process of aging—"the body's changing cruelties" and may reflect the young poet's fear of aging. (He has informed me that his views have changed with age!)

Just as modern health care is increasing our longevity, current technology allows us to keep alive babies who would certainly have died even five years ago. Neonatology is a growing field. During my pediatric surgery rotation, we routinely placed infants on respirators in the ICU, with precisely titrated fluids and medications. But once again, progress has inherent problems. Miller Williams describes *The Ones That Are Thrown Out* as being deformed, with "flippers," "a little tail," or "no dome at all above the eyes." In the medical literature they are called "monsters." This poem implicitly asks if they should be saved. When handicapped infants survive, we see their fate in Diana O'Hehir's poem, *The Retarded Children Find a World Built Just For Them*. In the self-contained institution, they can live their own enchanted but precarious lives. Even their shoes are fragile, and their songs parched: "They walk on the streets in crystal shoes," while they "sing and sing like all the birds of the desert."

Ever since Aldous Huxley's *Brave New World* was published, the world has debated the control of behavior through medical technology. Psychosurgical and hormonal manipulation of behavior have been tried recently with variable success but always with ethical controversy. Robert Veatch, a well-known ethicist, has succinctly summarized the complex issues involved: "the relation of subject risk to societal benefit, the degree of organization that qualifies a procedure as an experiment, the duty to continue a successful experimental procedure, the right of a patient to be an experimental subject, the problem of privacy, the researcher's responsibility for harmful consequences, and the publication of unethical research."[3] Etheridge Knight, in his poem *Hard Rock Returns to Prison from the Hospital for the Criminal Insane*, examines the problem of psychosurgery from the perspective of a black inmate. Throughout the poem, there is racial tension: "that's one crazy nigger," "a black son of a bitch." These references suggest that there may have been a racist element to the surgery. William Heyen depicts human experimentation in its ghastliest form, during the Holocaust in Germany. There can be no debates about right or wrong, only *Simple Truths*. The savage Nazi "physician" waits "some days for the boy's skull to knit" and then takes "up the club to strike the boy again." This is worse than torture; it is torture in the name of medical research. We cannot forget the lessons of the Holocaust.

The poet W. B. Yeats wrote that birth and death are two of the three major themes of poetry. (The act of procreation is the third.) These events are associated with the issues of abortion and of euthanasia. Abortion has inflamed proponents and opponents to such a pitch that it has had a major impact on American politics. The poems dealing with this question all show the emotional conflicts inherent in the procedure. None is able to clearly define a position on the subject; each approaches it from a different perspective.

Frank O'Hara's poem, *An Abortion*, brings out the conflicts in a direct manner. At first, before the procedure, the narrator of the poem urges the parents to "not bathe her in blood," but in the second stanza, says "Don't bathe / her in tears," discouraging excessive grief. The ambivalence of conception is figured in the opposing connotations of "she was a shad / a snake"; while both the shad (a fish) and snake can be phallic images, one is inoccuous but the other is malevolent. In a brutally moving poem by Ai, the question of *Abortion* is complicated by the condition of poverty, for the "poor have no children, just small people / and there is room only for one man in this house." The woman felt compelled for economic reasons to do the abortion herself, no doubt under unsterile conditions which may cause her death due to sepsis, or generalized infection. The poem uses no conventional poetic techniques, instead deriving its power from skilful description and unexpected statement.

In the preceding poems, the choice to terminate a pregnancy is agonizing and protracted. Other situations in medicine, however, do not allow time for reflection. Every hospital has its signal for a "code," a life-threatening emergency. My heart still beats faster on hearing a high-pitched tone which resembles the signal where I did my internship, though University Hospital gets our attention with an overhead page for "Dr. Standstill." Outside a hospital, the time before response to an arrest can vary. The luckiest victims suffer minimal brain damage, and children usually fare better than adults. After five minutes, the brain cells, starved of oxygen, begin to die and the intra-cranial pressure increases. In the hospital, the usual dilemma of resuscitation is when to stop, but outside, it often involves whether one should begin at all. The patient in John Stone's *Resuscitation* was lucky. Perhaps his young and pliable brain was able to tolerate oxygen deprivation, in spite of being dead "By all signs and proper science." Then again, his arrest may have been witnessed, as implied in the first lines: "When the heart coughed / and the lungs folded / like flowers / your eyes had barely closed." The patient in *Accident* by Karin Ash was less fortunate and is now "decerebrated." Dependent on a ventilator, he is reduced to the "animal posturing" typical of these patients who have lost "whole sections" of their brains. Seeing the victim of the motorcycle accident, the man who "had to save him" could not stop to think "how long [he] might have waited." This line subtly, but clearly, implies that the patient should not have been "saved," that there are *two* "accidents" in this poem. A patient in *Coma*, by Beth Bentley, is on the verge of death: "The bed's a monument." In fact, her tarot cards begin to take on a life of their own, and feel that the "virtue has gone out of her."

The poems by Ash and Bentley approach the issue of euthanasia in an oblique manner, unlike the final poems of this anthology. An article on withholding treatment in *The New England Journal of Medicine* states that "it is permissible, at least in some cases, to withhold treatment and allow a patient to die, but it is never permissible to take any direct action to kill the patient. . . . [But] the process of being 'allowed to die' can be relatively slow and painful, whereas being given a lethal injection is relatively quick and painless."[4]   Three of the four poems on euthanasia included here support the individual's right to choose his or her quality of life. (These were the only poems I could find on the subject, and do not reflect any bias in selection. In fact, I felt compelled to include Dylan Thomas' *Do Not Go Gentle Into That Good Night*, even though it was published more than twenty-five years ago, and is British.)

Writing just before his father's death, Thomas exhorts "old age" to "Rage, rage against the dying of the light." Repetitions of the title and the preceding line, along with multiple rhymes, give the poem a stirring rhythm; this is especially true in the final lines, where the refrains come together in a crescendoing effect. (The meter is primarily iambic, skilfully varied to give stress ("Rage, rage") or to speed up the line by juxtaposing unstressed syllables: "dying of the light.") Yet the poet recognizes the night is "good" and that "wise men at their end know dark is right." The poem's impulse arises from grief and anger, from denial tempered by the beginning of acceptance. In contrast, the speaker in May Sarton's poem *Of Grief* felt a great relief when her "father fell down / Dead in his splendid prime." Society finds it difficult to accept such emotions and considers them "heartless." In defending her reactions, she remembers the "slow death" of her mother, and how she "buried grief with her."

Interestingly enough, Thomas does not describe the patient's condition, unlike the poems by Denise Levertov and myself. *Death Psalm: O Lord of Mysteries* is about the speaker's mother, who appears ready to die, but "laggard death... shuffles / past the open gate, / past the open hand, / past the

open, / ancient, / courteously waiting life." Her mother may
have had a stroke, for she "lies half-speechless, incontinent,
aching in body, wandering in mind." Repetitions of "She
made ready to die" and "She did not die," along with the in-
cantatory rhythm of *She made, She tended, She gave, She
prepared* create a dirge-like atmosphere; *this* psalm is not one
of praise, in ironic contrast to the Biblical *Psalms*. My own
poem, *Lullaby*, was written for a patient with end-stage renal
failure who was delirious and appeared in great pain. At this
point, his heart, lungs, and brain were all affected, making his
prognosis dismal. I followed this patient for over two weeks,
watching him worsen each day, and hoping that he would
soon be freed from his pathetic condition. His medical record
is "Clamped / Between this hard plastic binder"; he is re-
duced to a series of numbers, "a sample / in a test tube." I
felt a helpless inevitability in the lines: "you keep on poison-
ing / Yourself, your kidneys more useless / Than seawings
drenched in an oil spill." Using the image of a deceased pa-
tient's file as a metaphor of euthanasia, I wrote, "Let me
take you in a wheelchair / To the back room of the records
office . . . And lay you down in the cradle / Of a clean man-
ila folder."

During my shift in the E. R., I had kept an eye out for
the smoker in his oversize tweed coat. When he hadn't arrived
at the desk past midnight, I decided to go looking for him.
The lobby was empty, except for the odor of stale smoke. I
tried picturing him in my mind's eye. Maybe he had taken a
bus and was touring the city, wearing his overcoat like a
shroud. Maybe he had gone back to whatever place he
called home. In any case, I was still waiting for him, and so
was his wheelchair.

THE MINNEAPOLIS POEM

1.

I wonder how many old men last winter
Hungry and frightened by namelessness prowled
The Mississippi shore
Lashed blind by the wind, dreaming
Of suicide in the river.
The police remove their cadavers by daybreak
And turn them in somewhere.
Where?
How does the city keep lists of its fathers
Who have no names?
By Nicollet Island I gaze down at the dark water
So beautifully slow.
And I wish my brothers good luck
And a warm grave.

2.

The Chippewa young men
Stab one another shrieking
Jesus Christ.
Split-lipped homosexuals limp in terror of assault.
High school backfields search under benches
Near the Post Office. Their faces are the rich
Raw bacon without eyes.
The Walker Art Center crowd stare
At the Guthrie Theater.

3.

Tall Negro girls from Chicago
Listen to light songs.
They know when the supposed patron
Is a plainclothesman.
A cop's palm
Is a roach dangling down from the scorched fangs

Of a light bulb.
The soul of a cop's eyes
Is an eternity of Sunday daybreak in the suburbs
Of Juarez, Mexico.

4.

The legless beggars are gone, carried away
By white birds.
The Artificial Limbs Exchange is gutted
And sown with lime.
The whalebone crutches and hand-me-down trusses
Huddle together dreaming in a desolation
Of dry groins.
I think of poor men astonished to waken
Exposed in broad daylight by the blade
Of a strange plough.

5.

All over the walls of comb cells
Automobiles perfumed and blindered
Consent with a mutter of high good humor
To take their two naps a day.
Without sound windows glide back
Into dusk.
The sockets of a thousand blind bee graves tier upon tier
Tower not quite toppling.
There are men in this city who labor dawn after dawn
To sell me my death.

6.

But I could not bear
To allow my poor brother my body to die
In Minneapolis.
The old man Walt Whitman our country man
Is now in America our country
Dead.

But he was not buried in Minneapolis
At least.
And no more may I be
Please God.

7.

I want to be lifted up
By some great white bird unknown to the police,
And soar for a thousand miles and be carefully hidden
Modest and golden as one last corn grain,
Stored with the secrets of the wheat and the mysterious lives
Of the unnamed poor.

—James Wright

COUNTY WARD

It begins in a corridor. A woman phones
Her uncle good-bye, the roster for ping-pong
Goes unsigned.
                    It continues,
And Leon naps hugging his shoes.
When he wakens he asks for water,
For rain to come in one door and leave by another;
He asks for the song of a woman
And hears a broom stroke.

Then onto Rachel and Maria, the dull mothers,
Who bandage, sponge dirt from cheeks,
Saying: *Go sleep, baby.*
                    And always
The old one who runs through rooms, cafeteria;
He is a plane watching the horizon
Where his son disappeared.

                    *

There is a pain that gets up and moves, like the night attendant,
Pointing to the cough
That rises like dust and is dust
A month later, pointing to the blond one
Who bites a smile and strokes
Under blankets, under the guilt of the one light
That never blinks off.

It comes to speak in the drugged voice
That ate its tongue, the cane tapping
Its way from window to TV,
And back again.
                    Outside,
Left of the neon glowing *Eat,*
Right of the traffic returning home,

This cold slowly deepens
The old whose bones ring with the coming weather,
The black children buttoning and unbuttoning their coats,
The stunned face that could be your father's—
Deepens the gray space between each word
That reaches to say you are alone.

Gary Soto

VETERAN'S HOSPITAL
(White River Junction, Vt.)

Bringing "only what is needed—essential
toilet articles" in a paper bag,
dressed as for dying, one sees the dying plainly.
These are the homecomings of Agamemnon,
the voyages to the underside of the web
that weaves and unweaves while the suitors gorge upon plenty
and the languishing sons at home unwish their warring
fathers, with strong electric fingers.
                              The fathers are failing.
In the Hospital Exchange, one sees the dying plainly:
color televisions, beach towels, automatic razors—
the hardware of the affluent society marked
down to cost, to match the negative afflatus
of the ailing, the bandages and badges of their status.
Under the sand-bags, rubber hoses, pipettes, bed-clamps,
tax-exempt, amenable as rabbits,
the unenlisted men are bleeding through their noses
in a perimeter of ramps and apparatus.

In that prosthetic world, the Solarium
lights a junkpile of used parts: the hip that caught
a ricochet of shrapnel; tattoos in curing meats;
scars like fizzled fuses; cancelled postage stamps;
automated claws in candy; the Laser's edge; and barium.
The nurses pass like mowers, dressing and
undressing in the razor-sharp incisions
and the flowering phosphorescence. The smell
of rubbing alcohol rises on desertions and deprivals
and divorces. It is incorruptible. A wheelchair aims
its hospital pajamas like a gun emplacement.
The amputee is swinging in his aviary.
His fingers walk the bird-bars.
                              There is singing
from the Ward-Room—a buzzing of transistors
like blueflies in a urinal. War over war,
the expendables of Metz and Chateau-Thierry,

the guerillas of Bien-Hoa and Korea,
the draftees, the Reserves, the re-enlisters,
open a common wave-length. The catatonic
sons are revving up their combos in the era
of the angry adolescent: their cry is electronic.
Their thumbs are armed with picks. The acid-rock guitarist
in metal studs and chevrons, bombed with magnesium,
mourns like a country yokel, and the innocents
are slaughtered.

On the terrace, there are juices
and bananas. The convalescent listens to his
heart-beat. The chaplain and his non-combative daughter
smile by the clubbed plants on the portico.

They shall overcome.

—*Ben Belitt*

NIGHT SCENE

The drunken man
On an old pier
In the Hudson River,

Tightening his throat, thrust his chin
Forward and the light
Caught his raised face,
His eyes still blind with drink . . .

Said, to my wife
And to me—
He must have been saying

Again—

Good bye Momma,
Good bye Poppa

On an old pier.

                    — *George Oppen*

DECEMBER 24 AND GEORGE MCBRIDE IS DEAD

You a gentleman and I up from the grime—
now wind has shut your dark, dark eyes
and I am left to hate this Christmas eve.
Christ, they're playing carols. Some crap
never stops. You're dead and I'm without
a goddam Wagner record in the house
to play you up to what for some must be
behind the sky with solid orchestration.

Rest in your defeat, you stupid jerk,
so fat your heart gave out, so sweet
you couldn't help but hear the punks.
"One gulp. The whole quart, Mac." That town
you died in—so unlikely—vineyards,
sunny valleys, stark white missions
and the pale priest summoning
brown sinners from the olive grove.
I'll not know your grave, though I believe
our minds have music that can lead us
through the tangle to the lost stone of a friend.

I get along, write my poems. Essentially
a phony, I try my feelings now
and know I fail. George, it's Christmas eve
and bells are caroling. I'm in the kitchen,
fat and writing, drinking beer and shaking.

—Richard Hugo

HERRICK HOSPITAL, FIFTH FLOOR
for a musician friend who
finally OD'd on Blackness

Well, so youve gone and overdone it again,
overdosed yourself this time on Blackness;
locked between Blue Cross, nurse-padded walls,
the unreliable air outside & beyond
shot up with softening Berkeley sunshine

Phrasing fails you, diction cramps,
words are a loss & reflection too costly
What color were you ever but infamous blue?

If your music werent sound & its realness
didnt cleanse, I know you could never walk
much less dance out of this white room again

                                        —Al Young

JIVE

Tomorrow some motel with a guy,
Who'd have thought my dreams would come to this?
It's better than junk.
At least in a clean bed.

Then movies with mother.
The cycle goes on.
It's two o'clock in the morning
Rain on street.

After all, this toughness only goes to state
I'm out for anything
And will settle for nothing less. A dollar bill
Blow in the wind.

                                        —John Wieners

IN THE WAITING ROOM

St. Gaudens would have known what would suit
this research institution: a tall,
stately figure of Science, proudly
undeterred, her plain draperies hung
in even rows to soften the cast
of her bronze body, one hand aloft
raising a hypodermic needle.

Before such images these six-month
check-ups would seem like a pilgrimage
in which unpardonable clerics
and unbathed wives had walked before me.
But in this vast, unadorned building
there's no distraction from my purpose
or the object for which I've journeyed.

With only the pages of *People*
and *Time* for amusement, who would not
feel afraid? For I am here as part
of a study on the life cycle
of the adult homosexual,
to see which of us will sicken next
in our group of twelve hundred odd

from this strange disease of yet unknown
beginnings that teaches the body
how to betray the life within it.
An endangered species, we are watched
to see how it makes its first appearance
and all the stages on which it acts
in our theatre of operations.

Sometimes two or three men are waiting
to be called—not by name—but number
to preserve our anonymity
(though who in the face of such cool
clinical detachment could retain
a sense of self?). Yet at times one might
see a friend or distant acquaintance

head down or looking at the wall
(there are no windows here) marking where
the plaster has given way. I stop,
exchange a few meaningless phrases
and perhaps he'll have a joke to tell
or news of someone known in common
until the silence descends once more.

And once, early for my appointment,
I was left alone when voices shot
through swinging doors. A man in a white
laboratory coat and another
clad in jeans were speaking, and I knew
that the man in denim had become
the person I feared that I might be.

And I hated him for having brought
his death so near that I could touch it,
and the room seemed to fill with the dread
odor of his dying, and I sat amazed:
for with his neat beard and curly hair
and the whiteness of his freckled face,
he might be taken for my lover.

Now the two were arguing in that
complicitous tone of handymen
faced with a machine that will not work.
What about this? Or that? they question,
uncertain which, if any, repairs
to undertake, running their cold hands
along the ailing anatomy.

"I'll never live through *that*," the patient
laughs, as though it were another's case
he were discussing. I asked myself,
can this be true? Can people withdraw
so far from their existence that life
and death become academic games
left to pique their curiosity,

a trivial pursuit that will not
bore when played for hours at a time?
Or is there some catharsis unknown
to me, when what you fear will happen
happens and there's nothing more to fear,
and one reaches that calm meadow where
the sacred few are allowed to rest

beyond the walled, polluted city
that cast them out? They are gone away
now out of sight through another set
of fire doors, but their voices still
can be heard faintly like a new spring
or the hushed tones of lovers careful
not to wake the disapproving crowd.

A nurse approaches, clipboard in hand.
Have I brought my paraphernalia,
samples of semen and excrement
which the study cannot do without?
And the old terror revives in me
of what they will find: the truth, perhaps,
that I like everyone else will die.

Bring him back, bring him back, the one who
gave me his healing touch. I'm ready
to embrace him now if he can stop
the pain of losing what was never
mine to keep. Bring him back
so that he can teach me how to be
content when I take his place at last.

                              —David Bergman

ELEGY FOR JOHN, MY STUDENT DEAD OF AIDS

In my office, where you sat years ago and talked
Of Donne, of how you loved
His persona, the bravado he could muster
To cover love's uncertainties,
Books still line the shelves, centuries
Of writers who've tried to make a kind of sense
Of life and death and, failing that,
Found words to stand at least
Against the griefs we can't resolve.

Now you're dead. And what I've got to say
Comes now from that silence
When our talk last fouled up. I allowed you less,
As always, than you wanted to say.
We talked beside the Charles, a lunch hour reunion
Of sorts after years of your postcards
(New York, San Francisco, Greece),
Failed attempts to find a place to live.
The warm weather had come on

In a rush. You talked of being the first born,
Dark-haired, Italian son. How you rarely visited
The family you so clearly loved.
I shifted to books, to sunlight falling
Through sycamores and the idle play of underlying
Shadows. When we parted,
All that was really left was the feeling
You deserved better. And yet I was relieved
Our hour was up, that we had kept your confusion

To yourself. We shook hands, you drove off to Boston.
Now you're dead and I wonder

If your nobleness of living with no one
To turn to ended in dishonor,
Your family ashamed. Or if your death had
About it a frail dignity,
Each darkening bruise precise as a writer's word,
Saying, at last who you were—exactly
And to anyone who would listen.

—*Robert Cording*

TARANTULA or THE DANCE OF DEATH

During the plague I came into my own.
It was a time of smoke-pots in the house
Against infection. The blind head of bone
            Grinned its abuse

Like a good democrat at everyone.
Runes were recited daily, charms were applied.
That was the time I came into my own.
            Half Europe died.

The symptoms are a fever and dark spots
First on the hands, then on the face and neck,
But even before the body, the mind rots.
            You can be sick

Only a day with it before you're dead.
But the most curious part of it is the dance.
The victim goes, in short, out of his head.
            A sort of trance

Glazes the eyes, and then the muscles take
His will away from him, the legs begin
Their funeral jig, the arms and belly shake
            Like souls in sin.

Some, caught in these convulsions, have been known
To fall from windows, fracturing the spine.
Others have drowned in streams. The smooth head-stone,
            The box of pine,

Are not for the likes of these. Moreover, flame
Is powerless against contagion.
That was the black winter when I came
            Into my own.

                    —Anthony Hecht

"AS MY BLOOD WAS DRAWN"

As my blood was drawn,
as my bones were scanned,
the People of Baha
were savaged were slain;

skeletons were gleaning
famine fields,
horrors multiplying
like cancer cells.

World I have loved,
so lovingly hated,
is it your evil
that has invaded
my body's world?

As surgeons put
me to the knife,
innocents
were sacrificed.

I woke from a death
as exiles drowned.
I called on the veiled
irradiant One.

As spreading oilslicks
burned the seas,
the doctors confirmed
metastasis.

World I have loved
and loving hated,
is it your sickness
luxuriating
in my body's world?

In dreams of death
I call upon
the irradiant veiled
terrible One.

—Robert Hayden

PLANE LIFE

TWA to Boston and
        a woman in 'Ambassador' Class having a
            heart attack while the
passengers wearing headphones are all
            laughing hilarious at
      a movie with
                Dustin Hoffman in
           which he
               impersonates a woman and
they bring in the oxygen tank and
      pump her up and
            when she comes to she
        starts crying and moaning over and over
        O I am going to die
           I am going to die
and the passengers all still roaring
      the woman weeping and moaning
            I am going to die!
                    but
she doesn't.
The movie continues
The passengers continue
The plane like life itself
        sails on
      carrying its helpless
           passengers.

              —Lawrence Ferlinghetti

GREAT INFIRMITIES

Everyone has only one leg.
So difficult to get around,
So difficult to climb the stairs
Without a cane or a crutch to our name.

And only one arm. Impossible contortions
Just to embrace the one you love,
To cut the bread on the table,
To put a coat on in a hurry.

I should mention that we are almost blind,
And a little deaf in both ears.
Perilous to be on the street
Among the congregations of the afflicted.

With only a few steps committed to memory,
Meekly we let ourselves be diverted
In the endless twilight—
Blind seeing-eye dogs on our leashes.

An immense stillness everywhere
With the trees always bare,
The raindrops coming down only halfway,
Coming so close and giving up.

—Charles Simic

TWO DEATHS

david stern
rfk
6 june 1968

the private grief and the public grief.
this old man is dead.
he was found in his private hell
by his children, unable to move or
call for help. and the other also
lay unconscious, and he died also.
all the time i bounce between the
private grief and the public grief.
it does not help much, but nothing
does that, these days. at least,
he had lived a long time, adamantly
refusing any help, anything that
would make him less of his own man,
and he was loved for that. the
apartment was filled with the pictures
that were his only intimates for
thirty years—his own grandchildren
had never seen the inside of this
room. he visited, he loved, he gave
of himself, but this much he held
for himself—pictures, a favorite
chair, the dining room table his
daughter was raised at. i mean
no complaint, but it does not help
that the death of the other was
a national tragedy, a national disgrace.

—joel oppenheimer

DEATHS

One will die   in a low little house in the snow.
One will die   on the mountain.
One will die   at a table. Red will spread on the white cloth.
One will die   on a trolley, will fall from the platform,
              rounding a curve. Soon after, the trolley will die.
One will die   in the bathtub. Slippery, heavy to remove. . . . Not die
              from cut veins or flooded lungs. From embolism
              at the end of the birthday party. The angel cake
              will hold 61 candles. . . . How do I know
              the number of the candles?
One will die   in a celebrated bed, where his grandfather died,
              where his father died, where his son will die.
One will die   in her wheelchair. She has lived there 50 years.
One will die   on a porch, on a summer day.
One will die   on the stairs of the same house, the same day, and
              robbers, with their gags and knives, will get clean away.
One will die   not knowing she dies, for three years suckled by
              machine, emptied by machine, made to tick and breathe
              by machine. Without moving, without speaking,
              she will grant 1000 interviews.
One will die   in the death of a plane, one in the death of a ship,
              another under a stumbling horse that breaks its neck.
One will die   in the hall outside his locked door, having forgotten
              the key inside.
One will die   made to die by one enraged, who will beg to die
              "like a man" by bullet instead of the hell
              of a lifetime in a cell. He will die a lifetime
              in a cell.
One will die   while driving a hearse. The coffin, spilled
              on the highway, will detour the traffic in which
              a cab containing one about to give birth will die.
One will die   about to be born.
One will die   in hospital, having gone to visit his friend, who,
              in eternal pain, has prayed to die, and envies
              that unexpected end. He, too, will die.
All will die   in the end.

                                                —*May Swenson*

NEAR THE OLD PEOPLE'S HOME

The people on the avenue at noon,
Sharing the sparrows and the wintry sun,
The turned-off fountain with its basin drained
And cement benches etched with checkerboards,

Are old and poor, most every one of them
Wearing some decoration of his damage,
Bandage or crutch or cane; and some are blind,
Or nearly, tap-tapping along with white wands.

When they open their mouths, there are no teeth.
All the same, they keep on talking to themselves
Even while bending to hawk up spit or blood
In gutters that will be there when they are gone.

Some have the habit of getting hit by cars
Three times a year; the ambulance comes up
And away they go, mumbling even in shock
The many secret names they have for God.

—Howard Nemerov

THE VERY OLD

The very old are forever
hurting themselves,

burning their fingers
on skillets, falling

loosely as trees
and breaking their hips

with muffled explosions of bone.
Down the block

they are wheeled in
out of our sight

for years at a time.
To make conversation,

the neighbors ask
if they are still alive.

Then, early one morning,
through our kitchen windows

we see them again,
first one and then another,

out in their gardens
on crutches and canes,

perennial,
checking their gauges for rain.

                    —*Ted Kooser*

THE OLD MUST WATCH US

The old must watch us as we walk the streets,
And ghosts of flesh must summon in their brains
    The autumns of a fallen past,
The lovers' wood in which no tree remains.

And then the memory of bits of leaf
Caught in the loosened hair; by heavy seas
    The wind that rasped across their skin,
And all the body's changing cruelties,

Must make them hate us as we walk the streets,
Hand in hand and brushing hip to thigh,
    And they must think we love, and know
That they can only watch and wait to die.

When skin hangs loose upon your shaken limbs,
Remember love you feared when you were young.
    Then read this on a weary night,
And roll these vowels on a shrunken tongue.

—Donald Hall

THE ONES THAT ARE THROWN OUT

One has flippers. This one is like a seal.
One has gills. This one is like a fish.
One has webbed hands, is like a duck.
One has a little tail, is like a pig.
One is like a frog
with no dome at all above the eyes.

They call them bad babies.

They didn't mean to be bad
but who does.

Miller Williams

THE RETARDED CHILDREN FIND A WORLD
BUILT JUST FOR THEM

The doors of that city are ninety feet high,
On their panels are frescoes of ships, of mountains.

Inside is the children's kingdom
Where the mad ones, the foot-draggers, garglers,

Askew as a tower of beads,
Are sustained by the air. Buildings, like great gold chains

Emboss themselves around
The crazy children, their jewels.

The children turn and turn like dancers,
Their sweaters whirl out at their waists, their long chopped hair

Scrapes the side of the archways,
They're happy, they're famous.

They walk on the streets in crystal shoes, lapis flows in the gutters;
Around the edge of each building there's a scarlet halo.

And those children with eyes like scars, with tongues sewed to the
                    roofs of their palates, with hands that jerk

Like broken-backed squirrels,
Feed the writing of light from the buildings;

They forgive us ninety times over;
They sing and sing like all the birds of the desert.

—*Diana O'Hehir*

HARD ROCK RETURNS TO PRISON
FROM THE HOSPITAL FOR THE CRIMINAL INSANE

Hard Rock was "known not to take no shit
From nobody," and he had the scars to prove it:
Split purple lips, lumped ears, welts above
His yellow eyes, and one long scar that cut
Across his temple and plowed through a thick
Canopy of kinky hair.

The WORD was that Hard Rock wasn't a mean nigger
Anymore, that the doctors had bored a hole in his head,
Cut out part of his brain, and shot electricity
Through the rest. When they brought Hard Rock back,
Handcuffed and chained, he was turned loose,
Like a freshly gelded stallion, to try his new status.
And we all waited and watched, like indians at a corral,
To see if the WORD was true.

As we waited we wrapped ourselves in the cloak
Of his exploits: "Man, the last time, it took eight
Screws to put him in the Hole." "Yeah, remember when he
Smacked the captain with his dinner tray?" "He set
The record for time in the Hole—67 straight days!"
"Ol Hard Rock! man, that's one crazy nigger."
And then the jewel of a myth that Hard Rock had once bit
A screw on the thumb and poisoned him with syphilitic spit.

The testing came, to see if Hard Rock was really tame.
A hillbilly called him a black son of a bitch
And didn't lose his teeth, a screw who knew Hard Rock
From before shook him down and barked in his face.
And Hard Rock did *nothing*. Just grinned and looked silly,
His eyes empty like knot holes in a fence.

And even after we discovered that it took Hard Rock
Exactly 3 minutes to tell you his first name,
We told ourselves that he had just wised up,
Was being cool; but we could not fool ourselves for long
And we turned away, our eyes on the ground. Crushed.
He had been our Destroyer, the doer of things
We dreamed of doing but could not bring ourselves to do,
The fears of years, like a biting whip,
Had cut grooves too deeply across our backs.

                                        —*Etheridge Knight*

SIMPLE TRUTHS

When a man has grown a body,
a body to carry with him
through nature for as long as he can,
when this body is taken from him
by other men and women who happen to be,
this time, in uniform,
then it is clear he has experienced
an act of barbarism,

and when a man has a wife,
a wife to love for as long as he lives,
when this wife is marked with a yellow star
and driven into a chamber she will never leave alive,
then this is murder,
so much is clear,

and when a woman has hair,
when her hair is shorn and her scalp bleeds,
when a woman has children,
children to love for as long as she lives,
when the children are taken from her,
when a man and his wife and their children
are put to death in a chamber of gas,
or with pistols at close range, or are starved,
or beaten, or injected by the thousands,
or ripped apart, by the thousands, by the millions,

it is clear that where we are
is Europe, in our century, during the years
from nineteen-hundred and thirty-five
to nineteen-hundred and forty-five
after the death of Jesus, who spoke of a different order,
but whose father, who is our father,
if he is our father,
if we must speak of him as father,
watched, and witnessed, and knew,

and when we remember,
when we touch the skin of our own bodies,
when we open our eyes into dream
or within the morning shine of sunlight
and remember what was taken
from these men, from these women,
from these children gassed and starved
and beaten and thrown against walls
and made to walk the valley
of knives and icepicks and otherwise
exterminated in ways appearing to us almost
beyond even the maniacal human imagination,
then it is clear that this is the German Reich,
during approximately ten years of our lord's time,

and when we read a book of these things,
when we hear the names of the camps,
when we see the films of the bulldozed dead
or the film of one boy struck on the head
with a club in the hands
of a German doctor who will wait
some days for the boy's skull to knit, and will enter
the time in his ledger, and then
take up the club to strike the boy again,
and wait some weeks for the boy's skull to knit,
and enter the time in his ledger again,
and strike the boy again,
and so on, until the boy, who,
at the end of the film of his life
can hardly stagger forward toward the doctor,
does die, and the doctor
enters exactly the time of the boy's death in his ledger,

when we read these things or see them,
then it is clear to us that this
happened, and within the lord's allowance, this
work of his minions, his poor
vicious dumb German victims twisted

into the swastika shapes of trees struck by lightning,
on this his earth, if he is our father,
if we must speak of him in this way,
this presence above us, within us, this
mover, this first cause, this spirit, this
curse, this bloodstream and brain-current, this
unfathomable oceanic ignorance of ourselves, this
automatic electric Aryan swerve, this

fortune that you and I were not the victims, this
luck that you and I were not the murderers, this
sense that you and I are clean and understand, this
stupidity that gives him breath, gives him life
as we kill them all, as we killed them all.

—*William Heyen*

AN ABORTION

Do not bathe her in blood,
the little one whose sex is
undermined, she drops leafy
across the belly of black
sky and her abyss has not
that sweetness of the March
wind. Her conception ached
with the perversity of nursery
rhymes, she was a shad a
snake a sparrow and a girl's
closed eye. At the supper, weeping,
they said let's have her and
at breakfast: no.

              Don't bathe
her in tears, guileless, beguiled
in her peripheral warmth, more
monster than murdered, safe
in all silences. From our tree
dropped, that she not wither,
autumn in our terrible breath.

—Frank O'Hara

ABORTION

Coming home, I find you still in bed,
but when I pull back the blanket,
I see your stomach is flat as an iron.
You've done it, as you warned me you would
and left the fetus wrapped in wax paper
for me to look at. My son.
Woman, loving you no matter what you do,
what can I say, except that I've heard
the poor have no children, just small people
and there is room for only one man in this house.

—Ai

RESUSCITATION

When the heart coughed
and the lungs folded
like flowers
your eyes had barely closed.

By all signs and proper science
you were dead

warm and dying
in one unmerciful
and unelectric instant.

Sweat hung
in my eyebrows
like a father's.

It is easier now
to reconstruct
your death in life.

Now four days later
as you play at trains

I can remember
when the blood began
to bump like boxcars
in the back of your eyes.

—John Stone

ACCIDENT

Decerebrated, a hole cut in your neck
the size of a quarter, you can only breathe and then,
only if I keep your trachea clean, hourly suction
the green strings of mucous that plug over the hole.
I go down and down with the metal-tipped catheter
until finally it pulls nothing back. You gag, choke,
turn blue and I click off the machine.

One arm stretches above your head, elbow flattened
and turned out; the other lies extended along
your hip and thigh and the fingers of your hands
are clenched as if they hold on to all you own.
All I know about you is this animal posturing,
the feel of your loose muscles when I turn you,
the steamy smell of machines pumping constantly
around your bed and that whole sections
of your brain are gone, lost in the minutes
you lay anoxic, waiting for someone to find you,
waiting for a stranger's fist
to beat your heart back alive.

He slammed on his brakes when he saw your motorcycle
crushed against the guard-rail, then saw the blood
congealed on your clothes, streamed from your mouth
across your cheek to your ear. He felt no pulse
on your damp neck. You look so young, even less
than twenty-five. What did he think, seeing you?
He had to save you, adrenalin so sprung
he never thought to check your pupils, never
thought how long you might have waited
and he saved you.

—Karin T. Ash

COMA

The bed's a monument.
Her body's been flung
so far into it, her shape's
impressed there, as on stone.
When her eyes are open,
they are blue stones.
I search for the word
that will make them eyes.
Her hands
have forgotten how to move.
They envelop mine,
anemones eating starfish.
The noise her throat makes
comes from the accumulation
of grievances in its cavities:
old sounds, primitive:
denials, curses.

Our years shuffle and reshuffle
themselves above her bed,
dog-eared cards, sticky
from handling, an abandoned
tarot pack. What is this body,
they ask, that played us
with such skill? We are ourselves,
now, four-square, complete.
Regard our infinite combinations;
do easy tricks with us; build a house.
The spirit that animated us
is disappearing into thin air.
The virtue has gone out of her.

                    —Beth Bentley

DO NOT GO GENTLE INTO THAT GOOD NIGHT

Do not go gentle into that good night,
Old age should burn and rave at close of day;
Rage, rage against the dying of the light.

Though wise men at their end know dark is right,
Because their words had forked no lightning they
Do not go gentle into that good night.

Good men, the last wave by, crying how bright
Their frail deeds might have danced in a green bay,
Rage, rage against the dying of the night.

Wild men who caught and sang the sun in flight,
And learn, too late, they grieved it on its way,
Do not go gentle into that good night.

Grave men, near death, who see with blinding sight
Blind eyes could blaze like meteors and be gay,
Rage, rage against the dying of the light.

And you, father, there on the sad height,
Curse, bless, me now with your fierce tears, I pray.
Do not go gentle into that good night.
Rage, rage against the dying of the light.

—Dylan Thomas

OF GRIEF

You thought it heartless
When my father fell down
Dead in his splendid prime,
Strong as a green oak thrown,
That all I did was praise
Death for this kindness,
Sang with a voice unbroken
Of the dear scholar's days,
His passion of a lifetime—
And my loss never spoken.

Judge of another's grief?
Weigh out that grief in tears?
I did not weep my father,
The rich, the fulfilled years.
What slow death have you known?
When no hope or belief
Can help, no loving care?
We watch and weep alone.
My heart broke for my mother.
I buried grief with her.

It is the incomplete,
The unfulfilled, the torn
That haunts our nights and days
And keeps us hunger-born.
Grief spills from our eyes,
Unwelcome, indiscreet,
As if sprung from a fault
As rivers seam a rock
And break through under shock.
We are shaken by guilt.

There are some griefs so loud
They could bring down the sky,
And there are griefs so still
None knows how deep they lie,
Endured, never expended.
There are old griefs so proud
They never speak a word;
They can never be mended.
And these nourish the will
And keep it iron-hard.

—*May Sarton*

DEATH PSALM: O LORD OF MYSTERIES

She   grew old.
She   made ready to die.
She   gave counsel to women and men, to young girls and
                                          young boys.
She   remembered her griefs.
She   remembered her happinesses.
She   watered the garden.
She   accused herself.
She   forgave herself.
She   learned new fragments of wisdom.
She   forgot old fragments of wisdom.
She   abandoned certain angers.
She   gave away gold and precious stones.
She   counted-over her handkerchiefs of fine lawn.
She   continued to laugh on some days, to cry on others,
                      unfolding the design of her identity.
She   practiced the songs she knew, her voice
                                          gone out of tune
                      but the breathing pattern perfected.
She   told her sons and daughters she was ready.
She   maintained her readiness.
She   grew very old.
She   watched the generations increase.
She   watched the passing of seasons and years.
She   did not die.

She   did not die but lies half-speechless, incontinent,
                      aching in body, wandering in mind
                      in a hospital room.
A plastic tube, taped to her nose,
          disappears into one nostril.
Plastic tubes are attached to veins in her arms.
Her urine runs through a tube into a bottle under the bed.
On her back and ankles are black sores.
The   black sores are parts of her that have died.
The   beat of her heart is steady.
She   is not whole.

She   made ready to die, she prayed, she made her peace,
        she read daily from the lectionary.
She   tended the green garden she had made,
        she fought off the destroying ants,
        she watered the plants daily
        and took note of their blossoming.
She   gave sustenance to the needy.
She   prepared her life for the hour of death.
But   the hour has passed and she has not died.

O Lord of mysteries, how beautiful is sudden death
        when the spirit vanishes
        boldly and without casting
        a single shadowy feather of hesitation
        onto the felled body.

O Lord of mysteries, how baffling, how clueless
        is laggard death, disregarding
        all that is set before it
            in the dignity of welcome—
laggard death, that steals
        insignificant patches of flesh—
laggard death, that shuffles
past the open gate,
past the open hand,
past the open,
        ancient,
        courteously awaiting life.

—Denise Levertov

LULLABY

Each morning I finish my coffee,
And climb the stairs to the charts,
Hoping yours will be filed away.
But you can't hear me,
You can't see yourself clamped
Between this hard plastic binder:
Lab reports and nurses' notes, a sample
In a test tube. I keep reading
These terse comments: stable as before,
Urine output still poor, respiration normal.
And you keep on poisoning
Yourself, your kidneys more useless
Than seawings drenched in an oil spill.
I find my way to your room
And lean over the bedrails
As though I can understand
Your wheezed-out fragments.
What can I do but check
Your tubes, feel your pulse, listen
To your heartbeat insistent
As a spoiled child who goes on begging?

Old man, listen to me:
Let me take you in a wheelchair
To the back room of the records office,
Let me lift you in my arms
And lay you down in the cradle
Of a clean manila folder.

—Jon Mukand

INTRODUCTION

1.   E.D. Pellegrino, "To Look Feelingly—the Affinities of Literature and Medicine," *Literature and Medicine*, v. 1, (1982), p. 19.
2.   D. Levertov, from *Healing Arts in Dialogue: Medicine & Literature*, ed., J. Trautmann, (Carbondale: Southern Illinois Univ. Press, 1981), p. 153.
3.   E.M. Forster, *Aspects of the Novel*, (New York: Harcourt, Brace Jovanovich, Inc., 1956).
4;   E.E. Gordon, "Case Reports: Appropriate Research," *The Archives of Physical Medicine and Rehabilitation*, 65, No. 7 (July, 1984), p. 355.
5.   C. Brooks and R.P. Warren, *Understanding Poetry*, (New York: Holt, Rinehart and Winston, 1976).
6.   E. Closs Traugott & M.L. Pratt, *Linguistics for Students of Literature*, (New York: Harcourt, Brace and Jovanovich, 1980.).
7.   C.L. Dana, *Poetry and the Doctors*, (Woodstock, Vermont: The Elm Tree Press, 1916).
8.   M.L. McDonough, ed., *Poet Physicians: An Anthology of Medical Poetry Written by Physicians*, (Springfield, Illinois: Charles C. Thomas, 1945).
9.   J. & H. Sergeant, eds., *Poems From Hospital*, (London: George Allen and Unwin, Ltd., 1968).
10. H. Sergeant, ed., *Poems From The Medical World*, (Lancaster: MTP Press, Ltd., 1980).

PATIENTS' VIEWS OF DOCTORS

1.   Geoffrey Chaucer, *The Canterbury Tales*, trans. N. Coghill, (London: Penguin Books, 1960).

PHYSICIANS

1.   W.C. Williams, *The Autobiography of William Carlos Williams* (New York: Random House, 1951).

FAMILY AND FRIENDS

1.   R.B. Salter, *Textbook of Disorders and Injuries of the Musculoskeletal System*, (Baltimore: William and Wilkins, 1983), p. 375.
2.   A.M. Freedman *et al., Modern Synopsis of the Comprehensive Textbook of Psychiatry*, (Baltimore: William & Wilkins, 1976), p. 518.

WOMEN

1.   *Modern Healthcare*, January 17, 1986.
2.   R.C. Benson, *Current Obstetric and Gynecologic Diagnosis and Treatment*, (Palo Alto, CA: Lange, 1978), p. 914.

MENTAL ILLNESS

1.   H. Leigh, ed., *Psychiatry in the Practice of Medicine*, (Menlo Park, CA: Addison-Wesley, 1983), p. viii.
2.   J.L. Weiss, "The Clinical Use of Psychological Tests," in *The Harvard Guide to Modern Psychiatry*, ed., A.M. Nicholi, Jr., (Cambridge: Harvard Univ. Press, 1978), p. 44.
3.   J.C. Nemiah, "Psychoneurotic Disorders," in *The Harvard Guide*, p. 186.
4.   D.V. Sheehan and T.P. Hackett, "Psychosomatic Disorders," in *The Harvard Guide*, pp. 328-329.
5.   C. Salzman, "Electroconvulsive Therapy," in *The Harvard Guide*, pp. 471-480.

SOCIAL ISSUES

1. T.L. Beauchamp and L. Walters, *Contemporary Issues in Bioethics*, (California: Dickenson Publishing Co., Inc., 1978), p. 89.
2. D. Lefton, "Hospitals Pressured to Tighten Their Belts," *American Medical News*, January 4, 1985, p. 25.
3. R.M. Veatch, *Case Studies in Medical Ethics*, (Cambridge: Harvard Univ. Press, 1977), p. 267.
4. J. Rachels, "Active and Passive Euthanasia," *The New England Journal of Medicine*, 292, No. 2 (January 9, 1975), pp. 78-80.

PERMISSIONS

Dannie Abse: reprinted from COLLECTED POEMS: 1948-76, with permission from the poet and Anthony Sheil Associates. Diane Ackerman: from WIFE OF LIGHT, Morrow, 1978, by permission of the poet. Ai: from CRUELTY, 1973, by permission of Houghton Mifflin. Karin Ash: by permission of the poet. John Mann Astrachan: from THE NEW ENGLAND JOURNAL OF MEDICINE, May 27, 1982, by permission of the NEJM. David Axelrod: from MYTHS, DREAMS AND DANCES, Despa Press, 1974, by permission of the poet. Michael Bachstein: from TOWARD SOLOMON'S MOUNTAIN, Temple Univ. Press, 1986, by permission of T.U. Press. Imamu Amiri Baraka: from SOUNDS AND SILENCES, ed. R. Peck, Delacorte Press, 1970, by permission of the Sterling Lord Agency. Marvin Bell: from A PROBABLE VOLUME OF DREAMS, Atheneum, 1969, by permission of the publisher. H.N. Beckerman: from TOWARD SOLOMON'S MOUNTAIN, by permission of Temple U. Press. Ben Belitt: from POSSES— SIONS: NEW AND SELECTED POEMS, David Godine, 1986, by permission of the poet. S. Ben-Tov: from DURING CEASE FIRE, Harper & Row, 1985, by permission of the poet. Michael Benedikt: from NIGHT CRIES, Wesleyan U. Press, 1976, by permission of the publisher. Beth Bentley: COUNTRY OF RESEMBLANCES, Ohio Univ. Press, 1976, by permission of the publisher. Stephen Berg: from IN IT, Univ. of Illinois Press, by permission of the poet. David Bergman: from POETRY, December 1986, by permission of the publisher. John Berryman: from LOVE ND FAME, Farrar, Straus & Giroux, 1970, by permission of the publisher. Elizabeth Bishop: from LIKE A BULWARK, Viking, 1956, by permission of the publisher. Leslie Blades: from THE NOW VOICES, eds. Carli & Kilman, Charles Scribner's Sons, 1971. Richard Blessing: from A CLOSED BOOK, U of Washington Press, 1981, by permission of the publisher. Michael Blumenthal: from DAYS WE WOULD RATHER KNOW, Viking, 1984, by permission of the publisher. Louise Bogan: from I HEAR MY SISTERS SINGING, eds. Konek & Walters, Thomas Crowell, 1976, by permission of Farrar Straus & Giroux. Harold Bond: from DANCING ON WATER, The Cummington Press, 1970, by permission of the poet. David Bottoms: from SHOOTING RATS AT THE BIBB COUNTY DUMP, Morrow, 1980, by permission of the poet. Philip Booth: from RELATIONS: SELECTED POEMS, 1950-1985, Viking, 1986, by permission of the publisher. Millen Brand: from HARPER'S, May, 1979, by permission of the publisher. Spencer Brown, from THE SEWANEE REVIEW, by permission of the publisher. Hayden Carruth, from FOR YOU, New Directions, 1970, by permission of the poet. Helen Chasin: from COMING CLOSE AND OTHER POEMS, Yale Univ. Pr., by permission of the publisher. John Ciardi: from POETRY, October, 1982, by permission of his literary executor, Miller Williams. Michael Cleary: from THE TEXAS REVIEW, Fall, 1983, by permission of the publisher. Robert Cording: from POETRY, December, 1986, by permission of the publisher.

Philip Dacey: from ST. LOUIS UNIVERSITY MAGAZINE, by permission of the poet. Marilyn Davis: from TOWARD SOLOMON'S MOUNTAIN, by permission of Temple Univ. Press. Peter Davison: from PRAYING WRONG: NEW AND SELECTED POEMS, 1957-1984, by permission of Atheneum Press. Carl Dennis: from SIGNS AND WONDERS, Princeton Univ. Press, 1979, by permission of the publisher. James Dickey: from BUCKDANCER'S CHOICE, Wesleyan Univ. Press, 1964, by permission of the publisher. Paul Dilsaver: from POETS WEST, Perivale Press, 1975, by permission of the publisher. Stephen Dobyns: from THE BALTHUS POEMS, Atheneum Press, by permission of the publisher. Alan Dugan: from COLLECTED POEMS, Yale University Press, 1969, by permission of the poet. Stephen Dunn: from LOOKING FOR HOLES IN THE CEILING, Univ. of Mass., Amherst, 1974, by permission of the poet. Richard Eberhart: from COLLECTED POEMS: 1930-76, Oxford Univ. Press, 1976, by permission of the publisher. Christopher Fahy: from THE END BEGINNING, Red Earth Press, 1978, by permission of the poet. Mary Farrell: from POETRY, September 1986, by permission of the publisher. Lawrence Ferlinghetti: from OVER ALL THE OBSCENE BOUNDARIES, New Directions Press, 1984, by permission of the publisher. Donald Finkel: from THE DETACHABLE MAN, Atheneum, by permission of the publisher. David Fisher: from THE BOOK OF MADNESS, Applewood Books, 1980. Brendan Galvin: from THE MINUTES NO ONE OWNS, U of Pittsburgh Press, 1977 by permission of the poet. Celia Gilbert: from QUEEN OF DARKNESS, Viking, 1977, by permission of the poet. Jack Gilbert: from MONOLITHOS, Knopf, by permission of the poet. Sandra Gilbert: from EMILY'S BREAD, W.W. Norton, 1984, by permission of the publisher. Patricia Goedicke: fromTHREE RIVERS POETRY JOURNAL, by permission of the poet. Albert Goldbarth: from POETRY, April, 1982, by permission of the publisher. Pamela White Hadas: from BESIDE HERSELF, POCOHONTAS TO PATTY HEARST, Knopf, 1983, by permission of the poet. Susan Hahn: from POETRY, June, 1984, by permission of the publisher. John Haines: from STONE HARP, Wesleyan Univ. Press, 1968, by permission of the publisher. Donald Hall: from EXILES AND MARRIAGES, Viking, 1955, by permission of the poet. Jim Hall: from POETRY, May, 1986, by permission of the publisher. Daniel Halpern: from SEASONAL RIGHTS, Viking, 1982, by permission of the poet. Michael S. Harper: from HISTORY IS YOUR OWN HEARTBEAT, U of Illinois Press, 1971, by permission of the poet. William Harrold: from WIN, 1975, by permission of the poet. Robert Hass: from THE NEW REPUBLIC, by permission of the poet. Robert Hayden from COLLECTED POEMS, Liveright Publishing Corp, 1985, by permission of the publisher. Anthony Hecht: from THE HARD HOURS, Atheneum Press, by permission of the publisher. Robert Hedin: from POETRY, April, 1982, by permission of the publisher. Judith Hemschemeyer: from VERY CLOSE AND VERY SLOW, Wesleyan Univ. Press, 1975, by permission of the publisher. William Heyen: from THE SWASTIKA POEMS, Vanguard Press, 1971, by permission of the publisher. Edward Hirsch: from WILD GRATITUDE, Knopf, 1986, by permission of the publisher. John Hollander from BLUE WINE AND OTHER POEMS, Johns Hopkins

Press, 1979. Edwin Honig: from SURVIVALS, October House Press, 1964, by permission of the poet. Richard Howard: from FINDINGS, Atheneum Press, by permission of the publisher. Langston Hughes: from THE SELECTED POEMS OF LANGSTON HUGHES, Random House, 1974, by permission of the publisher. Richard Hugo: from SELECTED POEMS, Norton, 1979, by permission of the publisher. David Ignatow: from SELECTED POEMS, Wesleyan, 1975, by permission of the publisher. Colette Inez: from THE WOMAN WHO LOVED WORMS AND OTHER POEMS Doubleday, 1972, by permission of the poet. Phyllis Janowitz: from VISITING RITES, Princeton U Press, 1984, by permission of the publisher. Randall Jarrell: from THE COMPLETE POEMS, Farrar, Straus and Giroux, 1969, by permission of the publisher. Erica Jong: from AT THE EDGE OF THE BODY, Holt, Rinehart & Winston, 1979, by permission of the publisher. Donald Justice: from THE SUMMER ANNIVERSARIES, Wesleyan Univ. Press, 1957, by permission of the publisher. Mary Karr: from POETRY, September, 1986, by permission of the publisher, Weldon Kees: from THE COLLECTED POEMS OF WELDON KEES, U of Nebraska Press, 1975, by permission of the publisher. X.J. Kennedy: from CROSS TIES: SELECTED POEMS, U of Georgia Press, 1985, by permission of the publisher. Norman Andrew Kirk: from SOME POEMS, MY FRIENDS, Four Zoas Night House Press, 1981, by permission of the poet. Etheridge Knight: from THE TREASURY OF AMERICAN POETRY, Doubleday, 1978, by permission of the poet. Ted Kooser: from SURE SIGNS: NEW AND SELECTED POEMS, U of Pittsburgh, 1980; and ONE WORLD AT A TIME, U of Pittsburgh, 1985, by permission of the publisher. Maxine Kumin: from THE NIGHTMARE FACTORY, Harper and Row, 1970 and from HALFWAY, Holt, Rinehart & Winston, 1961, by permission of the poet. Stanley Kunitz: from SELECTED POEMS: 1928-1958, Little, Brown, 1979, by permission of the poet. Sydney Lea: from THE NEW YORKER, August, 1983, by permission of the publisher. Philip Levine: from ONE FOR THE ROSE, Atheneum Press, 1981, by permission of the publisher. Robert Lowell: from LIFE STUDIES, Farrar, Straus & Giroux, 1967, by permission of the publisher. Thomas Lux: from HALF PROMISED LAND, Houghton Mifflin, 1986, by permission of the poet. Marcia Lynch: by permission of the poet. Norman MacCaig: from RINGS ON A TREE, Chatto & Windus and The Hogarth Press, by permission of the publisher. Rose Marcel: by the poet's permission. William Matthews: from A HAPPY CHILDHOOD, Atlantic, Little Brown, and from BLACK WARRIOR REVIEW, by permission of the former and the poet. Kirk Maxey: from JAMA, April, 1984, by permission of the publisher. Gloria Maxson: from TOWARD SOLOMON'S MOUNTAIN, by permission of Temple Univ. Press. Sandra McPherson: from ELEGIES FOR THE HOT SEASON, Indiana U Press, 1970, by permission of the poet and Ecco Press (second edition). James Merrill: from FROM THE FIRST NINE: POEMS 1946-76, Atheneum Press, 1976, by permission of the publisher. W.S. Merwin: from THE COMPASS FLOWER, Atheneum Press, 1976, by permission of the publisher. Josephine Miles: from KINDS OF AFFECTION, Wesleyan U Press, 1967, by permission of the publisher. Vassar Miller: from

VASSAR MILLER: NEW AND SELECTED POEMS, Latitudes Press, 1981, by permission of the poet. Lilian Morrison from: WHO WOULD MARRY A MINERAL, Lothrop, Lee, & Shepard, 1978; and from TOWARD SOLOMON'S MOUNTAIN, Temple U Press, 1986, by permission of the poet. Howard Moss: from NEW SELECTED POEMS, Atheneum Press, 1985; and from THE NEW YORKER, May 1983, both by permission of the publishers. Lisel Mueller: from SECOND LANGUAGE, Louisiana State U Press, 1986, by permission of the poet and publisher. Jon Mukand: from JAMA, April 1984 and from MEDICAL HERITAGE, Fall 1984, both by permission of the publishers. Ogden Nash: from BED RIDDANCE, Little Brown, 1969, by permission of the publisher. Leonard Nathan: from GLAD AND SORRY SEASONS, Random House, 1963, by permission of the publisher. Howard Nemerov: from THE WESTERN APPROACHES: POEMS: 1973-1975, U of Chicago Press, 1975; and from THE POETRY ANTHOLOGY: 1912-1977, Houghton Mifflin 1978, both by permission of the poet. John Frederick Nims: from THE SATURDAY REVIEW, by permission of the publisher. Jeremy Nobel: by permission of the poet. Joyce Carol Oates: from ANGEL FIRE, Louisiana State U Press, 1973, by permission of the poet. Frank O'Hara: from THE COLLECTED POEMS OF FRANK O'HARA, Knopf, 1969, by permission of the publisher. Diana O'Hehir: from THE POWER TO CHANGE GEOGRAPHY, Princeton U Press, 1979, by permission of the poet. Sharon Olds: from AMERICAN POETRY REVIEW, v. 14, No. 6, by permission of the poet. George Oppen: from COLLECTED POEMS, New Directions Press, 1975, by permission of the publisher. Joel Oppenheimer: from ON OCCASION, Bobbs-Merrill, 1973, by permission of the poet. Robert Pack: from FACES IN A SINGLE TREE, David Godine, 1984, by permission of the publisher. Dixie Partridge: from AHSAHTA PRESS, 1986 & from TOWARD SOLOMON'S MOUNTAIN, Temple U Press, 1986, by permission of the poet. Linda Pastan: from AM/PM NEW AND SELECTED POEMS, Norton, 1982, by permission of the publisher. Molly Peacock: from POETRY, February 1986, by permission of the publisher. Anne Perlman: from POETS WEST, Preivale Press, 1975, by permission of the publisher. Robert Phillips: PERSONAL ACCOUNTS, Ontario Review Press, 1986, by permission of the publisher. Marge Piercy: from STONE, PAPER, KNIFE, Knopf, by permission of the publisher. Sylvia Plath: from COLLECTED POEMS, Harper & Row, 1981, by permission of the publisher Felix Pollak: from TUNNEL VISIONS, Spoon River Poetry Press, 1984, by permission of the poet. David Posner: from THE NEW YORKER, 1972, by permission of the late poet's personal representative, Rick Lavelle. Susan Irene Rea: from FIRELANDS ARTS REVIEW, 1977, by permission of the editor. Janet Reno: by permission of the poet. Kenneth Rexroth: from THE COLLECTED SHORTER POEMS OF KENNETH REXROTH, New Directions Press, 1966, by permission of the publisher. Adrienne Rich: from POEMS, SELECTED AND NEW, 1950-1974, Norton, 1975, by permission of the publisher. Theodore Roethke: from THE COLLECTED POEMS OF THEODORE ROETHKE, Doubleday, 1963, by permission of the publisher. Robin Morgan: from MONSTER: POEMS BY ROBIN MORGAN, Random House, reprinted permission of the publisher. May Sarton: from SELECTED POEMS, Norton, reprinted by permission of the poet. Jim Schley: reprinted by permission of the poet. Peter Sears: from FIELD, v. 28, 1983, reprinted by permission of the publisher. Anne Sexton: from LIVE OR DIE, Houghton Mifflin, 1966; and from THE AWFUL ROWING TOWARD GOD, Houghton Mifflin, 1975, by permission of the publisher. Karl Shapiro: from COLLECTED POEMS, Random House, 1978, by permission of the poet. Jon Silkin: from POEMS NEW AND SELECTED, Wesleyan U Press, 1966, by permission of the publisher. Charles Simic: from CLASSIC BALLROOM DANCES, George Braziller Press, 1980, by permission of the poet. L.E. Sissman: from HELLO DARKNESS THE COLLECTED POEMS OF L.E. SISSMAN, Little Brown 1969, by permission of the publisher. Judith Skillman: from POETRY, September, 1986, by permission of the publisher. Tom Sleigh: from POETRY, February 1986, by permission of the publisher. W.D. Snodgrass: from HEART'S NEEDLE, Knopf, 1959, by permission of the publisher. S. Soloman: from BERKELEY POETS COOPERATIVE/18, Berkeley Poets Workshop and Press, 1980. Gary Soto: from THE ELEMENTS OF SAN JOAQUIN, U of Pittsburgh Press, 1977, by permission of the poet. Barry Spacks: from TEACHING THE PENGUINS TO FLY, David Godine, 1981, by permission of the publisher. Roberta Spear: from SILKS, Holt, Rinehart & Winston, by permission of the poet. William Stafford: from STORIES THAT COULD BE TRUE, Harper & Row, 1956, by permission of the publisher. John Stone: from IN ALL THIS RAIN (1980) & RENAMING THE STREETS (1986), Louisiana State U Press, and from THE SMELL OF MATCHES, Rutgers U Press, 1972, by permission of the publishers. Laurie Stroblas: from TOWARD SOLOMON'S MOUNTAIN, Temple U Press, 1986, by permission of the poet. Hollis Summers: from OCCUPANT PLEASE FORWARD, Rutgers Univ., The State Univ of New Jersey, by permission of the publisher. Amber Coverdale Sumrall: from KALLIOPE, vol. 7, No. 3, by permission of the publisher. May Swenson: from NEW AND SELECTED THINGS TAKING PLACE, Atlantic, Little Brown, 1978, by permission of the poet. Arthur Sze: by permission of the poet, from DESPITE THIS FLESH, ed. Vassar Miller, U of Texas Press, 1986. James Tate: from VIPER JAZZ, Wesleyan U Press, 1976, by permission of the publisher. Dylan Thomas: from THE POEMS OF DYLAN THOMAS, New Directions Press, 1952, by permission of the publisher. Richard Tillinghast: from SLEEP WATCH, Wesleyan U Press, 1966, by permission of the publisher. John Updike: from FACING NATURE, Knopf, 1985, by permission of the publisher. Constance Urdang: from THE LONE WOMAN AND OTHERS, U of Pittsburgh Press, 1980, by permission of the poet & the publisher. Jean Valentine: from THE MESSENGER, Farrar, Straus & Giroux, 1979, by permission of the publisher. Mona Van Duyn: from TO SEE, TO TAKE, Atheneum PRess, 1971 by permission of the publisher. Ellen Bryant Voigt: from CLAIMING KIN, Wesleyan U Press, 1976, by permission of the publisher. David Wagoner: from COLLECTED POEMS, Indiana U Press, 1973, by permission of the poet. Diane Wakoski: from COINS AND COFFINS, Hawk's Well Press, 1982, by permission of the poet. Alice Walker: from ONCE,

Harcourt, Brace Jovanovich, by permission of the publisher.
Jeanne Murray Walker: from POETRY, September, 1986, by
permission of the publisher. Ronald Wallace: from PLUMS,
STONES, KISSES AND HOOKS, U of Missouri Press, 1981,
by permission of the poet. Robert Watson: from SELECTED
POEMS, Atheneum Press, by permission of the publisher.
John Wieners: from SELECTED POEMS, Grossman Publish-
ers, 1972. C.K. Williams: from: TAR, Random House, by
permission of the publisher. Miller Williams: from DISTRAC-
TIONS, Louisiana State U Press, 1979, by permission of the
poet. William Carlos Williams: from COLLECTED EARLIER
POEMS, New Directions Press, 1938, by permission of the
publisher. David Wojahn: from ICEHOUSE LIGHTS, Yale U
Press, 1982, by permission of the poet. James Wright: from
WE SHALL GATHER AT THE RIVER, Wesleyan U Press,
1966, by permission of the publisher. Al Young: from GEO-
GRAPHY OF THE NEAR PAST, Holt, Rinehart & Winston
1976, by permission of the poet. Gary Young: from AN-
TAEUS, 1979, by permissio of the poet. Samuel Stearns: by
permission of the poet.

INDEX

Abse, Dannie: 141-144
Ackerman, Diane: 242
Ai: 375
Ash, Karin: 377
Astrachan, John Mann: 326
Axelrod, David: 244, 245

Bachstein, Michael: 327
Ballard, Rae: 249
Baraka, Imamu Amiri: 269
Beckerman, H.N.: 310
Belitt, Ben: 346
Bell, Marvin: 64, 84
Ben-Tov, S.: 130
Benedikt, Michael: 123
Bentley, Beth: 93, 378
Berg, Stephen: 178
Bergman, David: 352
Berryman, John: 281
Bishop, Elizabeth: 131
Blades, Leslie B.: 316
Blessing, Richard: 23
Blumenthal, Michael: 247
Bogan, Louise: 278
Bond, Harold: 300
Bottoms, David: 203
Booth, Philip: 262
Brand, Millen: 246
Brown, Spencer: 259

Carruth, Hayden: 288
Chasin, Helen: 232
Ciardi, John: 70
Cleary, Michael: 321
Cording, Robert: 355

Dacey, Philip: 297
Davis, Marilyn: 325
Davison, Peter: 126, 207
Dennis, Carl: 286
Dickey, James: 190-191
Dilsaver, Paul: 34
Dobyns, Stephen: 83
Dugan, Alan: 129, 323
Dunn, Stephen: 243

Eberhart, Richard: 80

Fahy, Christopher: 304

Farrell, Mary: 194
Ferlinghetti, Lawrence: 360
Finkel, Donald: 45
Fisher, David: 122

Galvin, Brendan: 63
Gilbert, Celia: 40
Gilbert, Jack: 273
Gilbert, Sandra: 25, 201, 202
Goedicke, Patricia: 221
Goldbarth, Albert: 42

Hadas, Pamela White: 264
Hahn, Susan: 261
Haines, John: 311
Hall, Donald: 366
Hall, Jim: 68
Halpern, Daniel: 87
Harper, Michael S.: 73
Harrold, William: 109
Hass, Robert: 224
Hayden, Robert: 358
Hecht, Anthony: 357
Hedin, Robert: 197
Hemschemeyer, Judith: 234
Heyen, William: 371-373
Hirsch, Edward: 85
Hollander, John: 186
Honig, Edwin: 205-206
Howard, Richard: 181
Hughes, Langston: 271
Hugo, Richard: 349

Ignatow, David: 108
Inez, Colette: 225

Janowitz, Phyllis: 180
Jarrell, Randall: 36
Jong, Erica: 228
Justice, Donald: 280

Karr, Mary: 230
Kees, Weldon: 82
Kennedy, X.J.: 277
Kirk, Norman Andrew: 306
Knight, Etheridge: 369

Kooser, Ted: 24, 313, 320,
        365
Kumin, Maxine: 117, 299
Kunitz, Stanley: 114

Lea, Sydney: 187-189
Levertov, Denise: 185, 382
Levine, Philip: 46-47, 65-66
Lowell, Robert: 267
Lux, Thomas: 51
Lynch, Marcia: 124

MacCaig, Norman: 32
Marcel, Rose: 275
Matthews, William: 48, 111
Maxey, Kirk: 223
Maxson, Gloria: 302
McPherson, Sandra: 226
Merrill, James: 263
Merwin, W.S.: 52-54
Miles, Josephine: 107
Miller, Vassar: 324
Morgan, Robin: 285
Morrison, Lillian: 301
Moss, Howard: 37. 67
Mueller, Lisel: 115
Mukand, Jon: 154, 276, 384

Nash, Ogden: 195
Nathan, Leonard: 21, 287
Nemerov, Howard: 274, 364
Nims, John Frederick: 110
Nobel, Jeremy: 119

Oates, Joyce Carol: 26
O'Hara, John: 374
O'Hehir, Diana: 368
Olds, Sharon: 175-177
Oppen, George: 348
Oppenheimer, Joel: 362

Pack, Robert: 112-113
Partridge, Dixie: 41, 305
Pastan, Linda: 35, 222
Peacock, Molly: 171, 240
Perlman, Anne: 236
Phillips, Robert: 121
Piercy, Marge: 241
Plath, Sylvia: 88
Pollak, Felix: 317-318
Posner, David: 270

Rea, Susan Irene: 173
Reno, Janet: 31
Rexroth, Kenneth: 209
Rich, Adrienne: 248
Roethke, Theodore: 91

Sarton, May: 380
Schley, Jim: 198
Sears, Peter: 272
Sexton, Anne: 89, 127
Shapiro, Karl: 76
Silkin, Jon: 183
Simic, Charles: 361
Sissman, L.E.: 94-95
Skillman, Judith: 231
Sleigh, Tom: 81
Snodgrass, W.D.: 30
Soloman, S.: 319
Soto, Gary: 344
Spacks, Barry: 200
Spear, Roberta: 74
Stafford, William: 174
Stearns, Samuel: 150-153
Stone, John: 145-149, 233, 376
Stroblas, Laurie: 322
Summers, Hollis: 77
Sumrall, Amber Coverdale: 303
Swenson, May: 363
Sze, Arthur: 312

Tate, James: 128
Thomas, Dylan: 379
Tillinghast, Richard: 125

Updike, John: 172
Urdang, Constance: 237, 250

Valentine, Jean: 50
Van Duyn, Mona: 28
Voigt, Ellen Bryant: 238

Wagoner, David: 39
Wakoski, Diane: 283-284
Walker, Alice: 204
Walker, Jeanne Murray: 239
Wallace, Ronald: 309
Watson, Robert: 22
Wieners, John: 351

Williams, C.K.: 192
Williams, Miller: 367
Williams, William Carlos: ix
Wojahn, David: 314
Wright, James: 341-343

Young, Al: 350
Young, Gary: 120

A NOTE ON THE EDITOR

The editor has a background in both Literature and Medicine. During college at the University of Minnesota, he majored in chemistry and English; while there, he was a researcher in Pharmacology at the Mayo Clinic. After two years of medical school, he took a leave of absence to earn an M.A. in English at Stanford. His M.D., with Honors in research, was at The Medical College of Wisconsin (Milwaukee). Currently he is a resident in Physical Medicine & Rehabilitation at the Boston University Medical Center.

The National Fund for Medical Education has awarded him a grant to write poetry about medicine, and he has received scholarships from the University of Wisconsin, Stanford University, the Alworth Foundation, the Joseph Collins Foundation, and the Breadloaf Writers' Conference. He has been a finalist in the Rhodes Scholarship competition, to study English. His medical research has been presented at national meetings, and a number of articles are in the process of publication in medical journals. Some of his poetry has been published in *Harbor Review, Medical Heritage,* and the *Journal of the AMA,* among other places.

This anthology was selected for presentation at a meeting of the Society for Health & Human Values. Parts of this anthology have also been presented at Loyola Medical School, Stanford, and Yale. An excerpt has been accepted by *Medical Heritage.*

Dr. Mukand is the co-leader of a discussion group titled *Viewing Medicine Through the Arts,* and offers a seminar which bears the title of this book, at the Boston University School of Medicine.

He is currently working on a book of literary criticism titled *The Physician in American Literature.*

ORDERING INFORMATION

Please send $ 18 .00 + $ 1.50 for postage and handling to:

AVIVA PRESS
P. O. Box 1357
Brookline, MA 02146

The editor may be contacted at:

Rehabilitation Medicine, F5
Boston University Medical Center
75 East Newton Street
Boston, MA 02118

OR

169 Nelson Court
Neenah, WI 54956